PAPERS IN ILLINOIS HISTORY

PAPERS

IN ILLINOIS HISTORY

AND TRANSACTIONS FOR THE YEAR 1937

THE ILLINOIS STATE HISTORICAL SOCIETY

SPRINGFIELD, ILLINOIS

1938

PRINTED BY AUTHORITY OF THE STATE OF ILLINOIS

CONTENTS

v

ILLUSTRATIONS

FOREWORD

Since 1900 the Illinois State Historical Society has been issuing an annual volume devoted in part to the official record of its annual meeting and in part to the publication of papers relating to various phases of Illinois history.

Without exception, these publications have been entitled *Transactions of the Illinois State Historical Society*—a title hardly likely to attract the attention of any appreciable number of readers. Their appearance, moreover, has generally been no less uninviting than their title. The combination has naturally repelled many readers who would have been delighted with the contents of these volumes had they had the hardihood to penetrate beyond the official reports with which each commenced.

The present volume is an attempt to eliminate these disadvantages. The title, at least in its short form, is believed to be less forbidding than formerly, and also more accurate as a description of the book as a whole. Official reports have been relegated to the last pages, where they can be found by those interested, but where they will not discourage the casual reader. Two features of preceding volumes have been omitted—the Society's constitution, and the annual list of acquisitions in genealogy. The former is always available; the latter has been compiled, and will be sent to inquirers in mimeographed form if an appreciable number of requests for it are received. Besides these changes, the physical appearance of the book has been greatly improved.

Most of the papers published in this volume were presented at the Society's annual meeting at Galesburg, May 13, 14 and 15, 1937. The exceptions are the articles "Illinois as Lincoln Knew It: A Boston Reporter's Record of a Trip in 1847," edited by Harry E. Pratt, and "Campaign Lives of Abraham Lincoln, 1860," by Ernest J. Wessen. These are contributions to Illinois history too long for publication in the *Journal*, but too important not to be made generally available.

PAUL M. ANGLE, *Editor*.

JOHN WENTWORTH

HIS CONTRIBUTIONS TO CHICAGO

By ANN STEINBRECHER WINDLE

To outsiders, in the year 1882, Chicago boasted three major attractions—the new three million-dollar courthouse, the Palmer House barber shop with its silver dollar floor, and "Long John" Wentworth. The elaborate architecture of the courthouse and the shining splendor of the silver dollar floor, however, paled into insignificance in the eyes of a boy visitor, when he caught his first glimpse of the man who had dominated Chicago's landscape for upwards of fifty years. Editor of Chicago's first successful daily newspaper, six times congressman from Chicago, and twice-term mayor, John Wentworth looked the part he played in the role of a Chicago Titan. William Campbell, who was later to become his private secretary, found Wentworth in the very center of his domain, the rotunda of the old Sherman House. Towering head and shoulders above the group of newspaper men who swarmed about him, he presented a striking figure. His colossal height of six feet, six inches, was well set off by a suit of finest broadcloth. He wore the well-known claw hammer coat with pointed tails, the low cut vest, showing an expansive pleated shirt bosom, a gold watch chain several feet long suspended from his neck, and, topping all, an enormous black felt hat. The massive features beneath the hat, the sharp, penetrating gray eyes, the large, determined mouth, and the square, smooth-shaven chin, revealed a nature, proud and intelligent, forceful and intellectually curious.

His dignified mien and commanding presence were Long John's birthright. His English ancestry dated back to one Reginald de

Wynterwade, mentioned in the Domesday Book, in 1066, as proprietor of the Wapentake of Strafford in the West Riding of Yorkshire. The family was a prominent and distinguished one, counting among its members Thomas Wentworth, Earl of Strafford. The first Wentworth to emigrate to America, the man from whom all of the American Wentworths are descended, was William, the Elder. Among the first settlers in Exeter, New Hampshire, he was one of the signers of that document known as the Exeter Combination, a fact which proves his arrival in America by the year 1639. Ten years later he established a permanent home in Dover, New Hampshire. Here he acquired much land, and became a leader in the community, frequently being chosen as one of the selectmen. He was the ruling elder in the church. At the age of seventy-three, he won lasting renown by a feat of which many a younger man might boast. In 1689, an Indian raid was made on five garrison houses. All were demolished except the one in which Wentworth lived. Wakened by the skirmish below, he dashed down the stairs, routed out the Indians, and lay on his back, setting his feet against the door of the stockade until help came.

From the year 1717, when John Wentworth, the grandson of William the Elder, was appointed Lieutenant Governor of New Hampshire, on through the period of the Revolution, the name of Wentworth signified in that state what the name of Winthrop signified in Massachusetts. Belonging to a family of statesmen and soldiers, Long John's own grandfather, John Wentworth, Jr., was a member of the Continental Congress and one of the signers of the Articles of Confederation. At the same time, his maternal grandfather, Amos Cogswell, served as a colonel in the Continental Army under the command of General Washington. Interest in local and national welfare, combined with an intense family pride and feeling of superiority above the rank and file of men which ran in all the Wentworth blood, was carried on to Long John. By an hereditary right, John Wentworth became Chicago's greatest "Democratic Aristocrat."

His own birthplace was an unpretentious New Hampshire farm-house. His parents, Paul and Lydia (Cogswell) Wentworth owned a farm just outside the town of Sandwich, in Strafford County, at the foot of Mount Israel. Here young Wentworth spent the greater part of his youth, gaining the hardihood which thrives on the rigors of New England climate and discipline alike. News of the Battle of New Orleans reached the Wentworth farm the day of John's birth, March 5, 1815. In 1827, educational institutions being as inefficient as the mail service, Wentworth went to Gilmanton, to attend the Academy of Asa Emerson Foster. In 1828, he changed to the Academy at Wolfeboro, where he uttered his first piece of oratory, declaiming Webster's eulogy on Adams and Jefferson. Thus his lifelong plea for "Liberty and Economy" had its youthful origin. He proved to be a precocious student, early becoming a facile reader in the classics, and he was an outstanding leader in the debating and literary societies of every school he attended. At the age of sixteen, he dropped his studies for a year to teach in a school at New Hampton, later resuming them at the Academy of South Berwick, Maine. Upon his graduation in the spring of 1832, he gave the valedictory address, and in the following autumn he entered Dartmouth College. An individual thinker and a fighting spirit, he clashed more than once in the next four years with those members of the faculty whose ideas were not in accord with his. His mind was not that of the average immature undergraduate, nor was it so considered. He was already taking an active interest in politics, and was made a delegate to the county convention to nominate a Democratic candidate for senator. He was appointed Chairman of the Committee on Resolutions, and his reports were highly praised by delegates and press alike.

In October, 1836, following his graduation from Dartmouth, this highly endowed young man set off across the Green Mountains to make his way in the great and unknown West. He carried with him several letters of recommendation from prominent New Hampshire men, and $100 in his wallet. From Schenectady to Utica, Wentworth took his first ride over a railroad. Going on to Tonawanda by canal boat, and to Niagara Falls by stagecoach, he traveled on a steamer from Buffalo to Detroit, where he hoped to find a position as school teacher. Receiving no replies to his advertisements in the *Detroit Free Press*, he made long walking trips to Ann Arbor and Ypsilanti. These met with the same ill success. He returned to Detroit, put his trunk aboard the brig *Manhattan* bound for Chicago, and took the stage for Michigan City, arriving there the afternoon of October 22. The next day he set out on foot for Chicago. With some twenty companions he spent the night in a shanty on the lake shore. Again continuing his march along the sandy beach, he rested the second night in Calumet. The following morning, October 25, 1836, John Wentworth walked into Chicago.

The picture of this tall, rangy youth, trousers tucked in his muddy boots, and wearing a brown hickory shirt and a great slouch hat as he made his entry into the town he was to grow up with, is best recreated in Wentworth's own words:

> Could you have been on the sandhills between here and Michigan City on the southern shore of Lake Michigan in the fall of 1836 you would have seen me stretched out like a leather shoe string tied up, just after wading a prairie marsh—all length and no breadth—leaning over the country at an angle of 45 degrees, with all my clothes under one arm and a jug of whisky under the other with which to bathe my blistered feet.

Upon his arrival, the first person he met was an old friend and former schoolmate from Northfield, New Hampshire, Matthew S. Maloney, of the leading mercantile house in town—Wild, Maloney & Co. Wentworth was advised by him to take up lodgings at the United States Hotel, on the southeast corner of Lake and Market streets. Originally, this had been the Sauganash Hotel owned by Mark Beaubien, but was now kept by John Murphy. On that first day, Wentworth dined at Mrs. Murphy's table, and from that day until his death he made it a point, whenever possible, to have dinner with "Mother" Murphy on each anniversary of his arrival in Chicago.

JOHN WENTWORTH

His first step was to make arrangements to study law under Henry Moore, one of the town's leading lawyers; but shortly after Wentworth's arrival, Moore was forced to return east on account of poor health. At this time, the *Chicago Democrat*, a weekly, was changing hands. John Calhoun, who had established the *Democrat* in 1833, as Chicago's first newspaper, was negotiating to sell it to Horatio Hill of Concord, New Hampshire. Hill, who was part owner and editor of the *New Hampshire Patriot*, was unable to remain in Chicago and was looking for someone to run his paper, when, happily, Wentworth walked into town. Within a month, the twenty-one year old boy had assumed the editorship of the *Chicago Democrat*.

He immediately set about to make it the leading paper of the Northwest. His first job was to move the office from its original site in the Jones, Walker & Company Building on North Water Street to the three-story wooden building at 7 North Clark Street. Having, usually, a shortage of hands, the physical work of printing a paper often fell to Wentworth. Even as late as the summer of 1838 he was turning out posters for Stephen A. Douglas with his own long arms, while the "Little Giant" inked the presses. Within a few months after he took over the *Democrat*, he had reorganized the subscription list and had increased the number of subscribers by more than two hundred. In his spare hours he attended to the literary side of the newspaper. His editorial policy, which aimed to avoid any factional prejudices within the party, stood for party usages, regular nominations and "pure democracy." His scourging editorials denouncing "wildcat" currency attracted the attention of readers all over the state.

Meanwhile, he was taking time off to attend the meetings held in the Old Saloon Building to discuss applying to the legislature at Vandalia for a city charter. The application was granted, and Wentworth was given the order to print the charter, thereby making a profit of twenty-five dollars for the *Democrat*, as he boasted in a letter to Hill. He was instrumental in the election of William B. Ogden as the first mayor of Chicago, and he was made the secretary of the first political meeting ever called in the first ward. In 1837, the Council appointed him first corporation printer of the city.

The date of John Wentworth's arrival in Chicago marked the passing of the pioneer stage of the city's history. He came just in time to catch the final reverberations of that romantic era. One of Wentworth's signal contributions to the future citizens of Chicago was the preservation of the spirit and legendary quality of that day in his notes, since published in the *Fergus Historical Series*. His young and active imagination was caught and held by the fragments of that early period, on whose trail he had so closely followed. Among his earliest recollections was one of seeing a line of caskets protruding from the ground along the beach, vivid reminders of the Black Hawk War and cholera siege of 1832. The cutting of the sand bar for the harbor had caused the lake waters to encroach and wash away the earth in which they had been buried. On December 29, 1836, Wentworth witnessed the final evacuation of Fort Dearborn:

> I saw the last sentinel withdrawn from the entrance, and the last soldier march out, and I heard the last salute fired from Fort Dearborn. For a while we missed the cannon's discharge at sunrise and sunset. And soon sunrise and sunset lost their significance in the measurement of Chicago time.

Although most of the Indians had departed for their reservation at Silver Lake, Shawnee County, Kansas, a few still roamed around the town prior to the final exodus. With the three most renowned Indians of the Middle West then living, Wentworth made fast friends: Billy Caldwell, known as Sauganash (the son of an Irish officer and a Potawatomi girl), a friend of the whites, and secretary to Tecumseh; Robinson or Chechepinqua, chief of the United Potawatomi, Chippewa and Ottawa; and Chamblee, the Ottawa who was at Tecumseh's side when the latter fell in battle. Wentworth spent many a long evening with these three before the fire in the log tavern of his hotel, listening to their description of battle after battle, including the massacre at Chicago and the Battle of the Thames, and their narration of personal interviews with, and characteristics of Tecumseh, General Harrison and General Wayne.

Keenly interested in all of the unusual figures of the community, Wentworth himself gave a heightened life and color to the rapidly growing town. An analogy between this struggling, dauntless, mud village and the bold, obstinate youth, just emerging from adolescence, was recognized by Wentworth in later life, when he told a newspaper man: "When I came to Chicago, I was a very small man. There was almost nothing of me. . . . I have grown with Chicago." He seemed to possess the key to the city's register. Chicago liked him. When the crowd gathered at the post office for the long awaited mail, Long John was frequently delegated to read the newspapers aloud while the letters were being sorted. His powerful voice made him a general favorite, and many a time he was escorted to the cracker box to match his vocal cords against the winds off Lake Michigan.

Chicago early discovered that Wentworth's mind was equal to his voice. Early in 1838, he was appointed school inspector, the first of his lifelong activities in connection with the Chicago School Board. He was one of the first and most arduous proponents of the common school system in the West. The following year, he was made one of Governor Carlin's aides-de-camp, from which office he derived a mingled satisfaction and embarrassment. Anticipating the fun his journalistic enemies would have at his expense, Wentworth stole a march on them by publishing the first cartoon ever to appear in a Chicago newspaper. It depicted Wentworth a gangling, beplumed warrior, astride a lean and paltry nag, surrounded by his political foes. The "balloons," which issued from their mouths, enclosed the same disparaging remarks they would have been expected to make in such a situation.

Within three years Wentworth had purchased the *Democrat* for $2,800, and he owned it free of all indebtedness. On February 24, 1840, appeared the first issue of the *Democrat* as a daily paper.

That same year he began his stump speaking throughout the state, and prepared an exhaustive article upon the relation of banks to government and their reciprocal duties. This article created widespread interest in the author.

Meanwhile, Wentworth had continued his study of law. In the spring of 1841 he went east to attend law lectures at Cambridge, with the intention of remaining a year. Hearing, however, that there was a strong possibility of his being nominated for Congress, he returned in the late fall of the same year. Soon afterwards, he was admitted to the bar. Because of the failure of the legislature to district the state, the election which should have taken place in 1842 was postponed until the following year. In May, 1843, Wentworth was the unanimous choice as Democratic candidate for Congress, and in August he was elected by a large majority.

December 4, 1843, he took his seat in the House of Representatives; he was the youngest member of the congressional body, being then only twenty-eight years old. His, the fourth district of Illinois, covered an area of 250 by 100 miles, comprising all the land from Wisconsin on the north to the Springfield district on the south, from the Indiana state line on the east to the Rock River Valley on the west. He was the first congressman ever to be elected from north of central Illinois, and the first who resided on the shores of Lake Michigan.

Before enumerating Wentworth's specific contributions to his community, while in Congress, it would be valuable to attempt an estimate of the far-reaching influence he wielded. His appearance in Washington immediately turned the spotlight of attention on Chicago. What kind of town had elected this young giant with such command of expression and fluency of tongue to speak for her? Wentworth did not wait long to answer. Chicago was the City of the Future, the gateway to the great Northwest. Prophesying that the South would ultimately yield first place as source of the nation's wealth, Wentworth predicted that Chicago, with its vantage point at the foot of one of the Great Lakes, would become the distributing center for that vast hinterland which swept from the Rocky Mountains to the very back door of the city. The prosperity of the United States, he pointed out, was dependent upon the facility with which western produce could be shipped, not only to various parts of this country, but also to foreign lands.

During his terms in Congress from 1843 to 1851 and from 1853 to 1855, Wentworth's efforts to modernize and render safe transportation on the lakes and rivers of the Middle West were unceasing. His first official act toward this end was almost coincidental with his entrance into the House. On December 20, 1843, he opened his congressional career, in behalf of Chicago, by giving notice that he would ask leave to bring in a bill to establish a port of entry in Chicago. From that day forward he was the chief agitator for harbor improvements, the erection of lighthouses and ports of entry on the Great Lakes, and the establishment of marine hospitals.

As a result of President Polk's veto of a bill for the improvement of rivers and harbors of the West and Northwest, he conceived the idea of the celebrated National River and Harbor Convention, which convened in Chicago, July 5, 1847. As Chairman of the Chicago Committee, which included George Manierre, J. Young Scammon, Isaac N. Arnold and Grant Goodrich, Wentworth drafted an address to the people of the United States, urging them to send delegates. In the closing paragraph he stated:

> Although the construction of harbors and the improvement of rivers will be the prominent subject before the Convention, yet, whatever matters appertain to the prosperity of the West, and to the development of its resources, will come properly before it, and all plans and suggestions will be freely entertained.

In response to Chicago's invitation, 3,000 delegates, representing eighteen of the twenty-nine states in the Union, assembled in the huge tent which had been erected on the Courthouse Square. The immediate effects of the convention proved of little value. But its tremendous significance was recognized by Thurlow Weed, who called it "undoubtedly the largest deliberative party that ever assembled." The presence of such men as Abraham Lincoln, Erastus Corning, Horace Greeley and Tom Corwin, gave a sparkle to this page of Chicago's history. A Convention City had been established. John Wentworth had brought the nation to Chicago!

In Washington, his absolute integrity and constant attention to his congressional duties were winning him a reputation among the capital's leaders. Chicago could not have boasted an abler or more striking representative on the floor. He was an ardent champion for preëmption and homestead laws, and was the first western congressman to introduce a bill advocating the bonded warehouse system. He was the chief instrument in passing the land grant bill for the Illinois Central Railroad through the House of Representatives. Stephen A. Douglas, continuing the work of Sidney Breese, had put the bill through in the Senate.

Probably no other man had the opportunity to view at close range so great a span of the nation's growth from the beginning of the nineteenth century on through the crisis of the Civil War. Two of the men with whom Wentworth was associated in Congress—John Quincy Adams and Benjamin Tappan—were born before the tea was thrown overboard in Boston Harbor. The former was fond of remarking that his earliest recollection was that of hearing the report of the guns at the Battle of Bunker Hill. During his six terms in Congress, Wentworth attended sessions with two members who served in President Monroe's cabinet, one in President J. Q. Adams', three in President Jackson's, one in President Van Buren's, five in President Harrison's, four in President Tyler's, four in President Polk's, four in President Taylor's, seven in President Fillmore's, four in President Pierce's, five in President Buchanan's, and six in President Lincoln's. He served with four future presidents of the United States—James Buchanan, Abraham Lincoln, Rutherford B. Hayes, and James A. Garfield. Four great statesmen of the period—John C. Calhoun, Daniel Webster, Henry Clay and Thomas H. Benton—were counted his personal friends. His sketches of these men, found in his *Congressional Reminiscenses*, show keen observation and analysis of character, and possess historical and literary value. He was an eyewitness to many of the dramatic events of his day. He was in Congress the day that John Quincy Adams fell in the House, and he was one of the committee appointed by Speaker Robert C. Winthrop to escort his remains to his home in Massachusetts. He was a delegate to the 1844 convention in Baltimore, which nominated James K. Polk for President, and also a delegate to the convention of 1848 which named Gen. Lewis Cass of Michigan as a presidential candidate. He was present at the inauguration of several presidents of the United States, including that of Abraham Lincoln. At Lincoln's death, he was one of the committee to receive his remains in Chicago.

At the close of the Thirty-third Congress, in which, under the census of 1850, Wentworth had represented a new district, the second, Chicago could no longer induce him to run again. It was during this term that he lost faith in the Democratic Party. In his estimate, the *idea* of the formation of the Republican Party originated in the House, when Colonel Benton made his great speech against the repeal of the Missouri Compromise in December, 1853. Following the passage of the Kansas-Nebraska bill, Wentworth, with other Democrats such as Judd, Palmer, Baker, Allen and Koerner, left the party to join forces with those Whigs and Abolitionists known as Anti-Nebraska men. From then on, the *Chicago Democrat* sounded the Republican cause, and through its channels Wentworth spread the antislavery creed. He supported the senatorial campaign of Abraham Lincoln, in 1858, and his presidential campaign in 1860.

Chicago recognized Wentworth's power and talent for leadership. Having reached the prime of life, he had acquired the characteristics this thriving, expanding, turbulent city needed. With firsthand knowledge and understanding of local and national issues, he was the man best suited to cope with the financial, social and political problems that faced Chicago. Possessing the suavity and dignity of a diplomat and the shrewdness and rough wit of the boisterous politician, he was big enough to be fervently admired and forcibly hated—altogether, the right man to control and direct the actions of so mixed a population as Chicago had. In 1857, Wentworth was nominated for mayor on a Republican Fusion ticket, and on March 3 of that year, in a hotly contested election, he won the office by a majority of over eleven hundred.

His first official act was to appoint a board of engineers to establish the grade of the city. He introduced the first steam fire engine into Chicago, appropriately named after him, the "Long John." Illustrative of his dispatch of executive duties was his prompt and decisive raid upon "the sands." This dilapidated section fronting on the lake shore was the most notorious part of the city. In one day Wentworth leveled it to the ground. Advertising a dog-fight on the outskirts of the city, he attracted most of the male inhabitants from the spot. Immediately, a deputy sheriff, accompanied by thirty policemen, began tearing down five of the disreputable shanties, and by four-thirty in the afternoon a fire had razed six more of the buildings.

In 1860, Wentworth was elected to a second term as mayor. Two more fire engines were introduced, the "Liberty" and the "Economy," the watchwords of his career. During this term he succeeded in rubbing off the word "deficit" from the records of the city treasury and writing the word "surplus" in its stead. His most spectacular act in 1860 was that of bringing the Prince of Wales to Chicago. He made the trip to Montreal to assure the Duke of Newcastle that if the Prince visited Chicago, he would receive a royal welcome. Wentworth personally superintended all the arrangements, and the visit was avowedly a tremendous success. After the Prince's departure, Wentworth received a letter of thanks from the Duke of Newcastle, and also a pair of Southdown sheep for his farm in Summit. In later years, asked by a young friend if he did not feel proud to be seated beside a future king of England as they rode in a carriage drawn by four horses through the streets of Chicago, his characteristic reply was:

I was not sitting beside the Prince. He sat beside me.

I felt no undue elation and the acclamations of the crowd were intended for me as much as for him. You are a good American citizen, and as such and on this principle, I should take more pride in having you as a carriage companion than if Queen Victoria sat by my side and the King of England on my knee.

At the close of his second term as mayor, Wentworth felt it was also time to bring to an end his long journalistic career. On July 24, 1861, he published in the final issue of the *Democrat* his farewell address to the patrons he had served for a quarter of a century. With the agreement that he would not publish a paper until after March 1, 1864, he sold to the *Chicago Tribune* his subscription lists, advertising, job work, and his patronage and good will.

Chicago, however, continued to call upon the services of Long John. In 1861, he became a valuable member of the Board of Education, and during the next three years strongly opposed all extravagance, and resisted the attempts of the banks to avoid the payment of par money for the School Board deposits. He was the originator and staunch defender of the Dearborn School, the first brick schoolhouse ever built in Chicago. When it became necessary for Illinois to revise her state constitution, Wentworth was made a delegate to the convention. In 1863, he made a dramatic and effective police commissioner. In this capacity, his tact and judgment averted two serious uprisings.

Aware that the speech of Clement L. Vallandigham, the antiwar Democrat, would arouse the anger of all Union men, he granted to him police protection; but when in turn the crowd called for Long John on the Courthouse Square, he prevented an interruption from the rebel sympathizers by reminding them of the courtesy their champion had received. He then broke into an impromptu speech, which, while adopting the sure-fire psychology of a Marc Antony, nevertheless contained a ringing challenge to the defenders of the Constitution. The following extract contains the political philosophy of Wentworth in regard to the Civil War:

If we want peace then, let us conquer. If the South want peace, let them lay down their arms and cease war. Then will I be willing to deal with them justly and generously. Then will I try to forget the rivers of Northern blood they have shed in their unholy struggle for slavery. . . . But while an arm wields a sabre, while the Constitution is defied and the laws laughed to scorn, I will uphold the authority whose solemn oath was, that the Constitution should be preserved and the laws maintained.

In that same year of 1864, Chicago was alarmed by the rumored uprising of the antiwar Democrats, known as the "Sons of Liberty." The plot to release 8,000 Confederate prisoners from Camp Douglas and to set fire to and pillage the city was disclosed in time, and with the assistance of Wentworth, Colonel Sweet was able to check the intended raid.

In 1865, Wentworth defeated Cyrus H. McCormick for the Thirty-ninth Congress. Under President Andrew Johnson, he was Chairman of the Ways and Means Committee, and was an advocate of the immediate resumption of specie payment. This, his final term in Congress, marked the close of his active political life, except for one year, 1880, when he was made Vice-President of the Republican National Convention.

Retirement from public life, however, did not mean in John Wentworth any decrease of interest in the city he had helped to build. Impressed by such estates as Mount Vernon and the Hermitage, and having a feeling in his own bones for the land, he had bought 4,700 acres at Summit, in Cook County, just fifteen miles from the Chicago Courthouse, on the banks of the Illinois and Michigan Canal, with a view to making it a refuge for his later years. But the activity and excitement of the city held too great a fascination, and the great stock farm remained unoccupied by its owner. Chicago, itself, was Wentworth's home. He knew no other. On November 13, 1844, Wentworth had married Roxanna Marie Loomis, the daughter of Riley Loomis, of Troy, New York. They, however, had never owned a home in Chicago. Always in delicate health, Mrs. Wentworth died in 1870. Of their five children, Roxanna was the only one who survived her father.

The later years of his life were spent at the Sherman House, except for the months of July and August, when he vacationed at Fountain Spring House at Waukesha, Wisconsin. He was a strong advocate of hotel life, declaring that there was the only place where the liberty bell was to be found. These were his words:

> I never was one of your bell-livers. I never did and never will live on time. Got no use for call-bells, dinner-bells, or alarm clocks, and I believe they do more for the general slaying of health and killing of people than either gluttony or intemperance. Now, my doctrine is this, eat when you're hungry, drink when you're thirsty, sleep when you're sleepy, and get up when you're ready.

Wentworth's manner of ordering his meals was original. The most desirably located table in the dining room was reserved for him. Though it had a seating capacity for five, it served Long John alone. Planning his menu in his room, he placed a cross before each dish that he desired, usually thirty-five to forty of them, and when he was ready to dine, he stalked into the dining room, expecting to find all the dishes on the table. Cold broth and melted ice cream did not matter; he insisted on everything being placed before him. If a desired dish was beyond his reach, he whirled the table around until it came within his radius. His favorite beverage was brandy, and his daily consumption from a pint to a quart.

His interests and hobbies were many. In 1867, he received a degree of Doctor of Laws from Dartmouth College, and in 1882-1883 he served as president of the Dartmouth Alumni Association. His greatest literary work was a three-volume *Wentworth Genealogy*, published in 1878. The subject closest to his heart, however, was the work of the Chicago Historical Society. The great sorrow of his life was his loss of manuscripts and papers, including a complete file of the *Democrat*, in the Chicago fire.

He made continuous efforts to collect information and anecdotes from the old settlers, in an attempt to reconstruct a picture of early Chicago for her future citizens.

John Wentworth's devotion to Chicago was twofold; he loved it as an actor in its development, and as a historian, evaluating its position in time. In his address on Fort Dearborn, he said:

> Chicago has ever been noted for its sensations, and that is one of the reasons why I have never liked to leave it. You can not find any other place that has so many of them. Why travel about when there is so much of interest transpiring at home?

The city quenched his thirst for drama and activity. His fundamental nature, however, responded to something deeper than mere excitement. A few lines from his *Reminiscences of Early Chicago* prove that:

> We often hear of different men who have done much for Chicago, by their writings, their speeches, or their enterprise. But I have never heard of a man who has done more for Chicago than Chicago has done for him. God made Lake Michigan and the country to the west of it; and, when we come to estimate who have done the most for Chicago, the glory belongs first to the enterprising farmers who raised a surplus of produce and sent it here for shipment; and second, to the hardy sailors who braved the storms of our harborless lakes to carry it to market. All other classes were the incidents, and not the necessities, of our embryo city. Chicago is but the index of the prosperity of our agricultural classes.

As his own life stretched out behind him, fifty years of which were coeval with the first half-century of Chicago's corporate history, Wentworth had glimmerings of what the future metropolis might be. Early in the fall of 1888, his health began to fail rapidly. The doctors could attribute the cause to nothing more definite than the general breaking down of the once powerful physique. Early on the morning of October 16, 1888, he died in his room at the Sherman House, surrounded by his family—his only daughter, Roxanna, his nephew, Moses J. Wentworth, his two brothers, Joseph and Samuel, and his sister, Mrs. Mary F. Porter.

The body lay in state at the Sherman House, where hundreds of Chicago citizens came to pay final tribute. Following the funeral from the Second Presbyterian Church, on October 18, the remains were taken to Rosehill Cemetery. A granite shaft, fifty-five feet in height, marks the final resting place of the man whose life was so entwined with Chicago's growth—John Wentworth, the outstanding actor in the annals of that city.

IMPRESSIONS OF LORADO TAFT

By TRYGVE A. ROVELSTAD

When I was asked to speak on the subject of Lorado Taft and his work, my mind reverted to a memorable day in the fall of 1922, when, in the Midway Studios in Chicago, I met the sculptor for the first time. I have often thought, since then, that I should like to give my impressions of Taft to the public, but in all probability I should never have done so had not the Illinois State Historical Society invited me to appear on this program.

Previous to my entry into the happy life of the Midway Studios, under Lorado Taft's able guidance, I had just received a glimmering of an idea of what sculpture was all about. This happened in the library at Elgin, Illinois, where I usually went during the extra moments of my lunch hour while attending the high school. Among the volumes on the Chicago Columbian Exposition of 1893, I found the first brilliant evidence of this man's work. Later I was fascinated by illustrations of "The Fountain of Time" which accompanied an article by Delia Austrian in the *International Studio Magazine* for March, 1921. Later, as I became personally interested in sculpture and its mysteries, my mother called my attention to an article in the *American Magazine* of April, 1922, by Neil M. Clark. This article, indirectly, gave me courage, later, to approach Mr. Taft in his famous studios.

In the meantime, I had attempted, in a naïve sort of way, to conquer the difficulties of modeling. I recall that one of my first attempts, in miniature form in clay, was that of a head of Lincoln. Following this came attempts, in the medium of plastilina, at a rearing horse, and also a copy of a primitive man I saw pictured in some history book. Later, happy chance sent me, with my small collection, to the estate of Mrs. Nellie Fabyan at Geneva, Illinois, and under her interest I attempted a larger conception of a doughboy, with rifle and fixed bayonet in one hand, and a torch in the other.

Just about this time I packed my suitcase and headed for Chicago, with the idea of finding work of some sort or another in this line. My first attempts were a failure. Unfortunately I approached a decorative plasterer, who was very considerate, but who had nothing for me to do. I have since recalled how very fortunate I was to have been refused work of this kind, for fate had a kinder surprise in store for me.

I believe it was on my third trip into Chicago that I arrived at the Midway Studios. Conquering whatever timidity I felt, I opened the folding doors into this interesting combination home and studio. I had with me, of course, my suitcase, filled with plaster pieces which I had painstakingly worked out. Mr. Taft happened to be in one of the inner studios. I do not recall at the moment, whether he was at work, or whether he was just reviewing some of his work. At any rate, he was informed of my presence by his secretary, and I was introduced to him.

I do not retain much of a first impression of the man, because I was too frightened to do more than open my grip and take out some of the plaster pieces. He looked them over with a twinkling eye, and the first few words which he spoke, and which I still remember, to the joyful recollection of my mother, were to the effect that a nude woman which I had copied at the Fabyan estate was a lady with a painful pose. I should like to have a picture of this figure, but perhaps it is as well that I have not. I was under the impression that Mr. Taft, although not impressed with my sculpture, realized that the same had taken a certain amount of patience. At least he went as far as to ask me if I was entering the profession for the money end of the same. As such an inquiry had been presented to me before, and as I was not particularly interested in the practical application of the art, I immediately answered to that effect. The result of this brief interview was an invitation to come and visit the Midway Studios for a week, and so to see how I should like the studio family, and how it would like me.

It was a happy day, and I returned home joyfully to tell my family the news, and to pack my things and return as soon as I could, to take advantage of this kind offer. The Midway Studios, at this time, were located on Ellis Avenue, with the main entrance back from the street. The inner court was down four or five steps below the level of the street. After passing through the main portals, one descended these steps through another door to the main court, in the center of which there was a fish pond sunken below the surface of the concrete, and flanked on either end by miniature copies of "The Fish Boy." This pool was of some interest to me later, for several of the studio cats had great sport jumping for the gold fish, sometimes successfully.

At the far end of this court was the heroic plaster model of "The Fountain of the Great Lakes," back of which, in a unique situation, was the studio kitchen. On either side of the court were groups from "The Thatcher Memorial Fountain"—Courage, Learning, and Love. On either side also were the main entrances into the various studios and adjoining rooms. It was in this court that I first met Lorado Taft.

One of the first figures of sculpture to impress my memory was in an adjoining studio, that of the heroic head of Labor, which adorns the "Alma Mater" group on the University of Illinois campus at Urbana. Mr. Taft caught me in the midst of my admiration of this piece. Some years later, when the group was being finished for bronze, I was asked to pose several times for this head.

As I have stated, the article in the *American Magazine* by Neil M. Clark gave me one of my first written impressions of Lorado Taft and his works. Perhaps I should also add it gave me something of the man himself in visual form, for one of the plates or cuts photographed the sculptor beside one of the heroic groups, "The Fountain of Time." A tall man with gray hair and beard, wearing a long smock—he stood by this spirited work. I recall that I pondered much over the picture. What were those huge figures all about, and what kind of man could he be who could create them? Lorado Taft has been something of a mystery and an enigma to most people. He had many friends, but I believe that there were very few who comprehended the real depths of his imagination, from which sprang the wraith-like figures and fantasies of "The Fountain of Time" and "The Fountain of Creation," and the numerous other allegorical works in bronze and in marble.

My stay in the Midway Studios lengthened from a week to a month, and then to nearly a year. If you can imagine yourself transformed into a place people call Heaven, that will give you some idea of how I felt. My dream had been realized. I was now working, not only amongst a happy group of people, but under a famous sculptor. I recall at this time that Lorado Taft was building up the first model for the work at Elmwood, Illinois, his home town. This was a pioneer group.

In a very friendly manner he asked me to pose for one of the figures in this group. Thus my acquaintance with his broad way of working and of handling a situation developed. Later I was asked to carve a small wooden gun for this group. Mr. Taft was so well satisfied with my crude carving, that he asked me later to do the enlargement for the full-sized group of the same weapon. I can recall the very kindly way in which I was treated at this time. There were no commands or orders. If I desired to do a thing, I could do so of my own free will. In a very thoughtful manner, I was later given a pay envelope, much to my suprise, for I had saved a small amount for an emergency, and even stood willing to pay for such an opportunity.

You can see, from this brief introduction, that my impressions of Lorado Taft were more in spirit form than in actual physical contact or memory.   Most of you, no doubt, are acquainted with the early facts in Lorado Taft's life, beginning with his birth in Elmwood, Illinois, in 1860.   In 1873, the Illinois Industrial University, now the University of Illinois, through the interest of its president, Doctor Gregory, and the professor of geology who was Lorado Taft's father, became interested in the subject of art, especially sculpture.   I am now giving a brief résumé of the above-mentioned article in the *American Magazine* entitled, "A Wonderful Thing Happened to This Boy."   Doctor Gregory asked for a subscription for a proposed museum, for which Mr. Taft, the father of Lorado, contributed fifty dollars a year from his meager salary.   A total of $3,000 was raised, with which Doctor Gregory went to Europe to buy copies of famous sculpture.

When he returned with the shipment, many of the pieces were found to be badly broken.   Young Taft's son was present at the time the boxes were opened, and watched his father and Doctor Gregory clumsily trying to fit the parts together.   Finally he tried it himself, and did it very successfully.   "I'm going to be a sculptor," he announced to them.

Thus began the career of Lorado Taft when he was only thirteen.   In 1879, he was graduated from the Illinois Industrial University with the best academic record ever made by a student there up to that time.   Having an insufficient amount of money to study in Paris, where he longed to go, he stayed at the University and studied for his master's degree.   By Commencement night in 1880, he had saved up $200, and with this and some more money which he borrowed from his father, he set out for Paris, where he entered the École des Beaux Arts.

Many were the hardships and limitations that he had to endure in Paris.   I can hear him now, telling us how he and a friend used to accept with considerable pleasure the invitation of an elderly lady out for lunch. He must have cut his allowance down to the limit, for food as well as for other necessities, because he stated that his expenses at the end of the first year had been only $252.   He remained in Paris for three years, and then, after a short visit at home, he went back for two more years. Returning to America, he settled in Chicago, where he managed to live by commission work and odd jobs, making numerous copies or statuettes of famous sculpture, and selling them to people who could not afford the originals. He tried competing his work, entering numerous designs into various competitions, but failed in all of them.

He also told us, laughingly, that he made a few soldier's monuments, and was quite thankful afterwards that he did not sign them. He spoke one time of building up a soldier's figure for an old gentleman who asked him to do the commission; after the first contact, he was never seen again, thus leaving Mr. Taft with the work on hand and no one to pay for it. Those were trying days for him. I recall that he told us that at this time he hit upon the idea of making a full cast of a model, which could be done in several hours, thus saving the many hours it would take for the model to pose. This casting was quite convenient, although he was somewhat criticized for using it. In the older Midway Studios we had many of these casts of legs and arms and other sections of the body, hung up in a certain part of the studio called the morgue.

For a Hallowe'en prank one night several of the boys and myself took a cast of a leg and placed it in the entry of one of the stores in such a manner that the leg protruded. We stepped back from the entry, waiting to see the impression it would have on our first victim when he sighted the grotesque object. Much to our delight, a man who was somewhat intoxicated came along and seeing the leg, veered out to the outer rim of the sidewalk, until apparently he grasped the idea that it was just a joke.

This first experiment of Mr. Taft's to save money and the patience of a model rested for many years in the basement of the Midway Studios, where I saw it often. It was cast in a position of despair. I believe it was the figure that he was working on one day when he received a visit from the Director of the Art Institute of Chicago. At this time his funds were characteristically low, but he refused to give this impression to the Director until at last he was obliged to confess that things were not going so well.

The Director asked him if he would like to teach at the Art Institute. He accepted, and this was a position which he held for many years, first as an instructor and afterwards as a lecturer. In later years he saw a great deal of the United States, as well as Europe, while lecturing. It was my good fortune to be one of his last assistants on the demonstrative clay talk which he gave; he told me that he had given this lecture over a thousand times, visiting practically every state in the Union. During the years 1928-1929, lecturing twice a day, we gave talks before more than forty different schools in the city of Chicago alone.

Mr. Taft's first real opportunity came with the World's Columbian Exposition. This was in the building of two large groups, flanking the entrance of the Horticultural Building. One was called "The Sleep of the Flowers," and the other "The Awakening of the Flowers." I can still remember one of the small models as it stood in the entry of the Midway Studios when I first arrived. Following that, contributions were made for the exhibitions at St. Louis—two groups with outstanding figures representing "The Mountain" and "The Prairie."

In the meantime, other works developed. One of these, which he told us happened more or less by chance, was the heroic group entitled "The Solitude of the Soul." This very beautiful group, which has stood many years in the Art Institute, depicts four figures, two male and two female, weaving their way in and out of the central core of the marble. Groping through eternity, they find each other's hands; thus we find, here and there along the pathways of life, our many or few friends. The next work was the design for "The Fountain of the Great Lakes." The model for this group was built up by pupils of his in the Art Institute. In fact, several years after I met Lorado Taft, I worked for one of these men. My understanding of the event was that each one of the best students was honored by the op-

Lincoln-Douglas Debate, Quincy

portunity to do one of these figures, thus lending an application of his studies to practical work.

One instance of heroism in this work was displayed by Lorado Taft. Someone had built up the armature or interior structure for the heroic figures in such a way that a certain point was weak. With many tons of clay thrown upon the work it began to sag, and would have fallen had not Mr. Taft stepped into the breach, placed his shoulder under the terrible weight, and held it up until someone, by means of a bit of engineering, released the weight from that section of the work. Only a sculptor can realize what it would mean, after many weeks of modeling, to have one's work come tumbling down. But Mr. Taft saved the day. I can imagine how the workmen who built up this structure must have felt at that moment. Later I witnessed the disastrous effects of a poorly constructed armature, from which many pounds of clay fell every other day, much to the modeler's disgust and Taft's expense.

The design of "The Fountain of the Great Lakes" is very beautiful. It contains the figures of five nymphs grouped on a pyramid of rocks, and pouring water from shells. At the summit is the nymph of Lake Superior, who pours water into the shells of Michigan and Huron below her, who in turn send their streams to Erie and Ontario at the base, whence the flow goes to meet the waters of the sea.

This group was erected by the Ferguson Fund, and now stands, in bronze, on the north side of the Art Institute. I can recall many happy hours spent in the older Midway Studios beneath the model of this group, where the cook, whom we teased for pastry, or whose pantry we "poached" in the later hours of the day, had her wee, small kitchenette. Elizabeth was a good-natured soul, and her cooking was excellent. I have forgotten to tell you of our noon-day lunches, in which each person in the studios participated at one long banquet table in one of the side studios, with Lorado Taft presiding. This was a rather painful occasion for me the first few times, as I was rather shy and not used to meeting so many people at once; but later, when I became acquainted, I enjoyed these occasions very much. During the latter part of my stay at the studios, it was my pride to take Mr. Taft's place at the head when he was out on a lecture tour. Sometimes there were as many as twenty-five or thirty people at this table; some of them were visitors of note, some were friends of the Taft family, and others our own personal acquaintances.

The boys and myself, that is Mr. Taft's students and assistants, lived across the alley from the main studio in what we called the Monastery. The girls, or women folks, inhabited a part of the main studio called the Nunnery. A bridge was constructed across the alley from the Monastery to the main studio. This formed a sort of sleeping porch, where I spent some of my time.

Following the completion of "The Fountain of the Great Lakes," came the group of "The Blind." This group has never been cast in permanent form, and still stands in the dark room in the Midway Studios, in plaster form. I do hope that at some time some individual, or group of people, will be inspired to bring this group out into the light, in bronze or in stone, and place it in some suitable surroundings where one can peacefully contemplate his thought and be inspired by this work as Taft was inspired to make it from Maeterlinck's great drama. Mr. Taft stated:

> After I had read the play, that wonderful tragedy whose symbolism expressed the great longing of all humanity for light in life, the group shaped itself in my dreams. It refused to vanish, and as it exhibited the concentration of a powerful emotion within the canons of sculptural composition, I made a small model to see how it would appear in the clay.

In the Maeterlinck drama, a company of the blind, old and young, men and women, sane and mad, are gathered in an asylum upon an island, watched over by nuns and an ancient priest. The latter takes his sightless wards to walk in the forest, and

THE PIONEERS, ELMWOOD

becoming weary (for he is very old), he seats the men on one side and the women on the other. Placing himself near them, he falls into eternal sleep. As the night comes on, members of the forlorn company question one another in a trivial manner, just as men so often deal with the problems of life. As the night grows chill and the snow begins to fall, the blind rise, and groping toward one another find the leader among them cold in death. The cries of the infant in the arms of the young blind mad woman awaken them to hope. They remember that the child cries when it sees the light, and the young mother, whom they call beautiful, exclaims: "It sees! It sees! It must see something, it is crying!" And grasping the child in her arms she pushes before the anxious ones seeking relief, and holds it aloft above their heads, that it may give token when help is near. Mr. Taft stated:

> It does not point to the hopeless note of Maeterlinck at the close. The hope that a little child shall lead them is one that all gladly accept as it keeps alive the light of faith that the race renews itself in young. It was a greatly absorbing creation. I felt for them, I experienced the deepest emotion while modelling the faces of the blind. The pathos of the helpless individual in the posture of the figures, the hands reaching upward into empty air, appealing to the great God above for guidance.

Following the group of "The Blind," came "Governor Oglesby," "General Logan" (Public Library, Chicago), then the colossal statue of "Washington" (University of Washington, Seattle). I do hope that at some time they will raise this figure upon an appropriate pedestal, for it is a grand conception of that broad-minded individual. I often saw this heroic conception of the father of our country while a student at the University of Washington.

Mr. Taft remained in the Art Institute as an instructor and lecturer from 1886 to 1907. He was a lecturer in the University Extension Department of the University of Chicago from 1892 to 1902, and a non-resident professor of art at the University of Illinois from 1919 until the time of his death. In 1903 he published *The History of American Sculpture*. Of this book, the *Chicago Evening Post* said: "[It is] a story of the deepest significance to American art, and one which as told by Mr. Taft is of fascinating interest."

The next two pieces he conceived were "The Funeral Procession" and "A Scene in the Temple." I should have stated that according to lists of Taft's works, "Black Hawk," the colossal concrete Indian statue for Oregon, Illinois, came after the purchase of "The Solitude of the Soul" by friends of American art in 1911. Following this, and previous to the completion in bronze of "The Fountain of the Great Lakes," came also the "Columbus Memorial Fountain" for Washington, D. C., in 1912.

Most of you, no doubt, are familiar with the "Black Hawk" statue, or have heard something about it. While planning this speech I received a telephone call from Mr. John Persuhn, superintendent of the erection of the heroic fifty-foot figure in its present location, under the direction of Lorado Taft. The following day, April 18, we visited the site of the statue and took some moving pictures, which I am going to show you at the end of this talk.

When I first visited the site of the "Black Hawk" statue, I was much impressed, not only with the majesty of the figure but with its location, high up on the bluffs of the Rock River, miles of beautiful Illinois scenery extending far to the west of it. A number of years ago while Mr. Taft was watching workmen build a reinforced concrete chimney at the Chicago Art Institute, the thought occurred to him of the possibilities of making a heroic statue with the same material. With this process in mind, a subject plausible for such material presented itself. For a number of years he had had a summer home and studio at Eagle's Nest, Oregon, Illinois, the summer place for the Chicago art colonies. Standing for the hundredth time at the highest point on the cliff, he remembered that it was here

Black Hawk, Oregon

that Black Hawk was finally driven out of Illinois, so he decided to immortalize this famous Indian chief.

One who knows the story of Black Hawk's last stand and who has viewed from this site the vast lands of Illinois territory which this Indian chief and his tribe had to give up, can realize the significance of Lorado Taft's heroic figure. The statue is immensely conceived and broadly treated, with the heavy folds of the garment surrounding the figure suggesting the anatomy beneath it without closely following its lines. With folded arms the Indian stands, head erect, the dignity, the stoicism, and the bitterness of the vanquished race in his face as he gazes across the river—a fitting memorial to a race that has passed from power.

This heroic statue was a gift of the sculptor to the people of Illinois, the expenses for it, it has been my understanding, having been raised by Mr. Taft through some of the first of his illustrated lectures or clay talks, of which the American public seemed so fond. The statue was unveiled in July, 1911.

While I was in Washington, D. C. in 1935, at work on the passing of our Elgin Pioneer Memorial coinage issue, I saw for the first time the "Columbus Memorial Fountain," standing before the Union Depot of that city. It was my first trip to Washington, and I was viewing the sights from the so-called "rubber-neck" or excursion bus. On the occasion of this brief glimpse of the fountain, among all of the other interesting and beautiful features of our capital, I was much impressed. Later I had a chance to view it more closely. Its design is characteristic of the sculptor's broad treatment of stone and bronze. As the story goes, it was one of his successful competitive pieces in later life. An assistant of his at the time, who is now quite a prominent sculptor at the Midway Studios, told me something of this work in its model form. She revealed to me that Mr. Taft was much discouraged about his model for the competition, but, as it happened, she had learned through influential sources that the committee was in favor of giving the commission to a midwestern sculptor. Naturally, this would be Lorado

Taft. So, as she stated, she kept him at the small model, working with him on it under his instruction, late at night, until the model was completed and ready for submission to the Washington Committee.

The design, of course, was accepted, and today we have in the heart of our capital city this most significant fountain. The principal feature of the fountain is a stone shaft about forty-five feet high, surmounted by a globe of the world. It forms the background for Columbus, who is represented as standing on the prow of a vessel, with arms folded, in an attitude of meditation. The figure is treated with grandiose dignity, throwing about it a great cloak, after the fashion of the discoverer's day.

Just below the statue of Columbus is the figurehead of a ship, a beautiful female figure of ample form and dignity, typifying the spirit of discovery. Below is the basin of the fountain with its abundant flow of water. On either side of the stone shaft are massive figures portraying the new and old worlds. The sculptor portrays the New World as represented by the figure of an American Indian, reaching over his shoulder for an arrow from a quiver. The Old World is represented by a figure of a patriarchal Caucasian of heroic mold and thoughtful mien. There is more to the composition of this design, but you must go to Washington yourselves sometime to see it. I spent many thoughtful and inspiring moments there under the two enormous lions which occupy the ends of the palisade.

About the time that I entered the Midway Studios, the model for "The Fountain of Time" had been standing just opposite from where the original is now. It was about this time that the Robert Early process of casting in concrete with a granite chip finish was brought before the public. The matter of completing "The Fountain of Time" in permanent form was then much under discussion. Robert Early, I recall, had several samples of this casting process made up for Mr. Taft and on exhibit in the studios. I also recall that a casting or piece mold had already been made from the plaster form of the fountain. For this

Alma Mater Group, Urbana

reason it was no longer necessary to allow the plaster models to remain out on the Midway under destroying conditions of the weather, where they had been for several years. So Mr. Taft set three or four of us to work taking down the models—that is cutting them up in pieces and storing them away in the alley behind the studios, under shelter. It is interesting for me to recall this time, as I had ample opportunity to study the great models, even though we were more or less in the process of the destruction of them. The opposite side of the Midway was, of course, to hold within a few months, the duplicate in the finished concrete, as done by Robert Early.

Most of you know the lines from which the inspiration for this great fountain was conceived. They are from the poem by Austin Dobson.

> Time goes, you say? Ah, no!
> Alas, time stays; *we* go!

Mr. Taft said:

These words brought before me a picture which speedily transformed fancy into a colossal work of sculpture. I saw the mighty crag-like figure of Time, mantled like one of Sargent's prophets, leaning upon his staff, his chin upon his hands, and watching with a cynical, inscrutable gaze, the endless march of humanity—in a majestic relief in marble, I saw it swinging in a wide circle around the form of the one sentinel and made up of the shapes of hurrying men and women and children in endless procession, ever impelled by the winds of destiny in the inexorable lock-step of the ages—theirs the fateful onward movement which has not ceased since time began. But in that crowded concourse, how few detach themselves from the grayness of the dusky caravan; how few there are who even lift their heads. Here an overtaxed body falls, and a place is vacant for a moment; there a strong man turns to the silent shrouded reviewer, and with lifted arms, utters the cry of the old-time gladiators—"Hail Caesar! We who go to our death salute thee!" —and presses forward.

Those of you who go to Chicago should make a point of going out on the Midway to see for yourselves this great group.

It is my personal regret that this famous sculpture could not have been carved into stone or cast in bronze, but as Mr. Taft said, it would have taken many more thousands of dollars and hard work to complete it in that material. The fountain, as it stands today, is quite impressive. I should like to see the South Park Board give it some night-lighting treatment. That would make it extremely effective during the evening hours to the thousands of motorists who are continually passing this attractive spot in Washington Park just off the Midway. If you are by chance driving there you will know what I mean.

The erection of the fountain was sponsored by the Ferguson Fund of the Art Institute, which fund, I understand, was aided materially by Lorado Taft's lectures and educational work in art. The fountain is about 112 feet in length and contains over 100 figures. Instead of signing this fountain, as is customary, Lorado Taft modeled among the figures in the rear, his own portrait, marching among the throng, with his hands behind his back, and his head bowed in thought. Behind comes Jellsomeno, his janitor, bent beneath the burden which is borne on his back.

Lorado Taft had a beautiful dream idea for the Midway Plaisance; this land became famous during the World's Columbian Exposition, under its landscape architect, Frederick Law Olmstead, who so named it. This was the same Mr. Olmstead who designed Central Park, New York. This proposed plan of Mr. Taft's consisted principally of three monumental bridges across the Midway, which at one time contained a canal running through its center. These bridges were to be ideals of grace and beauty. One was to be the bridge of Sciences, one of the Arts, and one of the Religions. They, as well as the walks of the Midway, were to be decorated with statues of the world's great idealists. I won't attempt to name them as the list is long. The other end of the Midway was planned for an accompanying fountain to "The Fountain of Time." This other fountain was to be called "The Fountain of Creation." Separate groups of this are still in the Midway. Some of them have been

ABRAHAM LINCOLN, URBANA

carved in sandstone. I have been fortunate enough to record some with my camera.

I should like to tell you more of Mr. Taft's work—of the "Shaler Memorial Angel" for Waupun, Wisconsin, completed in 1923; of the "Foot Memorial" for Jackson, Michigan; of the "Lincoln" for Urbana; of "The Pioneers" for Elmwood; of the important "Alma Mater" group for the University of Illinois; and many other examples of Mr. Taft's inspirational sculpture. I should like to go into some detail as to the "peep shows" he made of the famous sculptors of the past, and to tell something of his dream museum. But my time is drawing to a close. I should like also to tell you of the good times we had in the Midway Studios, of the parties and plays, and the bits of pageantry with which Mr. Taft delighted in entertaining his guests.

Lorado Taft died on October 30, 1936, and with his passing the world lost one of its great men. My last visit to Lorado Taft's studios was while he was at work on a relief of Lincoln for Quincy, Illinois. I had brought to him, for approval, my coin design for the Pioneer Memorial Half-Dollar. Mrs. Taft was in the studios at the time, and I remember with joy the interest that this great man and his wife took in my work.

My last letter from Lorado Taft was received while I was in the East, just after the occasion of the passing of our coinage bill and its signing by President Roosevelt. I had written to Taft of its passage, and thanked him in turn for a letter of introduction to one of our senators, which, no doubt, was instrumental in its passage. Here is the message I received:

THE MIDWAY STUDIOS
6016 INGLESIDE AVE.
CHICAGO, ILLINOIS
June 27, 1936

DEAR TRYGVE:

Good for you, Tryg! You do not know when you are licked! I wish I could look back upon anything so brave in my career.

Faithfully yours,
LORADO TAFT.

THE MISSISSIPPI RIVER AS AN ARTISTIC SUBJECT

By LUCIUS W. ELDER

The Mississippi River is a variable experience, depending on the manner in which it is approached. The traveler by train or by automobile crosses it by a bridge far above the water and catches a glimpse of only a limited expanse. The scene is complete in itself, no doubt. But it gives no impression of the totality, no feeling of the size and power of the river. A different experience awaits one who stands on the bank at water level; or one who sails out upon the current in a boat either great or small; or one who emerges from a tributary into the wide reaches of the main stream.

The extent to which, amid these variations of contact, there may be an experience of artistic value to the individual is a speculative problem which is difficult to answer. Explorers, pioneers and early settlers along the banks of the Mississippi may conceivably have felt its natural beauty in a restricted view or may have been awed by a realization of the sublimity inherent in a vast phenomenon of Nature. The fact that beauty and awe may unconsciously exert their proper stimuli on the emotions of men may not be overlooked nor denied. It may not be denied that many perceptions of beauty never come to expression. We are now, however, dependent on such evidence in verse or in sketch as may be assembled, to estimate the artistic value of the river for the pioneers and early settlers in the immediate vicinity of the great river.

Any assumption that the Mississippi River should, by some inherent power, or by like disposition of individual character, evoke artistic expression will be upset by results in the case of verse inspired by the river; and only moderately confirmed by rather more positive results in the field of pictorial art. These two phases of the theme must be dealt with separately, and with recognition of the fact that those Europeans who first explored the Mississippi were not engaged in a quest for beauty; and those who first built towns on its banks were primarily concerned with the means for securing mere existence.

The early explorer in the valley of the Mississippi came, undoubtedly, with an imagination fired by zeal in a great adventure: his objective was ease in economic relations, political power, or imperialistic grandeur, or some such temporal achievement. In the background of his mind there may have lurked memories of fairy tales concerning talismans and lost hordes of treasure; and in some cases we might be able to adduce the evidence. But certainly the exercise of the creative imagination in art would be quite foreign to his moods when engaged in exploration. There was, indeed, some feeling for the natural conditions of the prairie and the wooded banks of the river; some might see in the Mississippi Valley a paradise for the unspoiled child of Nature. Others might sense the opportunity for the metamorphic power of love and religion to raise the native to a higher level of civilization. These, and other great aims, depending on the times, and on the conditions whence the explorers came, must have predisposed them to a fairly fixed attitude toward Nature in this region.

We find an occasional adjective, in the written works of the original explorers, used with something more than rhetorical force. Father Marquette describes some things as grand or fine; La Salle had the size and beauty of the river which he had not yet seen described for him; and Hennepin refers to the Mississippi Valley as "the delight of America" and "nothing like it in the world." What we may infer from such references, however far extended, must be clarified by the reasons why the scenic value of Nature did not inspire them much further. Explorers coming from Europe in the seventeenth and eighteenth centuries would understand Nature when conventionalized; they would appreciate wild Nature as an abstract idea but they would hardly see artistic value in the vast, untamed reaches of river, prairie, or forest.

If the early explorer was able to see a vision of future empire in terms of Paris ruled over by a benign emperor, we may deduce that whatever was grand or fine in the scene had a large admixture of civilized resources. The scene had possibilities in spite of the tribulation of actual exploration; in spite of marshy stretches along the margins; in spite of nostalgia and illness. It is perhaps for just this reason that a legend of the West became more influential than any perception of natural beauty could be.

Pioneer civilization in the Mississippi Valley had to combat conditions which were recalcitrant and impervious to the artistic imagination. Travelers from the old world to the new, and especially those who, like Mrs. Trollope, penetrated to the West, deprecated the lack of softening and refining influences in this region: the lack of books, music, and similar expressions of the spiritual life. Not forgetting that Cincinnati, New Harmony, or St. Louis had these things in limited measure, Mrs. Trollope's remark about the ubiquitous newspaper had a large element of truth, no doubt. Pioneers were more likely to read newspapers than poetry: but that is still true. The literary development of the West has been told by Rusk and others and need not be repeated here. The one point that commands attention in this story of literary development in the Mississippi Valley is that pioneer days developed an era of oratory—an era that has faded away within our own memory. To recognize that the pioneers lived in an age of oratory is but to give the contemporary political structure of life its due emphasis.

The labor of clearing the soil, like that of pioneering in general, requires a type of mind, a physical vigor, and other qualities in keeping. It certainly could not be true that the early settlers were all of a rough and tumble type, both physically and mentally. At the same time, the testimony of such a man as Peter Cartwright, in his *Autobiography*, might lead one to infer that life was a battle with the rowdy and the trouble-maker. Peter Cartwright, a preacher, was able to hold his own amid the lawless and turbulent elements of pioneer society; but whether the artistic soul was equally successful is another question. Conditions demanding a definite type of character for successfully meeting life in general are found in the case of boatmen and *coureurs de bois*. They indeed had their songs, of which some examples have been cited by Hall. But we know too little about this subject to speak in general terms.

Specific cases of literary production, when we can cite them, stand out as sporadic examples. One such case is the *"Chanson de l'Annee du Coup,"* the famous song of Jean-Baptiste Trudeau in the year 1780. It was written in French; and, as so often happens, stands at the beginning of a national literature in a language other than that which finally prevails. The story of this song belongs to the colonial history of St. Louis; and you may take its prophetic value for whatever it is worth. Two other omens of literary development in the Mississippi Valley are startling but equally lacking in subsequent results.

John Keats, the poet, writing to his brother George in America, prophesied that the child of his brother, as yet unborn, would be the bard of the western world. That prophecy may be read in the poem beginning: " 'Tis the witching hour of night." The story of George Keats in America has not been completely told, I think; but it is at least correct to say that no fulfillment of the prophecy occurred. The male issue of George Keats is extinct, and the bard of the western world will not, perhaps, bear the name of Keats.

The second prophetic example is the proposed literary association of Edgar Allan Poe with E. H. N. Patterson at Oquawka. The proposal was abortive by reason of the untimely death of the former. This is not the place to tell that story; but the promise that, by their projected partnership in a literary journal, Oquawka might have become a great literary center, is a pleasant topic for speculation. The *Oquawka Spectator*, under Patterson's editorship, provides us with a fairly clear picture of what journalism could be on the banks of the Mississippi. And because its pages contain contributions in verse by local writers, some idea of the literary level of the region is provided. A glance through its pages will turn up a number of poems inspired by the river. Some candidate for a doctor's degree might find a thesis in so doing. In the course of a desultory search, I find a homesick cry from New Iberia, Louisiana, where even the majestic steamers do not relieve the uncongenial shores. In the issue for March 9, 1848, the ever-flowing river suggests pride and exaltation in freedom. On May 17, 1848, a poem appears in which Neptune asks the Mississippi why his waters are so muddy. The answer involves Miss Missouri and Miss Ohio in a somewhat bigamous relation; or, at best, in a confused poetic figure. Several examples could be cited in further illustration.

One more oddity may be noted. Charles Mead published in Philadelphia in 1819, *Mississippian Scenery; A Poem, Descriptive of the Interior of North-America*. The book called forth a notice in the *North American Review* for January, 1820, in which the reviewer said: "[It is] a production altogether without merit. . . which has no other claim to protection than that of insignificance." I wish he had not been so frank; or at least not so harsh. The book has no value as poetry, it is true; but it has the value of showing, by a modern voice, what some of the early explorers may have dreamed. I find nothing of the author or the book in the bibliographies and hence we must take it as it stands.

The difficulty which versifiers found in using the river as material is a rhetorical one, in the main. No fundamental image which brings the river as a whole to the mind of the reader is any more real and perceptual than is the actual experience of the object itself. Since one must acquire an idea of the object piecemeal or by a succession of experiences, the immensity of the Mississippi is a difficult concept. The same is pretty largely true of any other quality. One local poet likened the river to "some great thought Omnipotence has awakened in its depths" and so on. Such similes are really beyond the scope of fancy.

Longfellow's solution of the difficulty facing the poet of Nature seems to me satisfactory and final. In his *Kavanagh*,

Longfellow embodies a piece of literary criticism in an interview between Mr. Churchill and Mr. Hathaway, the latter demanding a national literature commensurate with Niagara Falls—something stupendous. "We want a national epic," Mr. Hathaway demands, "that . . . shall be to all other epics what Banvard's Panorama of the Mississippi is to all other paintings." Mr. Churchill holds his fire until the end and answers: "A man will not necessarily be a great poet because he lives near a great mountain. Nor, being a poet, will he necessarily write better poems than another because he lives near Niagara." If this principle has any merit, we may infer that the Mississippi River would not necessarily create poets, nor inspire poets; and the extent to which it would do either, on occasion, would depend not so much on the direct influence of Nature on man, as on the revelation which takes place in the spirit of man in reaction to Nature. For, as Mr. Churchill says later: "Literature is rather an image of the spiritual world, than of the physical."[1]

Relatively little can be said in words, then, of the grandeur of Nature: verbal description fails to interpret adequately except when employed by the highest art; and persons endowed with the highest art certainly were not prevalent in the western world at large. Nature can, however, be drawn with the pencil or painted with the brush of the pictorial artist. This is exactly what happened not only in the Mississippi Valley, but also in other parts of the country during the first half of the nineteenth century. The bibliography of illustrated travel books is enormous; and it indicates a widespread attempt to visualize, for the public, the glories of natural scenery and man's habitations in the midst thereof. As towns developed along the rivers, and steamships made travel even easy and comfortable, albeit at times extremely dangerous, attempts to show the growth of the country by picture developed amazingly. The human element, man and his works, gave needed inspiration to the pictorial

---

[1] *Kavanagh, Drift-Wood (The Prose Works of Henry Wadsworth Longfellow,* III, rev. ed., Boston, 1866), 115-16.

draughtsman; and the duplication by the lithographer and engraver made publication possible. Mere natural scenery of cliff and lake, island and river, was not neglected either. The artistry displayed is also of great range: some crude, and some of great excellence. Some work is highly individualized and expresses the interpretative power of the artist; other work, transformed by the lithographer or engraver, tends to become conventionalized in the technique of mechanical reproduction.

As an example of the crude but vivid illustration of the river, I refer to *Lloyd's Steamboat Directory*,[2] wherein wood engravings of New Orleans, Cairo, and St. Louis will be found. The glory of the book, however, is the series of cuts picturing explosions, sinkings, capsizings and burnings of steamships. Explosions are most satisfactory and complete; but undoubtedly the lugubrious tone of all of them rightly interprets the horror of disaster. The pictorial value of the river receives kinder treatment in the lithographs of Currier and Ives, several of which attempt to capture the color, sentiment and activity of life on the main current or on the bank. The steamboat race gives the artist his chance in dramatic force; and the views of steamboats, while not accurate in detail, express the human interest in the stately design of these craft. It is needless to cite examples: they must be seen.

The work of two men, Bodmer and Lesueur, goes further in illustrating the Mississippi, for they are artists in their own right. Charles Alexandre Lesueur (1778-1846) spent some years in America between 1816 and 1837. His drawings, made during that time, constitute some important early documents so far as the history of the lower Mississippi settlements is concerned. He was a draughtsman with the minute and accurate technique of the engraver, but more economical of line and more selective of detail. Charles Bodmer accompanied Maximillian, Prince of

---

[2] James T. Lloyd, *Lloyd's Steamboat Directory, and Disasters on the Western Waters, Containing the History of the First Application of Steam, as a Motive Power: the Lives of John Fitch and Robert Fulton, Likenesses & Engravings of their First Steamboats. Early Scenes on the Western Waters, from 1798 to 1812. . . .* (Cincinnati, 1856).

Wied, in the years 1832-1834 on his expedition through the upper Missouri Valley. From the sketches made by Bodmer as the official artist of the expedition, some eighty large engravings were published. Little of the work of Bodmer on this expedition is strictly pertinent to the Mississippi; but he did make a number of drawings of Mississippi scenery (such as that of Tower Rock) which have pictorial value. It is difficult to evaluate the work of an artist when it can be seen only through the medium of the engraved copy. In this respect, some of Bodmer's work gives the impression of being "over-exposed" to the engraver's tools. Some of his plates, on the other hand, approach the delicacy of Lesueur. I offer such judgments as these solely as attempts to relate these pictorial documents to the actuality of river scenery: they are not intended as critical *dicta*. I have, nevertheless, a predilection for the substantial truth of their work. Both lived for a time at New Harmony, Indiana; and both actually saw the Mississippi as it was a hundred years ago.

The era of the panoramas followed that of the expeditionary artists. I wish the works of Banvard, or of Lewis, if indeed they are still extant, could be recovered. In the storeroom of some museum, fragments of these panoramas or of some others may yet be turned up. Since the subject has so recently been covered by Bertha L. Heilbron in her account of motion picture making in 1848,[3] I have no need to enter into detail here. At present the nearest we can come to a recovery of the work of either is the series of lithographs made for Lewis: *Das Illustrirte Mississippithal*, first published in Dusseldorf (1857), and reprinted in Leipzig-Firenze (1923).

We must conclude, then, that the Mississippi River did not inspire the pioneers to any great literary heights, since only scattered examples of such production can be found, but it does seem to have been a source of inspiration to a number of artists. Many an expedition into this great valley included among its

---

[3] Bertha L. Heilbron, "Making a Motion Picture in 1848: Henry Lewis on the Upper Mississippi," *Minnesota History*, Vol. 17, No. 2 (June, 1936), 131-49. On Banvard's panorama, see also *post*, 184.

members, one who recorded the scenery of the region in pictorial form. We know, too, that there were some great panoramas painted of this region, portraying on vast stretches of canvas the succession of scenes to be found along the Mississippi River. It is to be regretted that these great panoramic works have disappeared, but fortunately, due to the work of lithographer and engraver, many of the above-mentioned sketches of the nineteenth century artists are available to us today.[4]

---

[4] At the conclusion of the address, the Society was invited to view exhibits of material illustrating the pictorial art of the Mississippi River. The main exhibit was made possible by the courtesy of Edward Caldwell of New York and consisted of a series of engravings arranged, in part, as a panorama of the river from Dubuque to New Orleans; the maps provided a cartographic history of the development of Illinois; and the portfolios of engravings by Bodmer and the drawings of Lesueur were on display in the Library of Knox College. The Currier and Ives lithographs were drawn from the Preston Player Collection, and the books on exhibit were from the Finley Collection founded by Edward Caldwell.

St. Louis

From a drawing by J. C. Wild; engraved by J. T. Hammond, about 1840.

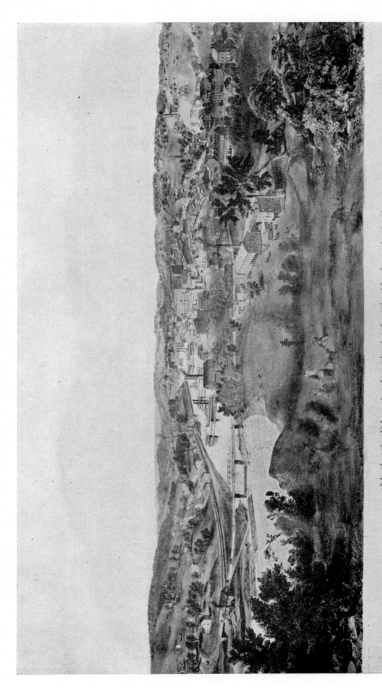

VIEW OF GALENA, ILL.

GALENA IN 1856

From a lithograph by E. Whitefield.

CAVE-IN-ROCK
From a drawing by Charles Bodmer.

CARONDELET, MISSOURI

From a drawing by Charles A. Lesueur.

MOLINE
From an early engraving.

QUINCY

Engraving from a drawing by R. B. Price.

QUINCY

From H. Lewis, *Das Illustrirte Mississippithal.*

BOUND DOWN THE RIVER
From a Currier and Ives lithograph.

LOADING COTTON

From a Currier and Ives lithograph.

COTTON BOAT
From a drawing by Charles A. Lesueur.

FORT ARMSTRONG

From a lithograph in H. Lewis, *Das Illustrirte Mississippithal.*

St. Charles, Missouri, on the Missouri River
From an engraving published by Herrmann J. Meyer.

KASKASKIA, ON THE KASKASKIA RIVER
From an engraving made in Germany about 1850.

NAUVOO

From a lithograph in H. Lewis, *Das Illustrirte Mississippthal.*

ALTON

From a lithograph in H. Lewis, *Das Illustrirte Misssissippithal.*

CAIRO

From a lithograph in H. Lewis, *Das Illustrirte Mississippithal.*

VIRGIN FIELDS OF HISTORY

By HENRIETTA L. MEMLER

Possibility of using the history of a small town, a small community, or a particular locality as a field for research has, until very recently, either been overlooked or neglected by all but a few historians. History departments of most universities and high schools have seldom suggested such local history as a proper field of research for the thesis or term-paper writer. The broader fields have always seemed preferable despite the difficulties and expenses involved in gathering material from sources which are likely to be widely separated.

As a result of this tendency the student of history has found the reference books and secondary materials of libraries his most promising field of research, rather than the fresher and infinitely more interesting sources which lie around and about him that have been hitherto untouched. This condition has existed, apparently, because students and teachers have failed to realize the possibilities, advantages, and actual values which accrue from a study of purely local history. They have been unaware of the vast amounts of material which are available for such a study and have failed to consider the possibility of doing valuable and comprehensive research on a subject which is strictly limited in its scope to one small locality or area.

Once one attempts to write the history of a locality, he discovers that both a quantity and variety of sources are available to him. The quantity is entirely sufficient to enable him to make a complete and comprehensive history, and the variety is as great as will be encountered in the study of a much broader subject. These sources may be rather roughly divided into two groups: the printed and public sources, and those which are more personal in their aspects.

In considering first the personal sources, it is well to begin by mentioning tradition, an extremely valuable source when properly used. Every locality has its traditions and one can be fairly sure that back of each tradition lies some fact. A fine experience in using the methods of historical criticism is afforded the student who endeavors to trace a story back through the generations until he arrives at the fact from which the tradition has sprung. The fact, when thus proved, oftentimes could be found in no other source and may prove invaluable in creating a complete history of the locality.

Together with tradition might well be mentioned the other oral source which is available in the memories of the residents of the community. In many communities will be found older persons who can remember back almost to the first days of settlement of their part of the state. So many towns in upper Illinois are celebrating their centennials in this decade, and a veritable treasure-house of information will be lost if the octogenarians and nonogenarians are allowed to slip away without recording their very vivid recollections of the pioneer days of the state. In many localities it is possible to find an old-timer who has retained full use of his faculties and whose memory of early dates and early events proves almost infallible as far as careful checking will show. Necessarily, careful checking and re-checking with other sources is imperative, just as in dealing with pure tradition; but what funds of information as to political sentiments and social habits and customs can be found in such a source!

Another personal source is that of the letters, diaries, and record books of one sort or another which have been handed down from generation to generation in the families of the community. A diary is, of course, a priceless source of information on all subjects, if the student is fortunate enough to find one in the locality. Interesting side lights are thrown on the social, economic, and political development of the people which never could be gleaned from newspapers or other public sources. Old letters are, perhaps, more often found than diaries, and even an isolated letter may contain valuable information; but a series of letters, consecutive over a period of time, is indeed a find for the local historian. Such sources are usually dependable as to facts, although the possible prejudices of the author should be carefully examined when dealing with controversial subjects.

Record books or household account books which have been kept over a period of years bring many interesting facts to light. In one instance, when using such a book, it was possible for a student to learn what materials the ladies were using in their dresses some seventy-five years ago, and how much they were paying per yard; what luxuries were being served on the family dinner table and how much they cost; the magazines to which the family subscribed through the years; how much it cost to go by stagecoach to the county seat; and even how much that particular family was contributing toward the support of the local church. By then establishing the fact that this one family was not one of extreme wealth, nor yet one of extreme poverty, the historian could be fairly sure what the average family of moderate income was eating, wearing, reading, and doing during those years.

Records of the various firms and business houses which have operated in the community at one time or another may also prove to contain valuable materials for the local historian. For instance, the volume of trade and business of the town would be fairly well shown by the account book of a grocery store. A comparison of the number of charge accounts and the amount of cash business done by the store from year to year would be an index to the business prosperity and growth of the community.

Many interesting details may also be found in such a source, details which help to complete a well-rounded history of the village. For instance, when examining the account book of a store in a small farming community in Peoria County, a historian discovered such interesting facts as the date on which canned fruit was first handled in the local grocery, when the first oysters were sold, and what was apparently the first appearance of commercial candy in the village.

Years ago in the same town an old mill had been operating, and, by writing to the last surviving member of the family which had owned the mill, it was possible to gain access to the account book of the firm. To the modern resident the amount of business which had been transacted there and the distance from which people came to have their grain ground at that mill was astounding. Through those records one could trace the growth of the business until it became the leading industry of the village. Then, with the advent of the railroad, the automobile, and improved roads, a sharp decline in the volume of business was clearly evidenced. The mill finally went into the hands of receivers and the building itself was torn down, after once having housed the main industry of the town. The history of similar business ventures could doubtless be duplicated in many an Illinois farming community of today.

Occasionally for political history, but more often for social history, the local historian can go to actual remains as sources. Heirlooms and antiques prove valuable for period history. It is also interesting to trace the various styles and types of architecture which have been used in the locality from year to year; and how better could this be done than by examining the remains—the homes, schools, churches, and other public buildings which have been erected through the years? The social historian might want to trace the styles in clothing, perhaps to see how his own particular community has kept abreast of the prevailing style trends through the years. How better could this be done than by going to the remains themselves, the remains in this case being the old wedding gowns, hats, suits, and dresses which have been stored away in many an attic through the long years?

Frequently the student can pick up interesting bits of information from a visit to the local cemetery. The birthplaces of the residents could there be established and hence the direction from which migration to that settlement was coming. By comparison of dates one might discover that at one time a dread disease struck the community and carried off a large percentage of the population. Or, if time and effort were expended, the life expectancy of the early pioneers might be established with some degree of accuracy through a comparison of dates.

In listing some of the more important printed and public sources which are available to the local historian, mention might first be made of the histories which have been written of the respective counties throughout the state. They are, of course, a help in establishing primary facts, although one must be exceedingly careful in checking for inaccuracies. Their chief advantage to the writer of local history, however, lies in the biographies of early residents of the county which these volumes almost invariably contain in conjunction with the history itself. It is here that the student is able to find the family names which are connected with the early history of his community, and it is only when one has such names that it is possible to start the long and tedious search for many of the personal sources.

To find the printed sources, obviously the student should visit a library. There it would be well to examine first of all a general history of the state, so that the student might get a background against which to paint the picture of his own community. The proceedings of the general assembly of the state could be examined to good advantage. If the particular locality which is being studied has at any time sent one of its own residents as a representative to the legislature, the student should by all means follow closely the stand taken by him on public questions, as his ideas would doubtless correspond to the ideas of the majority of the people from his community. If writing in certain areas of the state, the Military Bounty reports should be examined and, if dealing with a war period, the student should not overlook the Adjutant-General's reports on our nation's wars. The census reports, those comprehensive statistics compiled periodically by our government, should afford facts and figures not only on the growth of population, but for social and economic history as well. Travel accounts, biographies, and all such kinds of material are available from the printed sources in any good library, and many others will be encountered by the local historian as his work progresses.

For unprinted public sources, it would not only be interesting but absolutely essential for the local historian to pay a visit to his county courthouse. There he might first go to the office of the recorder where will be found on file the plats of the community in question. In connection with these might also be used the plats to be found in the office of the county surveyor, were one interested in checking as to how heavily forested the land was originally, what land was prairie land, where the settlement was made in relationship to forest and prairie, or where the first paths and roads were laid out.

At the courthouse can also be found old wills which have been placed on file. By using the names which have been found to be connected with the history of the locality, it is frequently possible to make use of the index and to locate old wills of early settlers of the community. The value of such documents does not appear on the surface, but these old wills may throw more light on social customs than almost any other available source. Many of them list the entire household equipment from the walnut four-poster bed upstairs, to the grandfather's clock in the sitting room and the six pewter plates in the kitchen. After reading such a will one can almost picture the household and its furnishings, as well as the residents themselves with their respective likes and dislikes as indicated by the bequests of the will. It proves to be an extremely interesting and valuable source in constructing social history, and is one which has been too often neglected or overlooked.

Many counties also have an index to the records of court proceedings which are on file at the courthouse. By expending no little time and effort, and again by use of family names, it is not at all improbable that the local historian may locate some court cases which pertain to the community which he is studying. Frequently, information regarding certain periods of social or political development may be gathered from such a source.

It is often worth-while for the student to endeavor to locate and examine the abstracts to the land on which his community is situated, as interesting and important facts may sometimes be learned from documents of that nature. For example, when studying the abstracts to a portion of the land of a central Illinois village, a student stumbled upon the fact that originally a town had been platted one-half mile south of the site of the present village. It was apparently laid out purely for the purposes of speculation. Sale of the lots waxed strong for a period of about eighteen months, some of the speculators realizing as much as $1,500 to $2,000 in two months' time from the sale thereof. The larger portion of the lots was sold to individuals in New York, Pennsylvania, Missouri or Kentucky, only a few going to actual residents of Illinois. So far as the records would show, no buildings were ever erected in the village; it was a "phantom" town existing only on paper in the office of the county recorder. Yet at one time a prospectus was printed which showed boats loading and unloading goods at the wharves of a flourishing city on the Tiber River—the Tiber River being a very small creek, not at all suited for the purposes of navigation! It is when the local historian stumbles upon facts such as these that the generalizations of most histories regarding the period of land speculation in the West become much more real and vital.

There should also be available to the historian of most localities a type of source which would pertain solely to that particular community. For example, if writing the history of a small town, one should have access to the village records and ordinances. For establishing specific facts and dates such sources are priceless, and they also make valuable contributions to social and economic history. When the student reads the ordinances

against dueling, ordinances closing the local saloon at 10:00
P. M., or ordinances forbidding the too rapid trotting of horses
through the streets, he can picture a day far different socially
from his own. The records of the tax levies and the lists of
delinquent taxes may be interpreted to some advantage for
economic history. There, too, it is possible to watch the coming
of modern improvements to the village. In the minutes will
be found the records of the bond issues to the various railroads
which at one time or another proposed to run through the village,
as well as the granting of charters to the first electric light and
telephone companies.

Another purely local source would be the minutes of the
various organizations which have had members in the town. It
is not at all unusual to find that such groups as the Grand Army
of the Republic, the Modern Woodmen of America or the
Knights of Pythias have kept a record of their proceedings
from the time of their organization. The minutes of the Protes-
tant churches may also be open for inspection. Such sources
give added details, all of which go to complete the picture of
the town's development.

The last to be mentioned, yet doubtless the most important,
and the source from which the larger portion of the material for
a local history will be taken, is the newspaper. Newspapers
vary considerably in their value as historical material and the
student will learn—perhaps to his sorrow—that what a newspaper
prints as news is no more reliable than the source from which
it comes. Nevertheless, it is from such a source that the framework of a local history can best be erected, the other materials
being used to fill in the framework and to bolster it up at certain
essential points. Practically every word printed in the local newspaper will prove of value to the student, if properly studied, criticized, and interpreted. The editorials, the voting returns, the
social items, market reports, and even the advertisements themselves will yield invaluable information.

Obviously, in writing local history, national events and movements cannot be entirely ignored. The effect which such events and movements have had upon the persons of the community can clearly be traced through the columns of the local newspaper. The ordinary general history would list the results of the Civil War in the North as being rising taxes, booming prices, increased demand for farm machinery, etc., and would overlook entirely the personal element; but when the scope of the study is closely limited to one small area it is possible to see how the lives of individuals themselves were affected. The student sees the sorrowing of some, the anxious waiting for news from the front, the little patriotic services of those who knitted, rolled bandages, or planted war gardens. He discovers to his surprise that what he had always thought of as a national event was simply a part of the everyday lives of the people in the community. From this perspective he will see movements of great historical moment gradually taking place entirely outside the realization of the individuals among whom they are happening. Perhaps the local historian will thus be better able to comprehend the issues and movements of his own time and to acquire a more accurate historical sense, and so to be a more constructive citizen of a rapidly changing democracy.

The writer of local history must be extremely careful not to become so interested in the personalities with whom he becomes well-acquainted as his work progresses that he will cease to write history and write only a series of biographical sketches. Names must be used only when history is being made—but the student will find history always in the making in his community, small though it may be. It is from the local newspapers that one will often see the small beginnings of movements which have later become sectional demands or even national issues. How better could one approach the true inception of the Grange movement than by tracing the agitation of the farmers in some Illinois community through the columns of the local newspaper? There can be found the reports of their local meetings, the articles which they submitted to the paper, the reaction of the editor to their ideas; and there, too, can be traced their gradual alignment with other county groups, and so on to merge with the larger sectional movement which is so well-known. It was not the entire group of farmers in a whole section who arose as if one man and voiced the demands which finally came to be the rallying point of a large political group with its hundreds of thousands of members. On the contrary, it was a small group of farmers in a small locality who came together to discuss their common problems. There, in that small meeting, the program of the Grange movement was first voiced. Doubtless many small groups of farmers made the same demands at approximately the same time, but it is when we can almost see the minds of those farmers working, as we read of their local activities, that we can reach the true beginning of the movement. All big movements have small beginnings, and one of the chief values of the study of local history is in searching out the origin of the issues which were later to loom so large on the national horizon.

From the sources mentioned above, it should be apparent that vast quantities and many varieties of material are available to the student interested in local history. It should also be increasingly obvious that strictly limiting the scope of one's study has many valuable results. The advantage to many students in being able to work with original sources which lie all around him, and the consequent saving of time and expense, is one which should not be overlooked.

To the question, "Has anything of value been accomplished when a local history has been completed?" the answer should unhesitatingly be "Yes"—providing, of course, that the work has been well and carefully done. There could be no better history of Illinois than a composite history of all the communities which make up the state and the individuals who have made up the communities. True history rests not upon nations or states, but upon individuals, and the local historian, by so limiting his study, is enabled to probe deep into the lives of individuals and hence to approach more nearly the production of an ideal history.

CONGREGATIONALISTS AND PRESBYTERIANS IN THE EARLY HISTORY OF THE GALESBURG CHURCHES

By HERMANN RICHARD MUELDER

It is hard to think of any phase of American life during the first half of the nineteenth century which is more complicated than the relations of the Congregationalists and the Presbyterians. Investigation of the intricacies of those relations, however, amply repays research. It reveals not merely the details of sectarian history, not only the devious distinctions of a forgotten theology, but also the process by which Puritan traditions were transferred to the physically and socially hostile frontier. In the issues of church government that were aggravated by the federation of these two denominations it is possible to discern that spirit of Jacksonian Democracy which not only disturbed civil institutions but troubled, as well, each of the larger sects. Furthermore, the connections between these Puritan bodies affected the religious sectionalism that eventually divided North and South.

Attention to local church history is particularly necessary in studying this problem. Congregationalism, which has never enjoyed the well-integrated national system developed by most of the other denominations, was, in the West, submerged in institutions which it shared with the more highly organized and aggressive Presbyterians, until the fourth decade of the nineteenth century. Its emergence as a distinct denomination, therefore, depended to a large extent on the action of the individual churches. Many churches which had been organized as Presbyterian during the thirties had become Congregational by the time of the Civil War.[1]   One of them was the church established by the Galesburg colony in 1837.

Study of the relations of the two sects in the Galesburg church is especially worth-while because its founders had in the East been intimately associated with such reformers as Charles Grandison Finney and Theodore Dwight Weld,[2] and in the West its founders at once became important figures in the early stage of the abolitionist movement.[3]   Moreover, the pastors of the church and the presidents of Knox College, with which the church was connected, were very prominent clergymen in the two denominations; four of them were moderators of the New School Presbyterian Synod of Peoria, which comprised all northern Illinois, in the seventeen years of its history before the Civil War.[4]

Before analyzing the history of the Galesburg church, it is necessary to describe briefly the connections which existed at large between the Presbyterians and Congregationalists at the time it was founded.   Since the opening of the century, what amounted to a religious federation had existed between the two sects.   Until the thirties, the Presbyterian General Assembly and the Congregational associations of New England exchanged "corresponding delegates," who were not only allowed to sit and deliberate in the bodies to which they were admitted, but were also allowed to vote.   Similar arrangements were also made

[1] G. S. F. Savage, "Reminiscences of Early Congregational Ministers and Churches in the Fox River Valley," *Illinois Society of Church History, Congregational, Historical Statement and Papers,* I:67; J. E. Roy, "History of Congregationalism in Illinois," *ibid.,* 24; Alonzo M. Swan, *Canton, its Pioneers and History, a Contribution to the History of Fulton County* (Canton, 1871), 38; *Prairie Mayflower* (Mendon, Illinois), Nov. 17, 1883; *History of the Presbytery of Peoria and its Churches, from 1828 to 1888, by a Committee of the Presbytery* (Peoria, 1888), 27.

[2] Photostatic copies of letters from George Washington Gale to Finney (in the collection of Oberlin College); *Letters of Theodore Dwight Weld, Angelina Grimké Weld and Sarah Grimké, 1822-1844,* edited by Gilbert H. Barnes and Dwight L. Dumond (New York, [1934]), *passim.*

[3] See *post,* 61-65.

[4] Records of the Peoria Synod (MS), *passim.*

between other Congregational associations and some of the Presbyterian synods. One of the results of such close communication was the formation of common denominational agencies for missions and education. Thus, the benevolent activities of both sects were merged in the following bodies: the American Board of Commissioners for Foreign Missions; the American Home Missionary Society; and the American Education Society. Moreover, after 1801, there was in effect between the two denominations an important ecclesiastical treaty, the Plan of Union. The purpose of this agreement was to facilitate the establishment of Presbyterian and Congregational churches in the West by avoiding wasteful duplications and by compromising differences in church government. According to the Plan of Union, Presbyterian ministers could serve Congregational churches, or Congregational ministers could serve Presbyterian churches, yet both parties to such an arrangement still retained their denominational affiliations with all the rights and privileges that were involved. Churches with a dual polity might also be organized, connected with presbyteries and synods on the one hand and with Congregational associations on the other. In some instances, Congregationalists were even sent as delegates to the Presbyterian General Assembly.

Nowhere was the connection between the two denominations more complicated than it was in New York, for there a supplementary Plan of Union in 1808 had resulted in the absorption by the Presbyterian tribunals of churches that remained Congregational in all but name.[5] The Galesburg colony was projected in this region. The leader of that colony, George Washington Gale, epitomized the confusion of the two sects. While still a young man he was delegate to a presbytery mostly

---

[5] *Minutes of the General Assembly of the Presbyterian Church, 1808*, p. 404; "The Records of the Middle Association of Congregational Churches of the State of New York," *Journal of the Presbyterian Historical Society*, XI:20-38, 49-68 (1921-1923); P. H. Fowler, *History of Presbyterianism Within the Bounds of the Synod of New York* (Utica, 1877), 62-63; S. J. Baird, *History of the New School and of the Question Involved in the Disruption of the Presbyterian Church in 1838* (Philadelphia, 1868), 160-65.

composed of Congregational churches. His ministerial labors, as a missionary on the New York frontier, were among what he termed members of the "Presbyterian, or rather the Congregational Church." He was ordained by a presbytery containing pastors of Congregational churches which still retained connections with Congregational associations, and his first regular pastorate was of the same description. He did persuade it to change its polity to the Presbyterian form, yet when he wanted a young man in his charge to be licensed to preach, he took him not to a presbytery but to a Congregational association, because the latter would not be restricted in its action regarding a candidate short on formal education, by a rather rigid denominational government. In this association Gale sat as a "corresponding member."[6]

The labels of the two sects were quite independable, and certainly were not mutually exclusive. The word Presbyterian became especially ambiguous.[7] The first church in Galesburg, for example, had, by 1857, deliberately severed its Presbyterian ties and formally dropped the word Presbyterian from its church name; yet its property was held until 1869 by the "Society of the Presbyterian Church."[8]

The alliance between the two denominations contributed much to their western expansion. Without their Presbyterian connections the Congregationalists were entirely regional in their organization, but in union with Presbyterians they enjoyed the aid of a well-organized and centrally directed ecclesiastical machine as well as the assistance of the national mission and educational enterprises which were operated in conjunction with the Presbyterians. The latter, on the other hand, profited by the consequent relaxation of their governmental system, the rigidity of which had aggravated the first unfortunate experiences of Presbyterians on the middle western frontier. The

[6] George Washington Gale, Autobiography (MS).
[7] *Report on Knox College, Presented to the General Association of Illinois,* May 24, 1861 (Quincy, 1861 [?]), 31.
[8] Minutes of the Society of the First Presbyterian Church in Galesburg (MS).

two schisms, in Kentucky and in the Cumberland Valley, during the decade of the Great Revival, were in large part due to the failure of the Presbyterian polity to adjust itself to the frontier.[9]

Had willingness to coöperate continued, perhaps the complicated connections between the two sects might have been simplified by complete coalescence. But the spirit of compromise which had generally characterized the first thirty years of the century gave way during the next three decades to a disposition for controversy. The time had not yet come when peculiarities of polity were regarded with indifference, and during the era of Jacksonian Democracy, church governments were especially subjected to the critical forces of democracy.[10] There were still those with sincere Congregational convictions who would not overlook the fact that Presbyterianism, though representative in its government, was not democratic; who objected that its lay officers had life terms; who complained that members of churches had only an indirect voice in the conduct of their affairs, legislative or judicial; and who disliked the powerful central tribunals of Presbyterianism. Presbyterians, on the contrary, feared the principle of independency practiced by their critics. They declared that it tended to popular government by mobs, was likely to be anarchical in large bodies, lacked means to discipline radicalism or heresy, and did not guarantee rights of individuals and minorities.[11]

After about 1820, Presbyterianism contained two contending parties, Old School and New School, differing somewhat over nice distinctions of Calvinistic theology, but more often over issues on polity. The chief of these last, due to the close connection with Congregationalism, was the intrusion of certain

[9] Hermann R. Muelder, "Jacksonian Democracy in Church Organization" (doctoral dissertation, University of Minnesota, 1933).

[10] Ibid.

[11] Minutes of the General Assembly, 1837, p. 460; Lew Cheeseman, Difference Between Old and New School Presbyterians (Rochester, N. Y., 1848), 208; G. N. Judd, History of the Division of the Presbyterian Church (New York, 1852), passim; S. Sawyer, Presbyterianism Proved by Revelation, Providence and Reason (Knoxville, 1852), 15, 25, 30; George Duffield, American Presbyterianism (Philadelphia, 1854), 20.

democratic and popular practices contrary to the Presbyterian constitution. The Old School feared that the power of the denomination to supervise and discipline its communicants was being weakened by decentralized or virtually independent units that had been formed within the sect. In short, they alleged that their denomination was being congregationalized, and they wished, therefore, to repudiate the Plan of Union and to desert the mission and educational agencies that had been shared with Congregationalists. The New School, on the other side, tolerated some of the changes that the polity was undergoing, and insisted on maintaining the alliance with the other sect.[12]

In 1837, the year that the Galesburg church was established, the Old School, having a majority of the General Assembly, pruned away certain presbyteries and synods in New York and the Western Reserve which were especially tainted with Congregationalism. This action led, in 1838, to the scission of the denomination and the formation of two separate denominations, one Old School, the other New School. The recently published Weld letters furnish further evidence that the slavery question, while it certainly did not cause, did aggravate the schism. Lyman Beecher expressed the opinion that the South was neutral in the controversy until the antislavery activities of New School partisans alarmed that region, and that it then cast its strength with the Old School. Significantly, the tribunals of New York and the Western Reserve, which were expelled on grounds of polity in 1837, were also those in which the most vigorous abolitionism prevailed.[13]

The independent New School continued the connections with Congregationalism. Furthermore, it decentralized its own organization by taking away the judicial powers of the General Assembly and by having it meet triennially instead of annually as had been the rule before. By 1842, a New School Presbyterian could declare that the modifications of the constitution had taken

---

[12] Muelder, "Jacksonian Democracy."
[13] *Autobiography, Correspondence, etc. of Lyman Beecher*, edited by Charles Beecher (New York, 1865), II: 427-29, 514.

from Presbyterianism "some of the prominent objections which were urged against it, and will enable the Presbyterians and Congregationalists to act more efficiently together than they ever could before."[14]

At this very time a movement was under way in Illinois to make the confederation of New School Presbyterians and Congregationalists even closer. In 1842 the New School Synod of Illinois urged a special Plan of Union with the Congregational Association of Illinois.[15] The Peoria Synod, set off from the Illinois Synod in 1843 to comprise Northern Illinois, continued the cordial relations with the other denomination. Dual membership of ministers in presbyteries and Congregational associations was specifically approved.[16] When a religious paper was proposed it was suggested that it should assume "grounds common to orthodox Congregationalists and Presbyterians."[17] In 1848, it was resolved to unite in a friendly correspondence with the Congregationalists and to send three delegates to the General Association of Illinois, George Washington Gale being appointed to the first delegation.[18]

In 1846, the presbytery of the Peoria Synod, to which the Galesburg church belonged, adopted a resolution revealing a strong feeling for the closest possible relations with Congregationalists:

> The Presbytery of Knox, having had under consideration the importance of a greater measure of union between the Presbyterian and Congregational churches, feel called upon to express their conviction that the cause of religion would be greatly promoted by a greater degree of unity among those denominations. While we are not prepared to say that the time has come in which a formal union may be effected, yet we hope that, by frequent interchange of labors, by more frequent attendance upon each other's ecclesiastical meetings, and by cooperation in all good and holy efforts to promote the cause of religion, a greater measure of real union and of brotherly love may be attained; and the time be

---

[14] *New York Evangelist*, I: no. 18 (May 5, 1842).
[15] *Ibid.*, no. 3 (Jan. 20, 1842).
[16] Records of the Peoria Synod, Oct. 12, 1844.
[17] *Ibid.*
[18] *Ibid.*, June 10, 1848.

hastened when a union in form as well as in substance may be consummated.[19]

When this resolution was adopted, forces were already forming, however, which strained the relations of the two sects. How cordial coöperation eventually gave way to conflict may be studied through analysis of what happened in the Galesburg church. It will help clarify the following discussion if the chief incidents in the history of that church are first briefly sketched.

It was organized in 1837, but almost immediately had to alter its ecclesiastical connections because of the schism of the Presbyterian denomination in 1838. In 1845 it adopted a compromise on church government. That same year, after the compromise, the Rev. Jonathan Blanchard came as president of Knox College, and from that time on the relations of the two denominations, not only in Galesburg but throughout the state, were influenced by his activities. In 1851 a large party left the Galesburg First Church to form a congregation of their own with a purely Presbyterian polity. Four years later another group left the mother church to form a purely Congregational organization. Within a few months of the last event the First Church itself severed the Presbyterian connections which it had maintained since its founding, retaining only the Congregational affiliations which it had assumed at the time of the compromise of 1845. Each of these developments will now be analyzed in greater detail.

The first church in Galesburg, as established in the spring of 1837, was wholly Presbyterian in polity. Most of the projectors of the colony who originally settled the village, founded Knox College, and organized the church were Presbyterians, but in the highly modified sense that they belonged to the New School— which meant that they desired alliance with Congregationalists and were not sticklers on the details of Presbyterian government. Though George Washington Gale used his influence against those who preferred the Congregational mode, he declared that he himself cared little for anything in the Presbyterian system above the

[19] *History of the Presbytery of Peoria*, 61.

presbyteries. He argued that the church had better agree to the name Presbyterian because it was "in better odor" in the East and would help bring aid to the college.[20] The Congregationalists were persuaded that the preference of the other sect should be heeded because it had taken the lead in forming the colony.[21] Finally, it was unanimously resolved that it was "expedient" to organize "fully" as Presbyterian.[22]

Almost at once the denominational split of 1838 was upon them. The Galesburg church sided with the New School, left the Old School Schuyler Presbytery[23] under which it had been organized, and joined the New School Presbytery of Knox which was constituted by order of the New School Synod of Illinois, in a meeting at Galesburg on November 7, 1838.[24]

At the beginning the church was agreed on an antislavery attitude. As soon as the colony was settled, some of its leaders, including Gale, became prominent figures in the Illinois Antislavery Society, which was organized the same year as the church.[25] Antislavery principles were a condition of membership in that congregation.[26] It is impossible to determine the degree to which their New School partisanship was provoked by simple ecclesiastical liberalism, and how much of it was

[20] *Rights of Congregationalists in Knox College: Being the Report of a Committee of Investigation, of the General Association of Illinois; with an Appendix* (Chicago, 1859), 66.

[21] H. E. Hitchcock to George Churchill, Feb. 11, 1887, *Semi-Centennial of the First Church* (Galesburg, 1887), 132.

[22] Records of the First Church (transcript of MS), Book A, pp. 3-4.

[23] George Washington Gale, *Articles of Faith and Covenant of the Presbyterian Church in Galesburg . . . to Which is Appended a Sketch of the History of the Church* (Galesburg, 1849), 36.

[24] *History of the Presbytery of Peoria*, 26, 33; *Peoria Register and Northwestern Gazetteer*, Oct. 27, Nov. 17, 1838.

[25] Carrie P. Kofoid, "Puritan Influences in the Formative Years of Illinois History," *Transactions of the Illinois State Historical Society for the Year 1905* (Springfield, 1906), 303-307; *Peoria Register and Northwestern Gazetteer*, July 17, 1840; June 17, 1842; Norman Wright Harris, *The History of Negro Servitude in Illinois and of the Slavery Agitation in that State, 1719-1864* (Chicago, 1904), 146; Verna Cooley, "Illinois and the Underground Railroad to Canada," *Transactions of the Illinois State Historical Society for the Year 1917* (Springfield, 1917), 87.

[26] *Galesburg Republican-Register*, March 5, 1887, p. 3; Records of the First Church, Book A, p. 11; *ibid.*, Book B, pp. 75-76, 126.

prompted by their antislavery sentiments, but a letter received by Gale from the Rev. John Frost throws some light on the problem. Frost had been, with Gale, the co-founder of Oneida Manual Labor Institute, the school attended by Theodore Dwight Weld and many of the other "Lane Rebels" before they went to Cincinnati. Frost, referring in this letter to the separation of the New School from the Old School which was already under way, expressed his joy at the prospect that the liberated New School could now become a tremendous antislavery influence. It is evident that he revealed this feeling to one whom he regarded as a sympathetic correspondent.[27] It is also significant that when the Knox Presbytery was instituted at Galesburg on November 7, 1838, the fact that the day was the first anniversary of Lovejoy's death was noted, and the event commemorated with strong antislavery resolutions, including a declaration that the denomination ought to "take speedy and decisive measures to purify itself from this long continued and enormous evil."[28]

Nothing more can be uncovered concerning the denominational relations of the local church until the middle forties. Then dissension attended the long delayed completion of the church building.[29] The Congregationalists asserted that in view of their large representation in the church, the polity should be modified somewhat in their favor. What brought the issue to a head is not clear. For a few months in 1844 a Congregational minister had served as the pastor, and in 1845 another clergyman of the same sect, Lucius H. Parker, became the minister.[30] Such pastoral arrangements were, however, quite common in New School Presbyterian churches. Whether Parker stimulated the discontent, or merely represented it, cannot be determined, but he did identify himself with the discontented element as over

---

[27] J. Frost to G. W. Gale, June 29, 1837, *Report on Knox College, Presented to the General Association of Illinois*, May 24, 1861, 47.

[28] *Peoria Register and Northwestern Gazetteer*, Feb. 2, 1839.

[29] *Semi-Centennial of the First Church*, 134; A. L. Bergen to J. P. Williston, July 16, 1845, *Report on Knox College*, 38.

[30] Gale, *Articles of Faith and ... History of the Church*, 19.

against the Presbyterians led by Gale.[31] Finally a compromise was arranged along the lines suggested by the Plan of Union of 1801 for mixed churches. The internal organization became both Congregational and Presbyterian, and dual denominational connections were established.[32]

It is possible, though not at all capable of proof, that the basic issue of church polity may have been complicated in this compromise of 1845 by the slavery question. The Reverend Mr. Parker was one of the "Lane Rebels" and a strong abolitionist. His father-in-law, William Holyoke, was the most prominent antislavery man in the community at that time and active in the Liberty Party. Perhaps the Congregational predilections of these men, and others like them, may have been strengthened by the action of the Congregationalist General Convention of Illinois, which in 1844 had made antislavery principles a condition of membership.[33] Such rather ruthless action the New School synods of Illinois, however antislavery their attitude, were not able to take without previous legislation by the General Assembly.

Gale seems to have expected the church to operate peacefully under the compromise of 1845.[34] Certainly if there had been any great abhorrence of Congregational influences, Gale would not have urged the coming of the Rev. Jonathan Blanchard as president of Knox College. The latter, though pastor of a Presbyterian church in Cincinnati, had expressed his intention of joining a Congregational church if he came to Illinois.[35] In fact, Gale expected the new president to use his influence with Congregationalists in the East for the sake of the college, and

[31] J. W. Bailey, *Knox College, by Whom Founded and Endowed* (Chicago, 1860), 56; J. Blanchard to G. W. Gale, Dec. 11, 1848, *Report on Knox College*, 49.
[32] Records of the First Church, Book B, pp. 59-61.
[33] T. C. Pease, *The Frontier State 1818-1848* (*Centennial History of Illinois*, II, Springfield, 1918), 420.
[34] G. W. Gale, *A Brief History of Knox College, Situated in Galesburgh, Knox County, Illinois with Sketches of the First Settlement of the Town* (Cincinnati, 1845), 4, 14; Gale, *Articles of Faith and . . . History of the Church*, 20.
[35] Bailey, *Knox College*, 52-54; *Galesburg Free Democrat* (weekly), IV: no. 33 (Aug. 7, 1857).

hoped he would be able to "unite the Presbyterians and Congregationalists in this part of the state."[36]

Blanchard no doubt proved to be more thoroughly Congregationalist than was anticipated. It was a matter of conviction with him that the day was at hand when there would be no more "crushing down anarchy with the ice-bags of human governments, and securing order by the frost work of law." He declared that "henceforth government must wax weaker and weaker, and truth stronger and stronger."[37] He preferred the weaker government of the Congregationalists to the firm government of Presbyterianism with its "principles of ecclesiastical power for the mastery of individual liberty in our churches."[38] Aside from its form of government, Blanchard approved of Congregationalism because of the more decisive stand which it had taken against slavery.[39]

In Galesburg he soon espoused the cause of Congregationalism so vigorously that strained relations between himself and Gale enlarged into a partisan quarrel including college and community. Basically, as Blanchard himself realized, the difficulty arose from Gale's conviction that his opponent was "promoting Congregationalism to the detriment of Presbyterianism," but the antagonism on that score was aggravated by Blanchard's antislavery activities, which went so far as serving on the Free Soil ticket in 1848 as presidential elector.[40]

Blanchard also engaged in a number of agitations, beyond the Galesburg scene, that so strained the relations of the two denominations throughout the state as to excite attention even

---

[36] Gale to Blanchard, June 5, 1845, *Report on Knox College*, 36; Hiram H. Kellogg to Blanchard, Aug. 22, 1846, *ibid.*, 33; Gale to Blanchard, Aug. 12, 1846, *ibid.*, 41–42; Bailey, *Knox College*, 69.

[37] Blanchard, "A Perfect State of Society," *Knoxiana*, IV: no. 5 (March, 1855).

[38] Jonathan Blanchard to Salmon P. Chase, June 30, 1849 (MS, Library of Congress). Other references on his opinion of Presbyterianism: Blanchard, "Christ Purifying his Temple," *Sermons and Addresses* (Chicago, 1892); *Report on Knox College*, 43–44.

[39] *A Debate on Slavery . . . October, 1845, in the City of Cincinnati, Between Rev. J. Blanchard . . . and N. L. Rice* (Cincinnati, 1846), 62, 76, 422–24.

[40] Blanchard to Chase, June 30, 1849 (MS, Library of Congress).

in the East.[41] Shortly before he came to Galesburg, he had affirmed the proposition that slavery was a sin; this was in a debate with an Old School Presbyterian which was later published and gave him national notoriety.[42] After he came to Galesburg he agitated vehemently for the principle that those guilty of the sin of slavery must be cut off from truly Christian churches. He earned nationwide prominence by leading the fight, in 1847, at the annual meeting of the American Board of Commissioners for Foreign Missions, to get that body to refuse to admit slaveholders into the mission churches.[43] He was very active in forwarding a national religious movement which had as a distinguishing characteristic the disfellowshiping of slaveholders, and in 1851 was elected president of the National Christian Antislavery Convention which was held in Chicago.[44]

In 1850 discontent manifested itself, among the more radical New School Presbyterians in the state, over the continued connection of their denomination with slavery, and certain clergymen of that following met with Congregationalists in a state convention to consider union. Such action, it was intended, would "deliver those of us who are Presbyterians from our ecclesiastical connection with slaveholders, through the General Assembly, and enable us to withdraw Christian fellowship from them."[45] To the fore in the endorsement of this convention were Blanchard and the Rev. Flavel Bascom, who since 1845 had been a trustee of Knox College and since January, 1850, the pastor of the Galesburg church.

Such ruthless pursuit of antislavery principles was sure to injure denominational coöperation, for the slavery problem was much simpler as an ecclesiastical matter for the Congregationalists than for their New School brothers. The former had no central tribunal, like the New School General Assembly, which could

---

[41] Separate Session Records of First Church (transcript of MS), 7-9.
[42] This is the debate referred to, *ante*, n. 39, p. 64.
[43] A. C. Cole, *The Era of the Civil War 1848-1870* (*Centennial History of Illinois*, III, Springfield, 1919), 222.
[44] *Ibid.*, 223-24.
[45] *Ibid.*, 223.

be expected to enforce the scruples of one section upon another. Furthermore, there were virtually no Congregationalists south of the Mason-Dixon line. The New School did have a considerable southern membership and it had a judiciary to coerce their communicants. Placing fellowship on an antislavery basis in their case required expulsion of several thousand Christians with whom they had no difference other than that over slavery. In brief, excluding slaveholders had no effect on the Congregational organization; to the New School it meant a division of their denomination.[46]

How the questions of church polity and slavery became entangled is clearly described by a report of the American and Foreign Anti-Slavery Society which was fostering the establishment of benevolent agencies which had no slaveholding connections, and which cited an address on that need by President Blanchard. According to the report, the problems of church organization and abolitionism were thus combined:

> Had the Northern, or New School division, even then [at the time of the separation from the Old School in 1838] assumed a strong, decided, and firm antislavery position, it might have maintained its ground and become strong. But it failed to do this.
>
> The peculiar machinery of the Presbyterian polity, instead of being wielded against the sin of slavery, was more commonly used to cripple and harass the opposers of slavery in the churches. By little and little, a disgust was created against the polity thus wielded. In large and important sections, (as in Central and Western New York, in Northern Ohio, and in Michigan,) a gradual abandonment of Presbyterianism for Congregationalism has been the effect, till, by the action of the Convention at Albany, new forms of ecclesiastical organization and activity, displacing to a great extent the old, have been witnessed.[47]

Examination of the records of the Peoria Synod shows clearly that on the New School side, so far as that body was concerned,

---

[46] History of the Presbytery of Peoria, 57.
[47] Thirteenth Annual Report of the American and Foreign Anti-Slavery Society, (1852), p. 87.

the antislavery sentiment was less aggressive, and the concern for integrity of organization more apparent in the fifties than it had been earlier.[48]   It is certainly true that in the case of George Washington Gale his antislavery sentiments moderated and at the same time his views on church polity became less broad.   The man who in 1837 had professed indifference to most of the Presbyterian system was in 1850 publishing his conviction that the time for being lax about matters of denominational government was past, and that it would be better if New School Presbyterians stayed close to their peculiar polity and deviated neither to left nor right.[49]   He also changed on slavery, the alteration being noted by one of the early benefactors of Knox College whose contributions to that institution had been attracted by its antislavery stand.[50]   In 1848 Gale had been a member of the committee of the Peoria Synod which brought in resolutions to the effect that it wished to take such action as would clear it "of all participation in the sin and guilt of slavery," and therefore asked the General Assembly to use all of its power to relieve the denomination from the just imputation of sustaining any such relation to the practice of holding slaves as "can fairly be regarded as implying approbation of it."[51]   But in 1853 he was chairman of the committee which brought in what was decidedly the weakest resolution on slavery that the synod ever adopted.[52] The petition of 1848, if fulfilled, might have split the church; that of 1853 was merely an expression of strong disapproval.

Like all questions of motive, the problem of what caused the change in Gale is not demonstrable of proof.   It may have been in part his coming to old age; it may have been partly the the influence of his third wife, whom he married in 1847.   She was an Old School Presbyterian before her marriage, and her

<hr />

[48] Records of the Peoria Synod, June, 1849, p. 79; Oct., 1851, p. 127; Oct., 1852, pp. 136, 141; Oct., 1853, pp. 161-62, 173.
[49] *Galesburg News Letter*, Oct. 10, 1850, p. 42.
[50] J. P. Williston to Southwick Davis, July 27, 1857, *Galesburg Free Democrat* (daily), Aug. 6, 1857.
[51] Records of the Peoria Synod, June 10, 1848.
[52] *Ibid.*, Oct., 1853, pp. 150, 157.

slavery opinions were such that she was admitted into the Galesburg church only after a special committee headed by Blanchard had investigated her case.[53] Moreover, about 1850, Gale became interested in the project of a Presbyterian theological seminary which he hoped to have connected with Knox College. Far from being antislavery, the seminary plan anticipated representation of certain southern presbyteries on its board.[54]

During 1849 and 1850 a definite cleavage appeared, both in the college and church, over the alleged anti-Presbyterian activities of Blanchard. The quarrel in the college was compromised,[55] but an attempt at reconciliation between Gale and his opponent was only partly successful, and the difficulties in the church continued. Two of the deacons refused to sign a minute denying Blanchard's alleged antagonism to Presbyterianism.[56] Another member was tried by the church session (the Presbyterian unit in the church) for certain strong charges he had made against Blanchard, and was convicted and suspended. The session refused, however, to pass on the truth of what had been said against Blanchard; and the presbytery, on the ground that it should have taken such evidence, changed the suspension to a rebuke.[57]

By that time a separation was under way within the church. In May, 1851, certain members of the church asked for a dismissal to organize a church of their own.[58] The request was granted and a purely Presbyterian church, called the Second Presbyterian Church, was established.[59]

After the departure of this group the mother church became even more Congregational. Furthermore, a boom of the town, attending the coming of the railroad, caused it to become over-

---

[53] Records of the First Church, Book B, pp. 75-76.
[54] *Rights of Congregationalists in Knox College*, 27, 81.
[55] *Galesburg Free Democrat* (weekly), Sept. 23, 30, Oct. 14, 1857.
[56] Separate Session Records of the First Church, 17.
[57] *Ibid.*, 33-41, 64.
[58] *Ibid.*, 47.
[59] Bailey, *Knox College*, 58.

crowded.[60] In 1855, another daughter church moved out of it because of this growth and organized as purely Congregational. The separation in this case was wholly amicable, and the new church, headed by a member of the famous Beecher family, maintained the most cordial relations with the original church.[61]

By the time that this second daughter church—the First Congregational Church as it was called—had been formed out of the original church, the latter was also in the process of becoming wholly Congregational. The causing factor in this instance was clearly slavery. Since shortly after the departure of the more Presbyterian faction in 1851, the mother church had been urging the Knox Presbytery to make its continued connection with the General Assembly depend upon that tribunal's repudiation of slavery.[62] This the presbytery was slow in doing. Finally, in 1855, the session of the First Church decided to stop sending delegates to the presbytery while it was in union "with a General Assembly in which slave holders are in fellowship."[63] On April 11, 1856, the Knox Presbytery erased the First Church from its rolls. The church thus ceased its dual denominational connections, retaining only the Congregational relations, and dropping the name Presbyterian from its title.[64]

Significantly, in 1856, the Knox Presbytery finally sent what amounted to a hint that it might not retain its connections with the General Assembly if it did not cut off slaveholders. The author of the memorial was the pastor of the Second Presbyterian Church which had left the mother church in 1851. The reasons set forth in the memorial for the need of such action read throughout like a list of the troubles that had afflicted New School Presbyterianism in Galesburg.[65]

---

[60] *Galesburg Free Democrat* (weekly), Feb. 1, 15, Apr. 19, June 21, 1855; *Galesburg Plain Dealer*, Nov. 12, 1880.
[61] *Semi-Centennial of the First Church*, 91; Records of the First Church, Book B, pp. 160, 169.
[62] Records of the First Church, Book B, pp. 138-39, 142-43, 145-46.
[63] Separate Session Records of the First Church, 77-78.
[64] *History of the Presbytery of Peoria*, 31.
[65] *Ibid.*, 57-58.

The final and bitterest phase of the contention between the sects broke out in Knox College in 1857. Here again, Blanchard and Gale were leaders of the factions, and here again they were divided on denominational lines which were made the more sharp by the slavery issue.[66] The paper weapons manufactured for this war[67] were still being published when more serious war on a broader front made this conflict much less significant, and it eventually became obsolete. After the Civil War, the strained relations of Congregationalists and Presbyterians, no longer perpetuated, soon became only bitter memories.

[66] Scrapbook of clippings and notes on the college controversy and other matters, compiled by Prof. George Churchill.
[67] *Rights of Congregationalists in Knox College; Report on Knox College;* Bailey, *Knox College.*

PHASES OF CHICAGO HISTORY

I

WRITING A HISTORY OF CHICAGO

By BESSIE LOUISE PIERCE

It is my purpose to outline very briefly the plan for the writing of a history of Chicago which has been going forward since the autumn of 1929. Other speakers will carry forward more specifically than I some of the aspects of research connected therewith. In the few statements which I shall make I shall therefore describe somewhat the background or history of the project which has been promoted by the University of Chicago Social Science Research Committee.

This Committee was organized in 1923 and received a grant of funds to plan and direct the social science research activities at the University. It laid out for itself a unique field for investigation in that it held that with the metropolis of Chicago at hand that area could provide an ideal scene of coöperative investigation. It was recognized that the metropolitan area offered opportunity for all social scientists to carry on researches in their special fields of endeavor, and that it also provided suitable subjects for investigation which could contribute to the whole pattern of social science. In this collaborative task the Committee felt that the historian played an important rôle. Besides dipping into sources which describe the backgrounds, the Committee believed the historian could cut across and synthesize the findings of all the other disciplines more specifically dealing with the contemporary scene and could demonstrate that the body of knowledge of all the social sciences is essentially the same. Because today the bulk of our population is shifting toward the great metropolitan centers, the importance of an understanding of the inner nature of cities becomes especially significant.

In the autumn of 1929, research on *A History of Chicago* was started. In order to define limits and to devise some workable scheme, it seemed desirable to set off, arbitrarily, chronological periods for the research activites to be carried on chiefly in the primary sources commonly used by the historian. Therefore, the following periods were established: 1673 to 1848, 1848 to 1871, 1871 to 1893, and 1893 to date. *The Beginning of a City*, which is represented in Volume I, recently published, covers the period from the early explorations of the French and the establishment of homes on the prairies by the first settlers down to the coming of the railroad. From 1848 to 1871, the period is representative of a growth of commercial life, until the fire laid low the city; this is the story which will be told in Volume II. The third period embraces the years 1871-1893, ending with the Columbian Exposition, which outwardly symbolized the attainment of an industrial competence. Since 1893, a fourth period shows the march toward leadership in all avenues of life.

It is only about forty years ago that Prof. Frederick Jackson Turner pointed out the significance of sections in the national life. Within the memory of all of us the expansion of cities has gone on with such rapidity that it now seems desirable to break sections into smaller units and set these in their national setting. Throughout our study, the history of Chicago has not been treated as an isolated local fact. Many factors in the development of the city are common to the growth of all urban communities. Where there are unique features these have not been overlooked. Biographies as such have played little part in the narrative although the leaders of community development have not been ignored. On the other hand, the part that the common man has played in the weaving of the fabric of community development receives much attention.

With these introductory remarks, I shall now ask three of the assistants who have been engaged in the search for material for the various volumes to present certain aspects of their study. Mr. Joe L. Norris who has assisted in the project since 1930 will discuss the land reform movement. Mr. Herbert Wiltsee will describe his researches on temperance and the humanitarian movement from 1841 to 1871, and Miss Dorothy Culp will set forth her conclusions regarding radical labor movements in what we have chosen to call our third period.

II

THE LAND REFORM MOVEMENT

By JOE L. NORRIS

The public land problem is an old one in the United States. No sooner had the national government come into possession of vast tracts of land than the question of their disposition arose. As it is not my purpose here to discuss the federal land policy, it will be sufficient to say that the system of surveying and opening the western lands to settlement did not keep pace with the westward movement of population. Many a family, at the time too poor to buy a farm, or impelled by a restlessness to move beyond the settled regions, squatted on unappropriated lands. In time, of course, these areas were surveyed and put on the market, and when such was the case the squatters began to demand preëmption rights.

This problem was more or less satisfactorily settled by a series of preëmption laws culminating in the general act of 1841. Such legislation protected the squatter but gave no permanent relief to those who wished to move westward, for in time the squatter had to pay for his land and speculators could still buy vast tracts and hold them for high prices. Even if the speculator did not own contiguous acres, the prospective buyer was, nevertheless, often dependent upon him for cash, since the government did not sell on credit. William B. Ogden, Chicago capitalist and frontier entrepreneur, often acted as agent for many easterners who had money to loan for such transactions. His favorite plan was to buy in his name, or that of the lender, the farm chosen by the would-be purchaser. The latter would then pay for each 160 acres, $60 a year for three years and $260 the fourth year, after which time he would be given the deed. Although the speculator over a period of four years received a return of 110 per cent on his original investment, Ogden assured him that this in no way violated the state usury laws. The property was in the speculator's own name and as owner he could sell on whatever terms he pleased. It was a safe investment, too, for should the buyer fail to meet his payments, the speculator still had the land.[1]

Thus to circumvent these evils and enable the poor man to have a piece of ground of his own and secure his ownership in it, there came the demand for land reform. The cry went up for free homesteads and land limitation. The movement gained considerable momentum after the panic of 1837. Free land for free white laborers was considered by many as a panacea for all the ills which led to the panic and the hard times following. Land reform soon became an integral part of the leading issues of the day—slavery extension, labor and capital, economic prosperity, and banks.

From the Atlantic seaboard, where George Henry Evans first organized the National Reform Association, to the western territories, the principles of free and inalienable homesteads and land limitation were adopted by portions of the Democratic, Whig, Free Soil, and Liberty parties. In the older sections of the country, the factory laborer and farm tenant accepted these ideas as a means of escape from the tyranny of employer and landlord. In the West, land reform was considered as a method whereby the newer sections could be settled by freemen, and thus bring prosperity to the territory or state. With lands to be filled with people, the West

---

[1] William B. Ogden to Obadiah Sands, Sept. 27, 1839, William B. Ogden Letter Books (MSS, Chicago Historical Society), II: 212-13.

was impatient with anything which checked its growth. Land monopoly, that is the holding of large tracts by speculators, was an evil of the most pernicious kind, said the editor of the *Chicago Democrat*. It rendered population almost stationary and checked the progress of agriculture. In fact, under its influence, the natural increase in population tended to diminish man's happiness, and therefore, under such circumstances, celibacy could not be called an evil.[2]

Not only did land monopoly hinder the growth of population, but it and its sponsor, capitalism, were dangerous to democratic institutions. This John Wentworth pointed out in one of his editorials in the *Democrat* in which he said the "dominion of capital" tended toward the "tenant system" under which "Republicanism" was impossible. It separated classes in society "to the annihilation of the love of country; and to the weakening of the spirit of independence." The tenant had "no country, no hearth, no altar, no household god." On the other hand, the freeholder was "the natural support of a *free government*." If the United States were to continue as a republic, then the public lands should pass into the hands of the people. "Let us," he concluded, "give to those who are unable to buy, *without money and without price*, that which the fact of birth entitles them to. By this means, we strike at the last foothold of the '*Money Monopoly*'—THE MONOPOLY OF THE SOIL."[3]

At the Industrial Congress, held in Chicago in 1850, the question of land monopoly was one of the most talked of evils, and an address stressing its pernicious influence was finally adopted. In substance this address said that land monopoly was the foundation of all the wrongs which afflicted civilized society.

> [It causes] over toil, and the loss of opportunities for study and self improvement and consequent ignorance and degredation; the poverty of the masses; the unjust accumulation of wealth and power by a privileged few; and the corruption of

---

[2] *Chicago Daily Democrat*, Oct. 10, 1848.
[3] *Ibid.*, Jan. 22, 1848.

the morals of the rich by luxury, pride and sensuality. . . . [It produces] intemperance, both among rich and poor, among the rich by conferring wealth upon them without meritorious productive industry, and thus exciting a depraved taste for vicious and animal pleasures; and among the poor by creating a want for a preternatural and artificial stimulus in place of the healthful stimulants imparted by moderate labor, and by moral and intellectual activity, and the studies of philosophy and natural science.

Lastly, it was the "root of the vast tree of selfishness and antagonism in society" which produced "the varied branches, flowers, and fruits of wickedness and discord and individual, domestic and national wars and calamities" which darkened "the world and shed a poisonous miasm over the minds and hearts of men," and there was no "effectual remedy for these ills of society, short of the extirpation of their great root and cause."[4]

Land reform, therefore, was not a farmers' movement, but was the common man's attack on uncontrolled capitalism, or—to use a more modern term—economic royalism. The engine of capital, explained John Wentworth, was the product of the commercial era. Through capitalism a privileged few of the present made possible an order worse than feudalism. "The *fear of want* does now," he said, "what the power of privilege did in former times."[5] Such conditions, of course, threatened the very existence of the nation. The tendency of money to accumulate in the hands of a few made the mere laborer the bondslave of the employer, and in times of stress the latter, in order to retain his profits, naturally reduced wages. This in turn "incited the poor against the rich, and stirred up revolutions" which threw down thrones and scepters. In America, however, such conditions could be avoided by enabling "every man to secure himself a home in the unappropriated lands of the Republic." Thus, by this means, the capitalist lost "his last stronghold, the monopoly of the soil." The laborer was then given

---

[4] *Chicago Daily Democrat*, June 17, 1850.
[5] *Ibid.*, Jan. 22, 1848.

a "security for the future" which would "forever place him in a position of impregnable strength."[6]

One must not think, however, that the land reformers were advocates of destructive measures. They were not fire-eating radicals. Rather, they thought of themselves as trying to save the old agrarian order. Capitalism was the revolutionary movement, because it tended to change society and institute a rule of aristocracy instead of one by the people. "We labor to save, not to destroy," wrote Wentworth. "We fully believe that the safety and perpetuity of our institutions rest upon the equitable division of the fruits of industry; upon the fact that labor will eventually be rewarded in proportion to the services which it renders."[7]

Closely allied to the problem of capitalism was that of free labor and slavery. To the land reformer, the slaveholder was as much of a capitalist as the northern factory owner or great landlord. If labor, therefore, was to receive its just share of this world's goods and happiness, slavery must be destroyed. The extension of slavery would tend to deprive the free laborer of his dignity. Wentworth, writing in one of his editorials of the men who would profit by the nonextension of slavery, said:

> And last, though not least, there are the laboring men of the North—the hardy sons of toil, who know that it is to labor they must look for every earthly thing of value, and that, therefore, it is their policy, and they believe it to be their duty, to elevate labor by every means in their power. They cannot fail to see that slavery tends to degrade their calling, and that the more slavery is extended, the stronger will be that tendency.[8]

To the land reformers, however, the problems of labor and capital could be easily settled by limiting the amount of land any one man could own and by granting free homesteads. If the western lands would be opened on these principles, not only would the "pauper laborer" of Europe and the American worker in the "tariff

---

[6] *Chicago Daily Democrat,* March 29, 1848.
[7] *Ibid.*
[8] *Ibid.,* Apr. 11, 1848.

protected" establishments of the United States come into "the possession of their own,"[9] but the whole question of slavery would also be solved.[10] But if capital persisted in its refusal to grant labor its just dues, Wentworth prophesied a great struggle.[11]

Although land reform was advocated as a means of aiding the laborer, the leaders and spokesmen of the movement themselves did not belong to the mechanic or tenant farmer classes. Instead they were men of responsible position and moderate fortune, and occasionally of great wealth. They considered themselves, however, as a part of the common people and envisaged a great free West, where every field was cultivated by its own proprietor and where every person who chose could become the owner of his field.[12] In addition to Wentworth, whom the *New York Globe* hailed as one of the greatest reformers in Congress, [13] a number of other Chicagoans espoused the cause of land reform.[14]

---

[9] *Chicago Daily Democrat,* Jan. 22, 1848.

[10] *Ibid.,* Feb. 12, 1850. "We think also that the freedom of the public lands will do more to calm the slavery agitation than any act of Congress or any constitutional enactment of any kind which will not have public sentiment for its basis. Slavery is the result of certain social organizations which must be dissolved by the action of land *reform* principles."

[11] *Ibid.,* Nov. 20, 1848. "Perhaps the most prominent feature of the present political agitation in the country is the question of the monopoly of the soil. The Wilmot Proviso is but a modification of the great principle, that the earth was given for the uses of man; and that, like the other essential elements to existence, no portion of its surface should be the subject of monopoly.

"All, to a greater or lesser extent, as they have perceived the evils of the accumulation of large landed estates, have felt the injustice of the present system of land tenure, and expressed their convictions accordingly. But few have seen their way clear out of the web into which the errors of civilization have cast the world. . . .

"Still no matter to what period of time the final issue may be delayed, from the question whether slavery shall monopolize the soil of the new States, to the question of monopoly by slavery induced by the power of concentrated capital, a great struggle is in prospect; and the merits or demerits of the principles advanced on both sides, are yet to be canvassed."

[12] *Ibid.,* Oct. 10, 1848.

[13] *Ibid.,* May 13, 1848.

[14] Dr. Carl A. Helmuth, editor of the *Illinois Staats-Zeitung*; James H. Collins, lawyer; Charles V. Dyer, physician; J. K. C. Forrest, of the *Chicago Daily Democrat*; Chauncy T. Gaston, printer; William B. Ogden, entrepreneur and president of the Free Soil League of Chicago; Fernando Jones, real estate operator and secretary of the aforementioned league; Nathan H. Bolles, real

To the reformers the problem of providing homesteads for the landless was, of course, a simple one to solve, since there were millions of acres of unsold public lands. In 1848 these amounted to 1,549,322,599 acres, out of which 241,391,138 acres were already surveyed and ready for sale.[15] In Illinois there were still 15,693,076 acres to be disposed of at the beginning of 1849—a little less than half the area of the state.[16] In the Chicago land district, there were 897,470 acres of public lands for sale on January 1, 1848. A year later Wentworth estimated that around 700,000 acres were still left and he wondered why more land warrants were not located there.[17]

By the late forties, therefore, there was considerable agitation for homesteads. In the Chicago newspapers appeared numerous poems on the subject, of which the following is typical:

> A billion acres of unsold land
>   Are lying in grievous dearth;
> And millions of men in the image of God,
>   Are starving all over the earth;
> Oh! tell me, ye sons of America,
>   How much men's souls are worth?
>
> . . . .
>
> Those millions of acres belong to man,
>   And his claim is, that he needs—
> And his title is signed by the hand of God,
>   Our God, who the raven feeds:
> And the starving soul of each famished man
>   At the throne of Justice pleads!

---

estate; W. B. Snowhook, dry goods merchant; John L. Scripps, publisher; William Sampson, real estate, and one of the vice-presidents of the Industrial Congress of 1850; and the Rev. William Barlow, pastor of the Trinity Episcopal Church. *Chicago Daily Democrat*, Apr. 29, May 19, 30, Sept. 8, 1848; May 9, June 7, 1850; *Chicago Commercial Advertiser*, Sept. 6, 1848.

[15] *Chicago Daily Democrat*, March 17, 1848.

[16] *Ibid.*, Jan. 3, 1849.

[17] *Ibid.*, Jan. 16, 1849.

Ye may not heed it, ye haughty men,
　　Whose hearts as rocks are cold—
But the time shall come when the fiat of God
　　In thunder shall be told!
For the voice of the great I AM hath said,
　　That the land shall not be sold![18]

In Congress, Wentworth and other members of the Illinois delegation constantly presented petitions and resolutions in favor of lands for the landless, and on December 27, 1849, Stephen A. Douglas introduced a homestead bill.[19] In fact, in March, 1849, the *Daily Democrat* claimed that more petitions had been presented to Congress that session "in favor of the freedom of the Public Lands than for any other measure save cheap postage."[20] The question of homesteads and homestead exemption was even debated in the legislature, and during the session of 1848-1849 a bill was presented providing for exemption from "foreclosure and forced sale for any debt contracted after March 1, 1849" forty acres of agricultural land or a quarter of an acre of a recorded town plat.[21] The bill failed to pass the House, however, and the *Democrat* remarked that the only thing to do was to "pick the flint and try again."[22]

In Chicago numerous public lectures were given on land reform, especially in the year 1848. Among the most prominent lecturers was H. H. Van Amringe of Wisconsin.[23] When the Industrial Congress met in Chicago in 1850, provision was made for popular lectures in the City Hall to be given during the sessions of the Congress.[24]

---

[18] *Chicago Daily Democrat*, Jan. 10, 1848.
[19] *Ibid.*, Apr. 11, 13, 14, 1848; Feb. 7, 1849; Feb. 9, March 11, 1850; A. C. Cole, *The Era of the Civil War 1848-1870* (*The Centennial History of Illinois*, III, Chicago, 1922), 90.
[20] *Chicago Daily Democrat*, March 20, 1849.
[21] *Ibid.*, Dec. 8, 18, 1848.
[22] *Ibid.*, Feb. 19, 1849.
[23] *Ibid.*, March 27, 1848 for example. Van Amringe was somewhat of a professional reformer and lectured also on women's rights, the ten-hour day, and other topics.
[24] *Ibid.*, June 7, 1850.

The first attempt to organize a National Reform Association in Chicago was in April, 1848,[25] and the organization was completed in May, with James H. Collins as president.[26] It was disbanded, however, after the presidential election of 1848, and was not reorganized until the time of the congressional election of 1850.[27]

At the convention of the Free Soil Party in Buffalo in 1848, the platform adopted did not satisfy many of the land reformers. In October, the Chicago National Reformers passed a long series of resolutions denouncing the Buffalo platform.[28] They put a ticket of their own in the contest, with Gerrit Smith for president and Charles C. Foote for vice-president, but the party polled only about a hundred and fifty votes in the whole state at the fall election.[29]

The land reformers, of course, met with some opposition in Chicago, chiefly from the Whigs. Alfred Dutch considered the movement as one led by "demagogues who spread their sales to catch every popular breeze in politics" and claimed it "humbugged" thousands "by the euphonious sound of free soil."[30] They were also accused of being Know-nothings, an accusation which they promptly denied, saying, however, that they did not intend that Sir John Murray, Louis Philippe, "and other foreign nabobs" should "hold land in this country, to speculate upon the same out of the hard earnings of the American laborer."[31] The differences, however, between those who opposed and those who advocated land reform were not over the ends to be achieved, but over the methods. Dutch, chief of the oppo-

---

[25] *Chicago Daily Democrat*, Apr. 15, 1848.

[26] *Ibid.*, May 19, 1848. C. A. Helmuth was vice-president, Charles V. Dyer, treasurer; J. K. C. Forrest, corresponding secretary; and C. T. Gaston, recording secretary.

[27] *Ibid.*, Dec. 12, 1848; May 9, 1850. The officers of the second association were: N. H. Bolles, president; C. T. Gaston, vice-president; William B. Snowhook, treasurer; and John L. Scripps, secretary.

[28] *Ibid.*, Oct. 2, 1848.

[29] *Ibid.*, Oct. 9, Nov. 3, 27, 1848.

[30] *Chicago Commercial Advertiser*, Sept. 6, 1848.

[31] *Chicago Daily Democrat*, March 31, 1848.

sition, said the "attempt to get land, without an equivalent, by political management," and by the same process, limit the amount of land others could hold, was "a much more difficult task, than to earn a sum to purchase it."[32]   A better way to break the money monopoly, or capitalism, he held, would be to pass a sound banking law which would "augment" the "circulating medium, and create so much rivalry that the producing classes" would not "be compelled to pay all their earnings and profits for the use of a little paper money" which they themselves furnished "the means to keep in circulation."[33]

The last great burst of enthusiasm for land reform in Chicago was in 1850 at the Industrial Congress. Here were considered the questions of land limitation, homesteads, the ten-hour day, and equal rights for women (social as well as political and legal).[34] After the Compromise of 1850 and the Kansas-Nebraska Act, northern and western fear of usurpation of power by the slave-holding oligarchy of the South tended to push land limitation and homesteads into the background and bring sectional issues to the fore. Although land reform principles were not forgotten from 1850 to 1862, it was not until the United States was engaged in the Civil War that the West was finally able to get its cherished homesteads.

III

THE TEMPERANCE MOVEMENT, 1848-1871

By HERBERT WILTSEE

In the 1830's and 1840's, the great Religious Awakening with which the names of Charles G. Finney and Theodore Weld are so closely associated, loosened the hold of orthodox predesti-narianism on the Calvinistic churches and substituted a spirit of humanitarian benevolence in its stead. The resultant impulse

[32] *Chicago Commercial Advertiser*, March 1, 1848.
[33] *Ibid.*, Sept. 26, Oct. 3, 1849.
[34] *Chicago Daily Democrat*, June 8, 10, 1850.

for social reform was directed in succeeding years primarily toward Negro emancipation, but the spirit of reform overflowed and made all social ills seem easily curable. Foreign and home missions, Bible and tract societies, conversion of sailors, and temperance reform were only a few of the movements taken up under the influence of the Great Awakening.

It is of importance to note that these reforms not only emanated from the churches, but that they were nurtured by and got their membership from the church element. And so close had become the intimate connection of temperance with revivals that the downfall of liquor and the conversion of the nation were a single object.[1] It was characteristic of the early temperance movement that its appeal was to earnest young people who were naturally predisposed towards high personal standards. Conversion for them involved a change of attitude rather than a change of life patterns, but the cause justified its existence in the eyes of its leaders "when it moved temperate people to denounce intemperance."[2]

In Chicago, during its first year of corporate existence, a movement was undertaken to control the sale of liquor. Growth in the number and strength of the evangelical denominations during the following years added the sanction which large numbers can give. By 1848, for instance, at least two hotels, the Lake Street House, and the City Hotel, were advertised as temperance houses where "men of principle . . . [can find] company and comforts of the right kind."[3] The United States Hotel at the corner of Canal and Randolph streets, in 1851, was also a temperance hostelry.[4] And almost twenty-five years before the Hillsboro, and Washington Court House, Ohio, ladies—founders

---

[1] Gilbert Hobbs Barnes, *The Antislavery Impulse 1830-1844* (New York 1933), 18.

[2] *Ibid.*, 25.

[3] *Watchman of the Prairies*, Jan. 2, 1849.

[4] *Ibid.*, Apr. 22, Aug. 26, 1851. This hotel, run by D. L. Roberts, observed the popular religious prejudice against breaking the Sabbath by announcing: "Omnibuses always in attendance (Sundays excepted) to convey persons to and from the house free of charge."

of the Women's Christian Temperance Union—conducted their prayerful picketing of local saloons and drugstores, certain of Chicago's druggists were advertising brandies and wines "*Expressly for Medical Purposes*," or for communion services only.[5] These, then, are but a few of the ways in which the growing temperance sentiment had forced a degree of conformity upon business as early as the beginning of the fifties.

In their attack on liquor, the churches did not hesitate to stigmatize drinking as sinful. This, again, was characteristic of that humanitarian-evangelical movement for social reform which regarded compliance with the high ends toward which it strove as "right" and failure to act in this manner as "wrong." Tippling was condemned again and again as a sin which led in due course to death "or an even worse fate." Hence it was that the term "temperance" as used by most of the advocates of this reform was really a misnomer, for in reality total abstinence was their goal.[6] The so-called Temperance Committee of the Chicago Presbytery of the Presbyterian church, reporting in 1849, advocated continual weekly pulpit exhortation as the most effective means of obtaining total abstinence on the part of the youth and adults. They declared that the first "social glass" was merely the inviting entrance to the downward path toward the "drunkard's grave," and stated unequivocally: "*No drunkard can inherit the Kingdom of God.*"[7] Calling on the clergy to stress the effect of liquor on the soul rather than upon the body, the editor of the local Baptist organ, who wielded a trenchant pen in the interests of antislavery, temperance, and other contemporary reforms, held that it was the welfare of the spirit that was placed in jeopardy by the use of liquor.[8] It was not long until advocates of the reform were attributing all forms of social

[5] *Watchman of the Prairies*, Jan. 8, 1850.
[6] In his *Lectures on Revivals of Religion* (New York, 1835), 413, Charles G. Finney drew an analogy between "backsliding" after revival, and intemperance: "Nine-tenths of those who become drunkards, are led on from small beginnings .... The only security is in adopting the principle of TOTAL ABSTINENCE."
[7] *Watchman of the Prairies*, Oct. 30, 1849.
[8] *Ibid.*, Feb. 12, 1850.

unrest to the liquor traffic, fortified as it was "by law, and strongly entrenched . . . in the indifference of . . . our citizens."[9] To the student of the more recent developments in temperance reform, cries that the depreciation of property values, the corruption of youth, depravity of public morals, and increase of taxation were the results of the liquor traffic, are singularly familiar. The extent to which the use of alcoholic beverages had become a moral issue can, perhaps, be best illustrated by quoting an editorial which appeared in a Methodist paper, admonishing housewives not to put brandy in their mince pies:

> It may revive the appetite for the poison in some one who is trying to get rid of it, or may form a taste for it in some one now innocent. . . . And who knows but that if one should eat your brandy pie he might be suspected of drinking brandy instead of eating it. Don't put the brandy in.[10]

To those who subscribed to the various temperance programs the liquor traffic had become "illicit" or "illegitimate," and the the use of spirits as a beverage had become a moral wrong.

The churches of Chicago, in conducting their attack upon drinking, used a wide variety of expedients. In addition to the regular sermons from the pulpit, temperance meetings were held, more often than not in the church buildings. Those for mariners, for instance, took place in the Bethel Mission Church under the auspices of the Marine Temperance Society.[11] Among the techniques most commonly employed at such meetings was the use of testimony of reformed inebriates. Particularly at outdoor meetings and for street-preaching were these men featured, since it was felt that as erstwhile drunkards they would be able to appeal to the unchurched and unreformed. The summer of 1848 saw a series of such sermons delivered on Chicago's main thoroughfares, and while it was believed "that much good was

---

[9] *Northwestern Christian Advocate*, Feb. 16, 1853.
[10] *Ibid.*, March 23, 1853.
[11] *Watchman of the Prairies*, Jan. 4, 1848. Among those who spoke in favor of temperance at one time or another was P. T. Barnum, "the greatest showman in the world." *Northwestern Christian Advocate*, Oct. 5, 1853.

done, as access was had to the very class of men the temperance reform [was] designed to benefit," it is impossible to determine to what extent success attended their efforts.[12]

The periodic meetings of 1849 were similar to those of the year before, although the cholera epidemic of the later year excited many to try to obtain real curtailment of the liquor traffic. The spread of intemperance as evidenced by police court indictments, and the fact that the majority of dispensers were of foreign birth led many Protestants to despair of obtaining real results unless the Catholic church would undertake a temperance movement, or unless the Common Council could be prevailed upon to pass restrictive ordinances. Agitation for the accomplishment of both was undertaken.[13] It was with considerable regret, therefore, that toward the end of 1849, it was seen that in spite of "all the warnings which God has given to the intemperate during the past season by the cholera, this vice abounds here more than ever."[14] The failure of the temperance forces to obtain greater success during this epidemic year seems to have convinced them that legal restriction was the most efficacious means of accomplishing their ends, moral suasion having been tried and found wanting. Thereafter greater emphasis was placed, both in temperance literature and on the platform, on the power of the ballot as the means by which the evils of the liquor traffic might be legislated out of existence. The meetings of the temperance groups, which began in the City Hall in April, 1850, took the lead from the Rev. L. Raymond and advocated legal restriction on the sale of spirits.[15]

The passage of the first such restrictive law by the Illinois legislature in early 1851, a law which set a minimum sale of one quart of hard liquor, and allowed no sale to minors under eighteen years of age, was highly approved by the temperance forces. They regretted, however, that a more stringent law had not been passed,

---

[12] *Watchman of the Prairies*, June 20, 1848.
[13] *Ibid.*, Jan. 2, 1849.
[14] *Ibid.*, Sept. 18, 1849.
[15] *Ibid.*, Apr. 23, 1850.

such as that of Wisconsin which made liquor retailers responsible for injuries resulting to purchasers.[16]

The great event of 1851, to temperance groups the country over, was the enactment in Maine of a law which wholly prohibited the sale of liquor. When, at the end of the first year that this law had been in force, it was seen that the results in decrease of crime and pauperism, as well as in the sale of liquor itself, were all that could be desired, groups in Chicago became highly ecstatic over the possibility of passing a similar law in Illinois.[17] When the Supreme Court of the United States upheld the Maine Law, and put an end to fears as to its constitutionality, real efforts began in Chicago.[18] Among the "hints" which one denominational newspaper of Chicago published to guide the arguments of the individual proselytizer was the following, of particular significance since a short two years before it had used the same reasoning to decry moral suasion and to defend restrictive legislation such as minimum liquor sales, or closing hours of saloons: "Raise no subordinate question, and be turned aside to no collateral issue. . . . Insist that under past legislation for partial restraint of the traffic in intoxicating drinks as a beverage, the evil has grown worse."[19] A similar stand was taken by the organ of the Congregational church when it first appeared in April, 1853.[20]

Up to and including 1853, the national temperance organization which had directed the reform activities, distributed literature, and sent speakers around the Union was the Sons of Temperance, famed in the song and verse of the day along with the Washingtonian total abstinence pledge. Originally an organization which sought to establish temperance through appeal to the individual and his conversion, climaxing in the signing of the "pledge," the Sons of Temperance, latterly, had been advocating

---

[16] *Watchman of the Prairies*, Feb. 18, 1851.
[17] *Ibid.*, Feb. 10, 1852.
[18] *Ibid.*, March 16, 1852.
[19] *Ibid.*, March 23, 1852; also issue of March 16, 1852.
[20] *Congregational Herald*, Apr. 7, 1853.

the wholesale methods of the Maine Law. When the National Division of the Sons, representing more than 300,000 members in the United States and Canada, met in Chicago in June, 1853, the Hon. Neal Dow, author of the Maine Law, dominated the entire proceedings. So completely had the Sons been won over that the many lectures which their representatives delivered in all parts of Chicago were categorically referred to as "Maine Law speeches."[21] During this assembly, Chicago had been thoroughly lectured on the fundamentals of the Maine Law, and meetings following the convention kept the subject before the people. It was Chicago, therefore, which took the lead in calling an interdenominational convention "of the friends of a prohibitory liquor law in the State of Illinois" to be held in the Clark Street Methodist Episcopal Church on December 7 and 8 of the same year. Some two hundred and forty delegates, of whom more than two hundred were clergymen, from twenty-four counties, attended, and following lengthy discussions adopted a set of resolutions and set up the Illinois Maine Law Alliance which pledged its members never to vote for a candidate who was "not unequivocally pledged to the Maine Law." In addition to adopting as their purpose "the entire suppression of the traffic in intoxicating drinks (as beverages) by efficient legal enactments," the Alliance set up a highly developed plan of organization for towns, counties, and the state.[22] A month later the local Cook County Maine Law Alliance was organized, the Chicago members taking the lead in the nomination of a temperance candidate for mayor in the forthcoming municipal elections. Their nominee, Amos Gaylord Throop, was badly defeated because of the concerted opposition (as a sympathetic Methodist paper explained) of the Catholic priests, the rum-sellers, Irish whiskey-drinkers, and German beer-drinkers.[23] To advertise

---

[21] *Northwestern Christian Advocate*, June 15, 1853; also *Congregational Herald*, June 18, 1853. A Cherokee Indian delegate was in attendance as the first representative of his race to attend a temperance convention.

[22] *Northwestern Christian Advocate*, Dec. 14, 1853.

[23] *New Covenant*, Feb. 13 (?), 1853; *Northwestern Christian Advocate*, Feb. 15, March 15, 1854.

their activities, the state Maine Law Alliance began the publication of a weekly newspaper, bearing the same name as the society, but this ill-starred venture, after several changes of management, was given up for want of subscribers.[24]

The political activity of the Alliance did not cease with its initial defeat, however, and with the election of Levi D. Boone as mayor on the antiforeign Know-nothing ticket in 1855, the city had an opportunity of witnessing the effect of enforcement of liquor restrictions. Sunday-closing laws and licensing ordinances, affecting the German population of the city, caused the "Lager Beer Riots" of April 21, during the course of which one man was killed and several wounded.[25] The Alliance at the time was preparing for an appeal to the people on a referendum for a state law similar to the Maine Law, the voting to take place on June 4. The state organization sent a number of eloquent speakers who addressed the citizens at weekly or daily meetings. With the hope of success near at hand, it is interesting to notice the extent to which the leadership of such meetings passed into secular hands. The clergy still appeared as speakers and were probably very important behind the scenes, but businessmen, editors, and politicians were selected as chairmen, secretaries, and other officers. Except for the participation of juvenile temperance societies, and their convention on June 2 in Dearborn Park, these meetings differed in no wise from the ordinary political rallies and mass meetings. In the voting on the proposed law, the prohibition forces were defeated by a wide margin in Chicago and by a somewhat smaller one in the rest of Cook County.[26] With this defeat, the Maine Law Alliance, as a political force in Chicago, seems to have disappeared

---

[24] *Ibid.*, June 7, 1854; also *Christian Times*, Sept. 6, 1854.
[25] *Standard Encyclopedia of the Alcohol Problem*, edited by Ernest H. Cherrington (Westerville, Ohio, 1925), II: 570.
[26] *Daily Democratic Press*, various numbers from April 27 to June 8, 1855. The issue of the last date gives the vote of June 4 as follows:

	In Chicago	In Cook County
For prohibition law	2,785	3,807
Against prohibition law	3,964	5,182

except for a union temperance movement which it sponsored at the time of the great revival of 1858 when practically every religious interest flourished.[27] That the friends of temperance had not given up hope of eventual victory is clear, however, for they continued their agitation until the eve of the war. In 1859, the Universalist organ, spokesman for the liberal element of Protestantism, demanded the embodiment in civil law of the responsibility of the liquor purveyor for all the damages occasioned through his "wicked traffic."[28]

While the Civil War diverted the attention of the entire country from customary concerns, it is certainly not true that the cause of temperance was deserted or that the moral censure of insobriety gave way to broad-minded tolerance while it was being waged.[29] Regular meetings of the societies such as those of the Chicago Temperance Legion continued to take place; new societies were set up, such as that at Bridgeport which had some two hundred members at its first anniversary in 1862; a number of Chicago churches coöperated with others in the state to hire the services of a famous lecturer and physiologist for temperance education; and when the Reverend Dr. Tiffany of Clark Street Methodist Episcopal Church got drunk while serving on Governor Yates's Sanitary Commission delegation after the Battle of Pittsburg Landing, the censorious cry which went up from the state and local secular press, to say nothing of the religious press, bespoke an aggrieved public opinion which was still highly sensitive to moral issues.[30] Relative to the high

---

[27] *Christian Times,* May 12, 1858.

[28] *New Covenant,* Feb. 5, 1859.

[29] *Chicago Tribune,* June 29, 1861. A movement was started at this time to solicit funds for distributing among the Illinois troops, copies of the *Illinois Temperance Journal* which were specially priced for this purpose by the editors at twenty dollars per hundred annual subscriptions.

[30] *Bloomington* [Ill.] *Pantagraph,* May 15, 1862; *Chicago Tribune,* May 17, 22, 1862. Immediately after returning to Chicago, Dr. Tiffany resigned his pastorate and his position as secretary of the Chicago Sanitary Commission, and also gave up his membership in the Methodist Episcopal Church, requesting to be put on probation. The *Pantagraph* revealed his reasons in a highly caustic article and made the whole affair a public scandal. The *Tribune* took the position that Tiffany had suffered enough already and should not be persecuted. Subsequently he was readmitted to full membership and reinstated in the ministry.

pitch reached before 1860, however, interest in temperance waned after that year, and did not regain its old strength until several years after Appomattox.

In 1869, a temperance mass meeting was held in Farwell Hall, concerning which meeting it was said that "the friends of temperance are waking, and issues, dropped on account of the war, are again to be vigorously pressed."[31] At this meeting, the Reverend Dr. Hatfield prophetically declared that the political parties were due for a surprise on the temperance question, suggesting that reëntry into politics, and on a national scale, must come.[32] The temperance interest, awakened this year, continued to grow as the old methods of revivalistic presentation were reintroduced. Saloon-preaching, for instance, came back into use when preachers invaded these places and prayed and preached for the besotted patrons.[33] In 1870, the perennial nonenforcement of ordinances restricting the hours and Sunday-opening of saloons, became a temporary focus point of which the temperance "host" availed itself.[34] When the mayor refused to close the saloons in accordance with the laws, and in spite of the petitions with 22,000 names which the temperance groups submitted, the salutary opposition which gave renewed vigor to the temperance movement appeared. The total abstinence pledges which obliged the signers to "touch not, taste not, handle not," were circulated in ever increasing numbers. Programs of child education in the Sunday schools were undertaken,[35] and temperance tract distribution went forward with a new impetus. Public meetings, such as those held each week in Farwell Hall, became the order of the day, and temperance "bars" where coffee and soup were available came into existence.[36] The

---

[31] *The Advance*, Nov. 28, 1867.
[32] *Chicago Tribune*, Nov. 22, 1867. The *Tribune*, on April 14, 1867, warned the prohibitionists that they would go down in defeat if they tried to erect a political party on the Maine Law experiment.
[33] *The Advance*, March 19, 1868.
[34] *Ibid.*, Jan. 6, 1870; also *The Interior*, March 17, 1870.
[35] *Ibid.*, March 31, 1870.
[36] *Chicago Tribune*, March 30, July 17, 1871.

Washingtonian Home, founded in 1863, expanded its work of curing drunkards of their taste for liquor, its income from the sale of liquor licenses guaranteeing its existence.[37]

By 1870 or 1871, therefore, the temperance campaign was again well under way in Chicago. The fire of the latter year did not put a stop to this activity, for the "Fire-Proof" ticket on which Joseph Medill was elected mayor was pledged to enforce the laws restricting liquor selling. This was the last important political success of the temperance groups in the line of municipal regulation of the traffic in spirits, however, for the victory of the foreign groups, and particularly the Germans, in 1873, put an end to the effective enforcement of the restrictive ordinances. While the temperance movement grew in numbers and strength from then on, political developments did not reflect this growth until the turn of the twentieth century.[38]

IV

THE RADICAL LABOR MOVEMENT, 1873-1895

By DOROTHY CULP

Chicago, in the last quarter of the nineteenth century, was the scene of a radical labor movement interesting not only from the local point of view, but also from the national, which it epitomized. Against the dramatic background of a city rising, in fifty years, from a frontier town to the center of a great commercial empire, the problems of the working men were brought into sharp relief. It was no accident that the three great crises of the labor history of the late nineteenth century centered in Chicago—the railroad riots of 1877, the Haymarket riot of 1886, and the Pullman strike of 1894.

What was this Chicago which was to be the scene of a movement which attracted national attention? In 1871 much of the

---

[37] *Chicago Tribune*, Jan. 14, 1868.
[38] *Encyclopedia of the Alcohol Problem*, II: 572.

city had been destroyed by fire, and many people believed that
the day of Chicago had passed, that some other middle western
city would become the capital of the great prairie section which
had looked to Chicago for leadership.[1] But the fire, terrible
catastrophe though it was, proved but an impetus to a development even more spectacular than the previous twenty years
had witnessed. In size Chicago grew, in the years between the
fire and the World's Fair of 1893, from thirty-five to over two
hundred square miles. Her population increased, in these two
decades, from a little under three hundred thousand to more than
a million people.[2] Such an increase would in itself have caused
vexatious problems, but other factors made the situation even
more serious. To a certain extent the growth in population was
due to natural increase; a part resulted from expansion from
more established communities of the United States; but a large
part resulted from immigration into the United States. During
the twenty years under consideration, the two main strains of
the immigrant influx into Chicago were German and Irish, and
these two racial groups alone accounted for over half of the
city's population.

Under any circumstances the adjustment of the immigrants to
the new society would have been difficult, but the situation in
Chicago only added to the complexity of the problem. Chicago
had become by 1871 the commercial capital of the Middle West
and was beginning to establish factories which were to make her a
manufacturing center of equal importance. In this maelstrom of
commercial and industrial activity, the immigrants found it difficult to adjust to the ethics and basic idealism of the dominant
middle class, whose will for power and quest for profit set the tone
for urban American civilization. In spite of the difficulties in-

---

[1] A. L. S., John B. Carson to Elihu Washburne, Nov. 8, 1871, Elihu Washburne Papers (MSS, Library of Congress), Vol. 76.
[2] G. H. Gaston, *The History and Government of Chicago: Its Expansion by
Annexations* (Reprint from the *Educational Bi-Monthly*, June, 1914), 10; *Ninth
Census*, Vol. I, *The Statistics of the Population of the United States* (Washington,
1872), 599; *Eleventh Census, 1890*, Part II: *Vital Statistics* (*House Misc. Docs.*,
52 Cong., 1 Sess., 1891-92, Vol. 50, pt. 18, Washington, 1896), 364.

volved, the vast majority of the newcomers soon accepted the ideology of nineteenth century America—believing that within their reach or that of their children lay the possibility of attaining the comfort, security and power of the middle class.

There were those, however, who could not accept the "great American dream," who could find no hope for themselves or their kind in the system they found in America. These men, largely German, espoused various of the anticapitalist theories current at the time and attempted to spread the teachings of these various schools of thought. There had been a socialist movement in Chicago even before the fire, but it remained for the panic of 1873 and the terrible distress which lasted for several years afterwards and found violent outlet in the railroad riots of 1877 to give the movement a degree of cohesion and the powerful motivating force of what Mr. Louis Adamic, with characteristic lack of delicacy but amazing aptness, calls "an underdog, belly-hunger movement."[3]

The first organization of anticapitalist thinkers among Chicago workingmen was that of the Universal German Workingmen's Association, whose members, affiliated with the International, were followers of the doctrines of Lassalle. In 1874 another organization of Lassalleans was begun under the name of the Labor Party of Illinois. Both of these organizations emphasized political action with but little success, and in 1875, discouraged by their failure to gain converts, they joined forces and turned their energies to trade union action. Meanwhile, another organization was growing up which, after several vicissitudes typical of radical organizations, emerged as the Socialistic Labor Party, and adopted a program of political action which had as its goal "to place the means of labor into the hands of the whole people, and thus establish a system of cooperative industry, by abolishing the present wage system."[4] By 1880, two diverse factions had grown up inside the Socialistic Labor Party, and the following year the trade

---

[3] Louis Adamic, *Dynamite, the Story of Class Violence in America* (New York, 1931), 44.

[4] *Report of the Special Committee on Labor*, 39 Gen. Assembly Ill. (Springfield, 1879), 39.

union faction split off from the political socialists. The new party formed by the trade union group came to be known as the International Workingmen's Association, and was thus described: "For a year and a half the character of this movement was very vague. There was loose talk of violence, dynamite, and assassination, but the party as a whole dangled self-consciously between Marxism and Nihilism, between theory and action."[5] The Chicago members of the group scoffed at the possibility of reorganizing society by political action, but they were perfectly willing to use this means of propagandizing their faith.

At the same time that a small but vehement group in Chicago was becoming convinced that anarchism was the ideal system to replace the capitalistic chaos, another more widespread change was making itself felt. It seems characteristic of the American labor movement that there be periodic swings from a belief in the efficacy of political action to a dependence upon direct action. Such a change was visible in the Chicago labor movement in the eighties. It was partly due to the fiery criticism of political action by the anarchist leaders, August Spies, Albert Parsons and others, for there were many who, although they were unwilling to accept the anarchist system, were still ready to believe with the anarchist that the vote offered no solution to their problems. And the anarchists could in this case back their criticism with facts. It had for years been apparent that the working classes could hope for little from either of the major parties. Nor had the attempts to form special workers' parties been particularly successful. Their greatest strength came in 1879 when they cast over 10,000 votes in the Chicago mayoralty election.[6] Generally they were unable to com-

---

[5] Adamic, *Dynamite*, 45. The national convention of the International Workingmen's Association in 1883 announced its belief in the destruction of class rule by "energetic, relentless, revolutionary and international action, the establishment of a free society based upon cooperative organization of productions without commerce and profit mongery; the organization of education on a popular, scientific and equal basis for both sexes; equal rights for all without distinction of sex or race, and the regulation of public affairs by free contracts between autonomous communes and associations resting on a federalistic basis." Nathan J. Ware, *The Labor Movement in the United States* (New York, 1929), 308.

[6] Lucy Parsons, *Life of Albert R. Parsons* (Chicago, 1903), xxvii.

pete with the older established parties for important offices, and were successful only in securing the election of one or two aldermen, who found themselves impotent against the organized party machines. The climax came, to the discontent of the radical workers for political action, with a particularly blatant action by which the Democratic machine in 1880 was able to prevent the socialist member of the council from taking his place in that body for almost the entire term for which he had been elected. After this time the number of votes cast for socialist candidates in Chicago steadily dwindled, until in 1884 they polled only some six or seven hundred votes.[7] This falling off was, of course, partly caused by the disgust of certain socialist groups with the possibility of attaining their goal by political action, and was partly due to the fact that with the return of comparative prosperity many workers who had previously voted socialist as a protest and not as a means of indicating their belief in the constructive program of that group, now returned to their old-line affiliations.

By 1885, anticapitalist thought in Chicago's labor circles was fairly well-advanced and divided into two schools: the old-line socialist and the anarchist. The Socialistic Labor Party and the Amalgamated Trades and Labor Assembly represented the former, and the International Workingmen's Association, the Progressive Central Labor Union and the *Lehr* and *Wehr Verein*, which were armed German drill organizations, represented the latter.

Already, however, just as the anarchist faction was establishing itself and gaining strength, the movement was beginning which was to result in the complete silencing of the anarchist movement in Chicago. It is a curious anomaly that the eight-hour movement, which resulted in the Haymarket incident and the ruthless suppression of the anarchists, was adopted only after hesitation by the anarchist leaders. Late in 1885 the Central Labor Union, organization of the anarchist faction, adopted the program of agitation for the eight-hour day. An eight-hour league

---

[7] *Report of the Senate Committee upon Relations Between Capital and Labor*, 48 Cong. (Washington, 1885), I: 585.

was formed in which this Union coöperated with the Socialistic
Labor Party and the Knights of Labor. Agitation was carried on
by means of mass meetings and May 1, 1886 was set for the inauguration of the campaign. May day passed without serious
trouble, much to the surprise of the worthies of the city who felt
sure that revolution and murder were imminent. But on May 3,
after a meeting near the McCormick Reaper works, where the
men were out on strike, there was a serious encounter with the
police, in which six men were killed. Angered by what they considered an unjustified assault upon a workers' meeting, the anarchist leaders determined to hold a large meeting in the Haymarket
which was to be at once a protest meeting against the McCormick
outrage and a demonstration in favor of the eight-hour day. Of
the events of that tragic evening, but little need be said. Parsons,
Fielden and Spies addressed the crowd, giving speeches not unlike
those that they had been giving for the past several years, advocating the overthrow of capitalism and the achievement of social justice. As the crowd was beginning to disperse, overzealous policemen appeared on the scene and ordered the meeting to disperse.
Immediately after the order was given, a bomb was thrown into
the ranks of the police, killing several and wounding many others.
Within the next few weeks, August Spies, Michael Schwab, Samuel
Fielden, Adolph Fischer, George Engel, Oscar Neebe, Louis Lingg
and Albert Parsons were arrested and charged with the murder
of Matthias Degan, one of the policemen who had been almost
instantly killed by the explosion. In an atmosphere of animosity
which was almost hysterical, the trial of these men took place.[8]
One commentator expressed it: "There is not a shred of evidence
to connect these men with the Haymarket bomb throwing. They
were anarchists and had talked wildly of violence and revolution
at one time or another, and on these grounds they were found
guilty. It was a case of Society against Anarchy with revenge as
the motive."[9] Viewed as a murder trial the case was a tragic

---

[8] Official Record of the Haymarket Trial (MS, Chicago Historical Society).
[9] Ware, *Labor Movement*, 315.

travesty upon justice. It emerges as a more understandable event when we realize that in the eyes of middle-class America the anarchists had—whether by deed or word is unimportant—destroyed the symbol of authority upon which their civilization rested. It was not to be expected that with the defense attorneys men of little experience, with both judge and jury at least predisposed in favor of guilt and with the added force of a hysterical public opinion, these men would be acquitted. Finally they were found guilty, one being sentenced to life imprisonment and the others to death. The sentences of Fielden and Schwab were commuted to life, and that of Oscar Neebe to fifteen years; Louis Lingg committed suicide in prison and the others were hanged.

The hysteria which the Haymarket incident caused among substantial citizens did not soon die away. Prominent businessmen of the city raised a fund of several hundred thousand dollars to convict the anarchists and to wipe out whatever survived of the anarchist movement. When Governor Altgeld pardoned the three surviving defendants, a storm of protest was unleashed against him, equalled only by the applause that came from those whom time had permitted to see the affair more objectively.

The incident had several important effects. It did undoubtedly silence the anarchists. Their great leaders, the ones who had believed sincerely in the constructive theory of anarchism, were imprisoned or hanged. But it would be a mistake to think that the labor movement as a whole was so affected. On the contrary it emerged from the 1886 hysteria in many respects stronger than it had been before that time. The diverse elements of labor, and the different organizations and nationalities were all drawn together by the realization that their common cause was more important than factional differences and theoretical disagreements among themselves. Furthermore, the labor movement really gained in practical strength with the removal of the radical intellectuals.

It was not until 1894 that labor in Chicago was faced with another such crisis as the one of 1886 which had been climaxed by the throwing of the Haymarket bomb. By this time the panic of

1893 had caused a serious amount of unemployment, wage cuts were being made and whole industrial plants were being shut down. The trouble this time centered about the Pullman Palace Car Company works. The paternalist system of Mr. Pullman's town, excellent though it may have been in theory, caused great dissatisfaction among his workers. Consequently, they welcomed the opportunity to join the American Railway Union which had been organized in Chicago in 1893 under the leadership of Eugene V. Debs. Dissatisfaction caused by the refusal of the company to recognize the union came to a climax in May, 1894, when the company announced a wage cut. The men walked out, and the company retaliated by closing the plant—a step it was not at all averse to taking, since conditions made operation at a profit difficult. It is unnecessary to discuss the details of the Pullman strike, already so familiar to modern American historians. Eugene V. Debs emerged as the leader of the labor forces, and directed the strike until the employer groups made use of the formidable weapon of the injunction, and Debs and his lieutenants were arrested and the strike broken.

These, then, are the highlights of the radical labor movement in Chicago in the years from 1873 to 1894. The period was one in which the organization of labor went forward at a rapid rate, when trade unions were increasing in numbers as well as in strength. At the same time a numerically small but vocal group was espousing anticapitalist theories, and in this group too, there was a period of organization and of definition. The course of the development is indicated by the mention of the great names of the labor movement of this period in the city—Parsons and Spies at the beginning and Debs at the end. As epitomized by these men, the socialist labor movement had changed from a thing of eloquent theorizing and idealism impossible of realization to the idea of evolutionary revolutionary socialism which Debs represented.

V

SUMMARY

By HERBERT A. KELLAR.

The story of the development of Chicago may be told in many ways. It can be regarded as the growing center of a great inland empire, the activities of whose citizens have reached, and continue to reach, intimately into the lives of the people of half a dozen surrounding states and beyond, and are in turn influenced by these individuals, and others, dwelling outside the boundaries of the city. Again it might be revealed in the record of the achievements and failures of its leaders in many lines of endeavor, portrayed against the background of the destinies of the remainder of the population. In another sense it forms an Exhibit A of the long struggle of labor for rights and privileges, as opposed to the functioning of unrestrained laissez-faire capitalism. Still another is the changing relation of the English speaking and the foreign language groups. Here may be noted such phases as the initial economic, political and social dominance of the latter by the former; the gradual political emancipation of the foreign language groups brought about by coöperation and the ballot box; the use of political control as a means of challenging the remaining economic and social prerogatives of their opponents; and lastly the partial amalgamation of the two groups with the gradual emergence of a social viewpoint on the part of both.

Suggestive is the fact that practically from the beginning of Chicago as an organized entity, three types of interest have been predominant, namely economic enterprise, intellectual activity along cultural and social lines, and concern with spiritual matters. Out of these has come at times a fourth phenomenon, the "I will" spirit, which has done so much to give Chicago her distinctive place among the great cities of her time. Tracing the individual growth and the relationship of these factors is fundamental to the understanding of the story of Chicago, past and present. So varied are the possibilities for analyzing and depicting the history of this great city that imagination continues to suggest others, but the above will suffice to illustrate.

The plan outlined by Dr. Pierce offers a further method of attack. Chronological division into periods and selection of topics within the period has obvious advantages, provided good judgment and imagination, as undoubtedly will be in evidence in this instance, enter into the choice of topics. In view of the emphasis placed upon the rôle of the common man, it would not be amiss to point out that impartial treatment would of course require that the mutual dependence upon each other of both leaders and the mass, should be duly shown.

Mr. Norris, Mr. Wiltsee, and Miss Culp have each in turn indicated the interesting and important data that they are uncovering in their research. Judging from the types of sources which they have cited (and this thought should also be held in mind for the history of Chicago as a whole), newspapers, periodicals and books should be liberally supplemented with manuscripts and other varieties of original material.

The project in which Dr. Pierce and her associates are engaged is both intriguing and important for American and world history. May their product in finality, equal in quality the zeal and enthusiasm which they are giving to their chosen task.

THE RUSSIAN COMMUNITY OF CHICAGO

By THOMAS RANDOLPH HALL

"The time has not yet come when the history of Slavic immigration can be written with any thoroughness. The preliminary work must be done by local antiquarian societies, state historical associations, writers of monographs, and mainly by members of the various nationalities themselves. Meanwhile, unless the work of collecting material is vigorously and systematically carried on, much will be irrevocably lost."[1] Little has been done in the period of some thirty years since Emily Balch made this appeal to the historical consciousness of American and Slav. The author, of course, could not foresee later developments, the prosecution of research projects on a large scale with public money, with the resulting preservation of sources too long forgotten.[2]

Until the W. P. A. Foreign Language Project began its work, Chicago's Russian colony remained neglected by the student. There had been no attempt to set forth in any connected form the life of the second largest Russian community in America. A few, greatly interested in the life of their people, had stored away handbills, letters, and copies of newspapers. It was to trace down these sources that the Russian section of the Foreign Language Project was organized, sending its investigators into damp basements and dusty attics, only to find with heartbreak-

---

[1] Emily G. Balch, *Our Slavic Fellow Citizens* (New York, 1910), 205.

[2] This paper is an attempt to give a general summary of the Russian colony as it appears from source material thus far collected by the W.P.A. Foreign Language Project of Chicago. It does not pretend to completeness, and is intended only to give students an idea of the problems which arise in connection with such a study.

ing frequency that the junkman had been there before them, or that carelessness, aided by fire and dampness, had destroyed records which could not be replaced. When some stray file of papers was found, its possessor often had to be persuaded that his material would not be used against him, that it was not the police who wanted it. However, it must be placed to the credit of the Russians, that, almost without exception, they have appreciated the necessity of such researches if their history is to be preserved in written form.

The early records of this Russian community are lost. The English language press informs us that a "Russian Mutual Aid Society" presented an address of welcome to President Cleveland upon the occasion of his visit to Chicago in 1887; there is to be found in the same source a reference to a Russian Literary Society, organized in 1890.[3] Beyond these there is little trace of the organized secular life of the Russians between 1871 and 1908. The Holy Trinity Orthodox Cathedral, founded in 1893, remains the oldest living Russian organization in the city.

The heavy immigration of the first decade of the twentieth century gave Chicago, for the first time, a semblance of Russian community life. Hull House was the early center, but new organizations soon began to rent and furnish their own quarters. In the period, 1905-1916, the first Russian paper, *The Russian in America*, a weekly, was established, existing about one and a half years.[4] Other efforts were made by liberal and socialist groups to publish small magazines; without exception, all expired after a few issues.[5]

In this same period there came a great growth of benefit societies. Immigrants working in factories for low wages, and suspicious of the life around them, began to band together to protect their families and their future. Organizations devoted to revolutionary, artistic or intellectual aims made provision to

---

[3] *Chicago Daily News* (morning issues), Oct. 5, 1887; Nov. 21, 1890.
[4] *Russkii v Amerike.*
[5] The Foreign Language Project has records to date of nineteen newspapers and eleven magazines published in Russian in Chicago since 1891.

pay their members sick and death benefits or to lend them small sums. The largest local society of this type, the Russian Independent Mutual Aid, was founded in 1912, following a quarrel among the parishioners of the Russian Orthodox Cathedral.[6] Around this society there has developed a church and a school. The Independent Church has become an intellectual center among the Russians of Chicago, vying with the Orthodox Church for leadership, and spreading its influence far beyond the city.

Intellectual ferment was the product of the war and its aftermath. Revolution in Russia was reflected in Chicago. Many saw their dreams come true and returned home to help build a new nation; those remaining behind in Chicago organized to give the Revolution moral and material support. The press grew rapidly. Several papers sprang up to debate the new Russia and the proper attitude of the colony toward it. There developed during this time the schism which has hamstrung the colony ever since. A growing distrust of the extreme policy of the Soviet government, together with an influx of refugee immigrants from the homeland, caused a majority of the community to cease their support of the new course of Revolution. Since 1921, the anticommunist sentiment of the colony has grown, and unceasing warfare with the more radical minority has become more bitter.

It is fitting that we draw the curtain with the year 1924. Events too recent cannot be seen in their proper perspective; we cannot yet correctly evaluate the effects of a decade of internecine strife. Clear it is, however, that the Russians of Chicago are erecting a new foundation for their community existence. Russians are entering the regular American parties in an effort to gain a foothold in the politics of city and state. At the same time an effort is being made to preserve the old traditions and transmit to the youth the language of their fathers. There is a lively consciousness, even among the more radical elements, of

---

[6] *Russkii Narodnyi Kalendar na 1929 god* ("Russian National Almanac, 1929"), edited by J. J. Voronko (Chicago, 1929), 78-81.

the need for schools to give this training.[7]   Among the young people there has arisen a movement to replace with English the Russian of the Orthodox Church service.   In a word, the Russians are much nearer assimilation, though let us hope that they will be able to synthesize the traditions of two great nations.

Sources of information for the more recent years, which are available to the Project, are much more abundant than for the early part of the century, although the newspaper files preserved are incomplete.   The dozens of societies which flourished have left their record in handbills, announcements and resolutions which throw light on the reactions of the colony to events abroad and at home.

The Russian press has been the Project's most difficult problem.   Russian journalism has never been highly successful in Chicago; lack of adequate finances, poor equipment, and untrained personnel have been the greatest restraining influences. The Russian-American newspaperman is often a drifter who has been unsuccessful in other professions.   Three types of paper have appeared in Chicago—the independent, the "front" or newspaper published to furnish prestige to its editor in politics, and that supported wholly or in part by an organization.   The latter has been most successful.   The Independent Society financed the publication of *Free Russia* in 1917 and has supported, at least in part, every important paper which has appeared since that date.   Despite this, it is obvious that the quality of Russian journalism is declining.   Too often the printed page becomes the scene of obscure intellectual battles; the editor's chief tool is a pair of shears, with which he acquires his daily budget of news from the local English language press.

Journalism and every other civic activity has obtained its inspiration from the "intellectual," and from the educated workingman.   Semi-illiterate masses have been forced to look to this minority to conduct them through the maze of difficulties arising

---

[7] *Novyi Mir* ("New World"), Apr. 4, 1936.   This newspaper is published in New York.

from American urban life, for which the old ways furnish no precedent. The intellectual is usually a professional man, a physician, lawyer, editor, or engineer, occasionally a writer, more rarely a business man. Though his professional training may be, and, in fact, often has been obtained in America, the learned man generally enjoys a Russian university education. Many of the Russian intellectuals of Chicago fled to America for political reasons. Before the war they were the heart of the numerous revolutionary circles and bands, of every political hue, which flourished in the colony. The intellectual in those far-off days kept his eyes on the tsarist state and worked feverishly to convert his backward peasant countrymen to the doctrines of social change.

Revolutionary reality greatly changed all this. Many, it is true, hurried home to join in the new life. Among them was Michael Berg who for almost a decade had been striving to educate the unlettered of his community. The world now knows him as Michael Borodin, adviser to Sun Yat-Sen, and mighty forger of revolution in China. He is the most famous of the scores who left Chicago to take an active part in the Revolution. The course of events and old political differences produced numerous quarrels among the leaders, the more conservative wing being strengthened by the influx of refugees between 1920 and 1924. Since that time there has arisen an interest in purely American politics; Russians, under the influence of their leaders, are taking their place in American public life.

All of the intellectual's talents have not been devoted to politics, however. No movement for the betterment of conditions among his people has failed to find him at the helm. Popular lectures on hygiene, art, music and literature have engaged the attention of the best forces of the colony for over three decades. Russian physicians conducted a campaign of education against venereal disease and quackery among their countrymen twenty years before these subjects became fashionable in the metropolitan press of Chicago. The Russian People's University of Chicago, founded in 1918, during its life of two years was a vital force in the intellectual and economic life of the entire community.[8]

It is tragic that these unselfish efforts have not been more successful. Unfortunately for the welfare of the colony, the Russian workingman's distrust of the learned has been much in evidence, and not entirely without justification. The tendency toward sectarian differences, personal quarrels and pettifogging has been prominent in Chicago. Many promising schemes have been ruined and the colony as a whole retarded by this suspicion of the well-educated. Until the level of the community as a whole is raised, no permanent solution of such serious problems as poverty and quackery can be attempted.

The study of the Russian colony is not yet sufficiently advanced to enable us to make any very definite pronouncements. The records available are so scanty that inevitably great gaps will appear in the complete story, particularly for the early periods. The years from 1924 to the present, however, will be well covered, and it will be possible to trace the recent history of the Russian settlement in full detail.

Chicago's Russians are making a valiant fight to maintain their individuality. The cessation of immigration will result eventually in their complete assimilation; meanwhile those who knew the homeland are struggling to inculcate in their children a love for its language and culture. It is very difficult to awaken the poorly educated to the great traditions of the old home. Among the masses, living on a low scale, the daily problems of food and shelter appear all-important.

Their failures in organization and community life are fully recognized by the Russians. Other peoples, more numerous or

[8] *Izvestiya Russkago Narodnago Universiteta v Chikago* ("News of the Russian People's University of Chicago"), No. 1, Chicago, 1919. This volume furnishes complete information as to the scope and influence of this institution. The Krasnow Scrapbooks, Vols. I and IX, owned by Dr. Henry R. Krasnow, 4601 N. Broadway, Chicago, Ill., contain newspaper clippings, handbills, and other materials covering the past thirty years of the Russian colony.

less torn by internal quarrels, have made a greater impression upon the city. So the Russians, unable to compete in numbers or in wealth, have been content to occupy an honorable place among the many nationalities that have had so large a part in the building of Chicago.

ILLINOIS AS LINCOLN KNEW IT
A BOSTON REPORTER'S RECORD OF A TRIP IN 1847

Edited by HARRY E. PRATT

INTRODUCTION

J. H. Buckingham, son of the founder and publisher of the *Boston Courier*, came to Chicago in July, 1847, as a delegate to the River and Harbor Convention and as a reporter for his father's paper. That Convention, which Horace Greeley said was the largest meeting ever held in America up to that time, convened on July 5 and adjourned two days later. Its purpose was to register a protest against President Polk's veto of a bill making appropriations for river and harbor improvement, and to strengthen the general cause of internal improvements by federal action. Chicago was an appropriate meeting place, because Polk's veto had deprived it of an anticipated $8,000 for the harbor improvement which had been in progress since 1833.

One of the Illinois delegates to the Convention was Abraham Lincoln, who had been elected to the national House of Representatives the preceding year but had not yet taken his seat. So far as is known, this was Lincoln's first visit to the Illinois metropolis. Buckingham made no mention of Lincoln's short speech before the Convention, but when they became fellow passengers on the stage between Peoria and Springfield a few days later, he was greatly amused by the Whig Congressman and described his antics in several of the most interesting passages of this narrative.

Buckingham was fascinated by Chicago and the West, and decided to proceed to St. Louis. His route took him by stage and steamer through Peru, Peoria, Springfield, Jacksonville and Alton.

Returning, he traveled up the Mississippi to Galena, stopping for a day at Nauvoo. His description of the famous Mormon Temple is one of the most detailed on record. From Galena, he followed the lower route through Dixon to Chicago.

Buckingham's letters to the *Courier*, which appeared at intervals in July and August, 1847, are first-rate travel literature. But they have a broader interest than most travel literature, for the state which they describe so accurately and vividly was the Illinois of Lincoln's time. Here are the towns as he saw them, the inns in which he slept, the people whom he knew—and, for good measure, a pencil sketch of Lincoln himself.

CORRESPONDENCE OF THE COURIER

CHICAGO
July 5, 1847

This city, with a permanent population of nearly twenty thousand inhabitants, is, to-day, occupied by at least forty thousand. It is a beautiful place, the most beautiful, at first sight, of any I have seen since I left New-England. Its streets are broad and long, and all lined with trees. It is bordered by the Chicago or Skunk River and Lake Michigan, and by a ten-mile prairie. The prevalent winds are from the North, blowing over the lake, and they keep everything healthy.

To-day, the great, long-talked of, and very important River and Harbor Convention, met in this place, and this fact, with the additional fact that the day was set apart for the celebration of our National Independence, has caused a great crowd. All the hotels,—and Western towns and cities, are famous for the number,—if not for the excellence of their hotels and taverns, have been full to overflowing for more than a week. I arrived here yesterday morning, in five days from Buffalo, in the steamer *Baltic*,[1] with two hundred and fifty passengers, but no hotel

---

[1] The *Baltic*, Capt. A. T. Kingman in charge, had left Buffalo, New York, for Chicago on June 29, 1847; it remained there until July 8. It was an 825 ton steamer, launched in Buffalo earlier in the same year. It was 221 feet in length, and had a 30 foot beam, with a 12 foot depth of hull.

accommodations could be had that were comfortable, and we all, men, women and children, remain on board the boat, by invitation of Captain Kingman, who keeps temporarily a hotel for our accommodation. Five other large steamers are lying in the river with their passengers also on board, and in the same situation. The citizens have been very liberal, and have put themselves to great expense and inconvenience to accommodate strangers;—every private house where there is a spare bed, has been freely offered to the strangers who are here, and I understand that all the houses are full. I have just declined an invitation to a spare mattress on the floor of the office of a lawyer in Lake street, because I am well accommodated on board the *Baltic*, and have no doubt some stray stranger will be glad of it before bedtime.

At early dawn to-day, or rather at early dark last evening, crackers, and squibs, and guns "begun to be fired," and they have been "being fired" for at least twenty-four hours. I miss the merry sound of the bells which are used to usher in our sunrise, noon and sunset, on such occasions in Boston; but in other respects the celebration of the day has been much as such celebrations are wont to be all the world over.

The procession was formed at nine o'clock, and escorted by a company of Light Artillery. Our Boston boys would have laughed to see the guns, which were longer and heavier than a majority of the volunteer militia of Massachusetts would be able to handle if they should try. But they looked as if made for service, and the men who carried them looked as if they were capable of doing service with them; there were no boys in this company, or if there were, they were boys with beards, and hard heads, and hard frames.

Next followed the Fire Department, and a more tasteful, and in fact a handsomer show was never got up in the Eastern country. The Chief Engineer is a Boston Boy, and he has Boston tastes, much improved, and with views enlarged to suit the boundaries of this noble Western World. He got up the procession, or his part of it, in a manner that would do credit to any body. The engines were mounted on cars and drawn by six and eight horses; the members of the different companies were dressed in appropriate costume, and a band of music accompanied each. The wheels and the brakes were garlanded with flowers, and while one was covered with a bower, another was covered with an open tent, and all had some appropriate decoration.

Next followed the Illinoisans, marching by counties, with banners,—Long John Wentworth, seven feet in height, being in the front rank.[2] The Massachusetts delegation was formed at the head of the column of foreign delegates, and were twenty-eight in number. Then came the delegates from other states. After marching some distance, the escort opened to the right and left, and the foreign delegates passed into a large pavilion, followed by the rest of the procession, so far as was practicable. This pavilion was said to be calculated to seat three thousand people, and half the number of persons who were in the procession could not get seats. The Mayor[3] of the city, in a brief address, gave us a welcome; and the Executive Committee, who have had the arrangement, the getting up of the Convention, then came forward and proposed Col. Barton of Buffalo as President *pro tem.*, and two gentlemen from the farther West as Secretaries. This being agreed to, we had prayer, and then the Committee proposed a plan of proceeding that was calculated to facilitate the operations of the Convention. After some preliminary discussion as to the details of business, the Convention adjourned until afternoon.

---

[2] John Wentworth, 1815-1888. He was born in New Hampshire, and was a graduate of Dartmouth College; he came to Chicago in 1836 and within a month had become editor of the *Chicago Democrat*. From 1839 to 1861, he was its sole owner, editor and publisher. He was admitted to the bar in 1841; member of Congress from 1843 to 1851, 1853 to 1855 and 1865 to 1867; and mayor of Chicago from 1857 to 1863. In public, as in private life, his motto was "Liberty and Economy." He was influential in bringing the River and Harbor Convention to Chicago. Wentworth was a striking figure, being six feet, seven inches in height, and weighing some three hundred pounds.

[3] James Curtiss, a Democrat, was elected mayor on March 2, 1847.

Among the arrangements of the morning was one, that in disputed votes, each delegation should be entitled to vote in states, and each delegation should choose a person to cast the votes. Another was, that each delegation should elect a person to act for it, and that the persons so elected should compose a committee to nominate officers for the Convention, and to make rules and orders and other arrangements to be observed. We chose B. B. Mussey of Boston as chairman, and authorized him to vote for the Massachusetts delegation. We chose Artemas Lee of Templeton as member of the nominating committee, and also elected a Secretary.

The Convention then adjourned until four o'clock. This afternoon the nominating committee are in session, and at the time I am writing, six o'clock, have not agreed upon their report. In the mean time, the Convention itself is in session under its temporary organization, and speeches have been made by several gentlemen. I was not able, without too much trouble, to penetrate the mass, and so have not heard the talk of this afternoon; but I heard enough from Mr. Corwin of Ohio to be satisfied that he is for political action, and disposed to make political capital out of this Convention.

People are here from all parties, but I cannot disguise the fact that the majority appear to be Whigs. They talk Whig, and they don't pretend to be any thing else than Whigs. What will be the effect, time will tell; but the West is aroused and will assert its right to a share of the public plunder—will have appropriations for the improvement of its lakes and rivers, let who will be President.

P. S. Since the foregoing was written, the committee has reported a list of officers, Judge Bates of Missouri being President,[4] and each state having a Vice-President; William T. Eustis of Boston is one of the latter. When the report was made, a

---

[4] Edward Bates, 1793-1869, was born in Virginia; he moved to St. Louis in 1814. He was a Representative in the Twentieth Congress and presided over the National Whig Convention in 1856; a leading candidate for presidential nomination in 1860; Attorney General of the United States, 1861-1864.

member of the committee stated that the minority of the same was in favor of Thomas Corwin of Ohio for President of the Convention, and proposed his name in opposition to the name reported; but Mr. Corwin declined, and the Convention, as I think they would have done without his declination, voted down the proposition at once.

The mail is about to close, and I will write you more for to-morrow.

CHICAGO
July 6, 1847

In my hurried letter of yesterday, I could not give you one hundredth of the actual information with which I am burthened respecting this place, and the convention which is now in session. For particulars of the latter, I must refer to the newspapers, for without taking a reporter's desk on the platform, and working all the time, it would be impossible to give any thing like even a sketch of what is doing.

There are men here who have come to make party capital, and there are men here who have come with a single eye to the professed objects of the gathering. But the majority is of the latter class, and the politicians find themselves trammeled, or if not trammeled, find that the leading sentiment is in opposition to all the professed Democratic doctrines of Mr. President Polk and his predecessors. The consequence is that while Whiggery, if I may use such a word, is predominant, the Locofocos feel a little uneasy, talk of their disgust at the "management," which they see so clearly, and try to mar where they cannot make.

Clergymen, of all other classes of men, are the most unfit to be sent on political missions, and if they have not discretion enough to stay at home of their own accord, their friends and neighbors ought not to make other people suffer by sending them into conventions, where they are entirely out of place. New-England stands high in the estimation of the Western people, but yesterday she was rendered ridiculous, if not contemptible, by the intrusion of a clergyman, before the thousands of people assembled, with a *written* speech of adulation and praise for the Puritan fathers and their descendants. I am ready to render all due credit to the gentleman who placed New-England, and in particular the Massachusetts delegation, in such a mortifying position, for his honesty of purpose, and for his good intentions, but I cannot but regret, in common with others, that he did not keep his sermon for ears that could better tolerate self-glorification. When he concluded, Mr. Corwin of Ohio was called for, and the withering sarcasm with which that gentleman politely agreed to all the fulsome twaddle of the Rev. Mr. Allen, was enough to have killed any one not wrapped up [in] self-conceit as with a coat of mail.

The greater part of the afternoon, yesterday, was spent in discussing some trifling matters of proceeding, and resulted in following the recommendations of the business committee. It was Mr. Charles King of the New-York *Courier* and *Enquirer,* who proposed to make Mr. Corwin the President of the Convention, and his movement was one injurious to any desire that he may have to increase his political or personal influence. Mr. Corwin's friends were much disappointed, and in proportion to their disappointment is their tone of complaint. They even talk of ill-usage, and intimate that Mr. Corwin expected the situation, in consequence of promises held out to him in advance. Mr. Corwin made an able speech yesterday afternoon, and was listened to with great attention.

To-day a committee of two from each state was appointed to draw up resolutions for consideration, and at half-past four o'clock they reported a long series, and much to the astonishment of every body the chairman stated that they had been agreed to unanimously. They are very strong, and were received with marks of favor, and were much applauded. When I left the tent, at five o'clock, Mr. J. C. Spencer of New-York was on the stand, explaining and advocating their passage. I see no reason now, why the convention should not close its deliberations to-morrow forenoon.

If I appear enthusiastic in my notices of the new world which has been opened to me, not only here, but in New-York state, I can offer no excuse, for I am filled with the wonders and the capacities of the West. A person living in Boston, and having experience of our hard soil, and the hard work which the people of Massachusetts have to undergo to produce even moderate crops knows nothing of what is to be opened to us by the extension of our railroad communications, without coming to see for himself. I consider that the Ogdensburg[5] Railroad is but joining us on to the string of western lakes, for it must be apparent to every one who looks at things as they are, that Boston is the natural market, on the Atlantic shore, for the whole country. New-York can never compete with us for this trade, to our injury, and while there must always be enough for both, we must, by force of natural circumstances, take the lion's share. It is incredible to me that we should so long have delayed building the road through Northern New-York, and it would be incredible to all our readers if I should show them what I know must be the immediate result of its being built at this present time. People are absolutely suffering for want of the accommodations which we are about to offer them by that line, and when we can say that the cars are in running order, we shall wonder how they have lived so long without it.

I saw to-day in the street casks of nails manufactured at Plattsburg, N. Y., which, on inquiry, I ascertained had arrived at this place after a long voyage down Lake Champlain, to Whitehall and Troy, thence through the Erie Canal to Buffalo, and then through the lakes to Chicago. Look at the map, and see how much of transportation would have been saved, if these nails could have come by railroad from Lake Champlain to Ogdensburg. As the newspapers say—comment is unnecessary.

Chicago is destined, some day hence, and no very far-off day neither, to be one of the largest cities in the Union; and the

---

[5] Ogdensburg, New York, located on the St. Lawrence River, is the terminal of deep water navigation on the Great Lakes.

wisdom of its projectors, in laying out its wide streets, is every where apparent. The streets are all lined with trees, and the Acacia and Maple and Elm are abundant; the Acacia, in particular, grows very thrifty and beautiful. The soil, even in its worst places, after you go a few yards from the shore of the lake, is nothing but the richest garden earth to the depth of many feet, and its capacity for yielding produce is unfathomable.

The latitude of Chicago is about the same as that of Boston and the climate, as regards heat and cold, is about the same. The prevalent breezes are from the North, and blowing over the pure fresh water of Lake Michigan, are very healthy and invigorating.

To-day I stood in what is called the Old Fort, a spot occupied by barracks, with a square in the centre, the whole occupying not more space than the Common on Fort Hill, in Boston; and in that spot, in 1832, Gen. Scott collected for safety, and to protect them from the Indians, every inhabitant that lived within a circuit of thirty miles. In the space of that thirty miles, are now living nearly fifty thousand people! Twelve years ago, one hundred and fifty inhabitants was a large estimate for the census of Chicago, and to-day the residents are estimated at twenty thousand![6]

A large proportion of the people of this city are of eastern origin, mostly from New-England, and one would hardly be aware in the intercourse with the town's people that he was not in a New-England village. But the persons who come into town from the country, and from other States, are strongly marked with the characteristics of the West. The procession of yesterday exhibited these hardy countenances and sturdy frames to great advantage, and if nothing else results from the Convention but a knowledge, by personal inspection, of the traits of character existing in each and all of the different classes of the East and the West, the North and the South, who are here assembled, enough

---

[6] Chicago had a population of approximately thirty in 1829; in 1835 the census figure was 3,265, and by 1847 it had increased to 16,859.

will have been accomplished to pay for all the cost and labor of individuals, and of this community.

The weather is intensely hot, and the roads are dusty. Chicago has no stone, and consequently the streets are not paved. Every street, however, to the end of its settlement—for some of them run out for miles into the prairie, beyond where there are houses,—is accommodated with a wide wooden sidewalk, which is pleasant to walk on. The crossings, too, are generally accommodated with a plank foot path, which is very fortunate, as some times one might run the risk of getting lost by sinking into the rich and fruitful looking earth. The dust is not sand, and the mud is not clay, but it looks more like the soil of a hot-house garden bed, than like any thing else.

CHICAGO
July 7, 1847

The Convention has adjourned, *sine die*, after passing the resolutions reported by the committee, voting thanks to the citizens of Chicago, and to the President, and listening to a long and eloquent speech from the President in reply. Judge Bates has acquitted himself during his term of office with great ability, and earned the respect of the thousands who have been in attendance. His speech this morning was singularly appropriate, modest, Christian and patriotic, and the three times three cheers with which he was saluted on concluding were well deserved. I must refer you to the Chicago papers for particulars of the proceedings, with the single remark that every thing has gone off harmoniously, and every body is now satisfied and pleased. The disaffections and the quibblings of a few Locofocos, to which I have before referred, appear to have been but the effervescence of a soda bottle, and better counsels, calmer judgment, soon settled all bickerings. I believe that now every body thinks that the Convention has done good, and I am satisfied, as I said yesterday, that the mere collection of so many people together, in this place, will be a national good, even if nothing results from our deliberations.

After the Convention adjourned, the mass went into committee of the whole, and we were entertained with speeches from different gentlemen from different places. You never saw so happy a multitude, nor so uproariously orderly and determinedly happy a set of men. They called for one after another of the prominent men known to be present, and would take no excuse; Western men wanted speeches, and speeches they would have at any rate. Among the rest, our friend Burlingame[7] was loudly called for, and the Badgers of Wisconsin, and the Wolverines of Illinois, would not be put off. He tried to turn them over to another gentleman of the Massachusetts delegation, but they would not be turned over to any body. They told him he must speak first, and they would hear his friend afterwards. He spoke for a few minutes in his usual eloquent manner, and his speech was received with great attention and most loudly applauded. He then introduced E. H. Allen of Boston, who made a short speech, which was well received, although it did not attract the attention it deserved. It is always unfortunate for a stranger to follow a known and popular speaker, and Burlingame is so well known to the boys of the West, that they were not attentive to any one else for some time.

All day, forenoon and afternoon, the tent has been full, and one after another has been made to mount the stage and air his vocabulary for a while. The day winds up with a bright sky, a burning heat, and lots of fun of all kinds. An old-fashioned country muster never exhibited any thing to be compared to the scenes of the last three days, and nowhere else could such an occasion pass off so well and so noisily, so rowdyish and so good-naturedly, as here in the West.

The more I see of Chicago, the more I am impressed with the value of its increasing trade with Boston,—for Boston is the Atlantic sea-port of this great country. Everywhere one meets with something new to astonish and delight him, and the only

---

[7] Anson Burlingame of Boston, who later became the celebrated American minister to China.

wonder soon gets to be, that we have not sooner made efforts to secure it all to ourselves. To-day I have had a ride on the prairie, and although new to me, I was coolly told that I had seen nothing at all. The flowers growing wildly beautiful, the roads running through miles and miles of unfenced grounds rich with soft black loam, the young trees growing thriftily and luxuriantly, the tall grass,—all, I am told, are nothing. Well, we shall see in a few days, for I am off, to-morrow, for the interior of the state, where I am to find "something" worth looking at.

I could write columns about Chicago, and give statistics upon statistics, to show that it is the greatest place of its age, and is destined to be still greater; but *cui bono?* You would not believe half I should tell you, and instead of writing notes from a plain diary, I should be set down as a romancer. This is a great place for the pork trade, in which article it is destined to rival Cincinnati, and its beef is said to be the finest in the world. Our steamer is now taking on board, as freight, two hundred casks—hogsheads of hams, which are to go through the lakes and the Erie Canal to Troy, and perhaps to Boston. Hundreds of barrels of beef and pork are also going on board, all bound East. Even at this season of the year the store-houses are filled with produce, and I this morning went into one where there were stored twenty-eight thousand barrels of wheat.

On one side of the river is the Lake House,[8] which was built in the "times of expansion," as they are called, of 1836 or 1837, for a public house. It is well kept, well furnished, and very comfortable. In its vicinity and for some distance around, are scattered numbers of elegant private dwellings, surrounded by gardens, and the streets are all wide and regularly laid out. One street on this side skirts the river shore, and has on it a few warehouses, and a large number of retail shops, mostly occupied by foreigners,—Dutch and Irish. On the other side of the river is now the principal business, and Lake-street is filled with retail stores of as much beauty of

---

[8] The construction of the Lake House was begun in 1835 and completed during the following year.

LAKE STREET, CHICAGO, ABOUT 1852

arrangement, and with as valuable stocks of goods, as can be found in any city in America. In fact, Chicago is now, with its present population, as much of a business place as I know of, after our own city. Hundreds upon hundreds of wagons are in its streets, drawn by the finest horses in the world, and laden with every sort of commodity. In the fall of the year they have their wheat brought into the city from the country in immense wagons, called prairie schooners, which hold two hundred bushels at a time, and these may be seen stringing out through the roads for miles and miles.

This is a great place for the lumber trade, although no lumber grows in this neighborhood. The boards, &c., are brought from the Sault St. Marie and Lake Superior, in different kinds of vessels, and stored in the lumber yards, to be transported by wagons into the country. A canal is about being built which will soon afford great facilities for internal transportation.

One of the principal features in the procession of Monday, was the appearance of the fire department, and I have made many inquiries concerning its composition. It consists of four hundred men, all volunteers, and they all pay their own expenses and the expense of their machines and decorations. The chief engineer is Mr. Gale,[9] a gentleman who served his apprenticeship with Hilliard, Gray & Co. in Boston. There are four engines, to which are attached sixty men each, and a hook and ladder, and a hose company. The department is limited in number, and none but the best and finest young men in the city are admitted into its ranks.

The military escort for Monday's procession was a company of volunteer flying artillery, who came from Cleveland, Ohio, bringing their horses, cannons, &c,—a hardy set of men, who certainly must have felt much patriotism and great interest in the objects of the Convention, to come so far and at such an expense of time and money. To-day I saw them manoeuvre, going through the different evolutions as practised by Bragg's and Ringgold's troops,

---

[9] Stephen F. Gale served as chief of the fire department from 1844 to 1847. He was the first president of the Fireman's Benevolent Association, and a member of the first Board of Directors of the Chicago, Burlington and Quincy Railroad.

which we have all heard so much of. They certainly went through with their exercises with a rapidity that was astonishing.

The drays used here are the short drays in the New York style, but they are drawn by good horses. In fact I have not seen a poor-looking horse in the place. The pleasure carriages, of which there are an extra number for a place of this size, are of the most approved Eastern city style, and drawn invariably by such horses as would make envious our gentlemen and ladies of taste in Boston, where we generally have better carriage horses than they have in other places.

The city is beginning to grow thinner, and the steamboats that left last night and to-day have gone crowded with passengers. But even in its desolation from the mob, it is a populous place, and the streets are filled with people who go about for pleasure and business.

CHICAGO
July.

History tells that many years ago, I believe in 1812, serious fears being entertained that the Indians would destroy the small party then resident at this place, the commanding officer concluded to move away, and join a larger party at Fort Wayne. Previous to going he destroyed all the stores on hand that he could not carry, and particularly all the spirit. The Indians were very much incensed, after his departure, that they could not find the rum, and took to drinking the water of the river, into which the rum had been poured, pronouncing it to be "very good grog." They could see for themselves that the waters of the river, and the lake into which it empties, do not amalgamate at once, and they may have thought that the rum remained. However that may be, it is very apparent that the waters remain of different color and of different taste, to this day. Chicago is so low that there is no good water for drinking, except that which is brought from the lake, and the latter is very pure and wholesome; it is easily procured, and furnishes the drink for the inhabitants; the former, which is brown and muddy, is extensively used for washing, and for other ordinary domestic purposes.

Our friend Degrand some years ago called the Worcester depot in Boston the end of "Worcester Longwharf." I know no reason why I should not christen the Fitchburg depot the "Chicago Long wharf," for by whatever channel of communication the trade from Ogdensburg reaches Boston,—whether by the Vermont Central or the Rutland route—it must all go to Boston, or most of it by the way of Fitchburg. The directors are in duty bound to make me and my family free passengers for the rest of our lives, for giving them so good and appropriate a name. Any one who looks at the map, and every one who comes out here and sees the business that is transacted on the lakes and in this part of the Western country, must be convinced that all this trade must go to Boston. A gentleman who is extensively engaged on the Fox river, thirty miles from this place, tells me that now, round-about as it is, he sends all his supplies, even his New-Orleans sugar and molasses, from Boston,— now it comes through the Erie Canal; but when Ogdensburg Railroad is completed, it will come more directly, and at a saving of some hundreds of miles of transportation. Perhaps I have mentioned this latter circumstance before; but I write at great disadvantage, with no opportunity to revise and correct, and as the printers are by this time satisfied, with no conveniences for stationery. All I aim to do is to state facts, and if time and opportunity were given me, I could multiply my record of facts almost innumerably. Never yet did Yankee go out from home with a more inquisitive disposition than myself, and I never saw but one man, and he was an esteemed member of the original party with which I left Boston, that asked so many questions. I shall be very happy if I ever become half as valuable a member of society, and retain but half as much statistical knowledge, as he is noted for.

When our Massachusetts delegation assembled, on Monday morning, on board the steamboat *Louisiana*, for organization, there was a general feeling of regret as well as disappointment, that we had not one distinguished man among us, no capitalist, and no one whose name was known to the world. It was apparent that the Western people had expected to see some great man, and that

Massachusetts was looked to particularly for something that we could not supply. But we put up with the disappointment as best we could, and determined to do our duty. The selection of Messrs. Eustis, Lee and Hobart, for prominent candidates for the offices we might be called upon to fill, was well and judiciously made, and gave satisfaction. Now that the Convention is over, and we have mingled with the thousands of strangers assembled here, I am not only disposed to give up my regret at the absence of those to whom we had a right to look for countenance on this occasion, but also to be rather glad of the result. As I said before, much was expected of Massachusetts, and I doubt whether any delegation, from any part of the country, met with more consideration and respect than we did. Gentlemen were continually claiming introductions, and continually offering their hospitality, and proffering their services to make known to us what we most wanted to know, to show what we most wanted to see. If we had had with us a prominent man, he would have absorbed a great part, if not the whole, of the attention which was now disseminated among the twenty-eight members of the delegation; and although the state might have been more distinguished, I have strong doubt whether as much good would have been effected. We had with us men of sound sense, men of business, and men with dispositions to encourage and increase the general desire for greater intercourse between the East and the West. We shall find hereafter that the association of intelligent men from different sections of the country is of quite as much advantage as the notoriety of a political or very rich delegation.

The mass of strangers is now about separating, and although the hopes and the expectations of some may have been disappointed, there is the best feeling prevailing, the utmost satisfaction expressed by every body. Politics have been dropped, after an ineffectual attempt on the part of a few unquiet and ambitious aspirants to do something—they did not themselves know what; the resolutions adopted, which are mostly from the pen of Mr. John C. Spencer of New-York, if they are not as strong and as startling as some people expected, are expressive of sentiments in which all parties agree. The closing speech of Judge Bates, the President, is spoken of on all sides with great and undisguised admiration, and the subsequent speeches in the informal mass meeting, of which Horace Greeley was chairman, served to let off the gas with which many gentlemen were filled, as well as afforded an opportunity to the curious to hear the eloquence of those who, from circumstances, were not able to mingle prominently in the doings of the Convention.

This place is the terminus of the Illinois and Michigan canal, of which so much has been said for the last twenty years. It was first surveyed in 1821, and in 1827 Congress appropriated a large quantity of the public lands in aid of its construction. Of its late history, the failure to complete it, its pecuniary troubles, &c., the capitalists of the country are well advised. Its fortunes have been chequered, and at times its fate has been doubtful.[10] But better days have come, and now there is a reasonable prospect of its speedy completion. It will not be long before the resources of the Illinois will be doubled by its means of easier transportation, and another link will be added to the chain which extends to the Atlantic market in Boston harbor.

I could spend much time here, in learning the sources of wealth which are to be opened to our New-England people, and in enjoying the hospitality of the inhabitants who are so closely connected with us by ties of the nearest kind. The business men are nearly all from our section of the country, and have brought with them and retained their New-England affections. The feelings and the

---

[10] In January, 1836, the legislature authorized the Governor to borrow $500,000 on the credit of the state, to begin the Illinois and Michigan Canal. Ground was broken July 4, 1836. Loan after loan was authorized as the work progressed, but the money did not come in fast enough and work ceased. In 1845, three trustees representing the state and the bondholders were chosen, loans were secured, and the work advanced rapidly. On April 23, 1848, the *General Thornton* passed through the entire length of the canal.

The state debt in July, 1847 was over $14,000,000. This amount was divided into Internal Improvement Debt, $8,000,000 and Canal Debt, $6,000,000. Between the opening of the canal in 1848 and October, 1870, the receipts were $4,360,419, and the expenses $1,828,790.

habits tend to connect them still with the places from which they emigrated, and Boston, as the head-quarters of business, must, by and by, be the recipient of most of their trade.

I believe that there is not a single bank in Illinois now in existence. There was a State Bank, located at the seat of government in Springfield, but it has shared the fate of many others, and now only lives to wind up its affairs. The money in circulation is of all sorts, including New-York, Canada, Wisconsin, and New-England bills; but there is money enough, and much more of the business is transacted for cash than would, under the circumstances, be supposed. There are agents or brokers here, who draw on New-York and Boston when wanted, who are in good standing, and are quite able to supply cash drafts at all times. How far business would be facilitated by the establishment of local banks with small capitals, as in Massachusetts, I am not prepared to say, and that is a serious question, which is now undergoing consideration at a State Convention to revise the Constitution, which is now in session at Springfield.

SPRINGFIELD, ILLINOIS
[July 9, 1847]

If any one had asked me, six weeks ago, to take a journey into the interior of Illinois, I should have hesitated, and should have been appalled at the task. Yet here I am, having been almost irresistibly led along from point to point, through states and lakes and rivers, and with a promise on my hands to go still further. A few hours, only, before the time appointed for leaving Chicago, on my way home, I was induced to join a party to this place, to inspect the interior of the country, to see the Illinois canal, and to learn from personal observation whether the extravagant assertions,— for they appear extravagant to a stranger,—which are made by the people of the West, are borne out by facts. Accordingly, as the *Baltic* started to go in one direction, I started in a stage-coach to go in another. Our party was composed of nine persons inside, three of whom were ladies. Three only were acquainted—that is to say, two only were known to me, and they were strangers less than a week ago, and they knew no one else of the company. We get acquainted strangely on such occasions, and in this western country, quite readily. One lady was from Vermont, and lived at Dresden, in this state. She was traveling alone, fifty-six miles, to her present home. One man was a Bostonian, now residing in Wisconsin, who came away to seek his fortune with his young wife, eighteen years ago. His wife and her sister, both natives of Bangor, Me., were with him, having been on a pleasure tour to the lakes. They have neither of them been in New-England for more than five years. One was from Connecticut, one from New-Hampshire, and two from Massachusetts. All were from New-England, and I was the only one who had seen his native state for years. These facts came out in the course of the day.

We left Chicago at nine o'clock in the morning, and took our way across the prairies. At first the road was uneven, dusty and uninteresting, exhibiting some cultivated farms, and but little wooded country. Soon we came upon the line of the canal, which we followed, at a short distance, through its whole extent. I have not time, nor inclination, to give a description of the few places we stopped at on the first day, nor to tell of the gross deception, and swindling actions, and gross impertinences of the stage-drivers, of which I could, if so disposed, fill a column or two, and then not tell half. The public houses were worse than the worst taverns ever seen in New-England,—dirty, and ill-found in every respect. An old lady furnished, at short notice, a dinner of boiled eggs, fresh fried pork, and tolerable coffee, which was much more palatable in the participation than in the appearance.

The prairie, where not cultivated, and in many places where it is, remains without fences, for wood is scarce for many miles after we leave Chicago, and the few houses to be met with are sadly lacking in many of the necessary boards and timbers. Corn and wheat grow luxuriantly, and large droves of cattle are to be found grazing at different places. Hogs are numerous, and I can easily conceive that Chicago may, by and by, become a great pork mar-

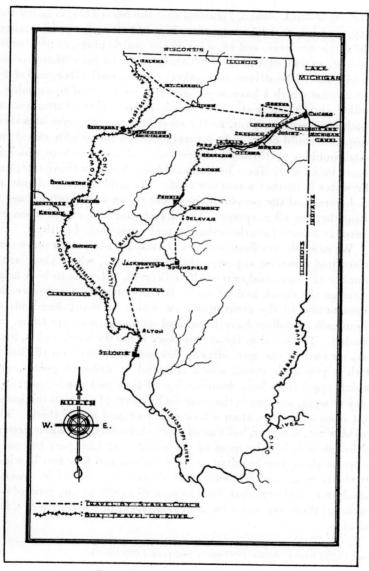

BUCKINGHAM'S ROUTE

ket.[11] When at Chicago, I learned that the beef of this country was very superior, and I had opportunities of testing its good quality. The cattle are large, and grow fat on the prairie grass, at little or no expense, except of the time which it takes to raise them to the proper age to be driven to market. At a small place, called by some name which I have now forgotten, we stopped to examine a boiling spring, the water of which is as bad to the taste, and as much filled with sulphur, as the most enthusiastic lover of watering-places could desire. At several places in the neighborhood the water bubbles up through white sand, and the pool into which it comes looks more like a boiling cauldron than any thing else; but the water is neither warm nor cold. The driver gave it freely to his horses, and the people of the house in the neighborhood use it altogether for all purposes. The driver said it operated upon his horses as a sort of gentle cathartic, and made them healthy.

We came to no village until we arrived at Lockport, a place that is not laid down on any map that I have seen, where there are a number of stores and two or three taverns. Here is to be a large basin on the canal, and we had a fine opportunity to observe the construction of the great work, on which so many hundreds of thousands of dollars have been, and so many more are to be, expended. The canal as far as this place is nearly level, and is, for a greater part of the way, already finished; it is faced on the inside with a yellowish stone, which is found at different points, and which appears to be a combination of lime and sand-stone; it is easy to work, and lies in the quarries in layers of unequal thickness, but none of it more than a foot or a foot and a half thick. The canal is not, however, built up of stone throughout its whole extent, although it is for the most of the route. At Lockport the canal must be about two hundred or two hundred and fifty feet in width at the bottom, and the locks and abutments are laid in smooth, handsome masonry, that would do no discredit to any part of our country; there are seven locks in this place, in a distance of a few miles.

[11] The exports of the port of Chicago in 1845 were: wheat 956,860 bushels, flour 13,752 barrels, beef 6,199 barrels and pork 7,099 barrels.

We then passed over to a town called Joliet, which was named after an old Frenchman who originally settled here and owned a great part of the land. By some mistake it was originally called Juliet,[12] but the name was changed by act of the legislature a year or two ago, to conform to the proper title of the old original settler. Here are several blocks of stone stores, evidently built with a view to a large trade, which is to come at some future day. The village is laid out on a plain, and on the side of a hill, with a handsome stone bridge crossing the canal; and here, too, is a large, broad basin. The projectors of this canal, and the original directors and engineers, appear to have had in view the immense business which it will take and which it will create, or they must have been very extravagant in their notions. It is probable that they knew what they were doing, what the future was to accomplish; but they were then, in a manner, before the age; they spent too much money, and by their financiering, their want of prudence, involved themselves and others in difficulties from which better counsels are now re-lieving the state. Now it is certain that the canal will be finished, the bonds will be paid, and nothing that I can imagine, not even another revulsion in the financial condition of the country, can prevent the stock from being a paying investment, except some mismanagement take place before the work is finished. The pro-duce raised in the interior of the state is incalculable, and the pro-ducers must consume other articles in their turn, both of which, the exports and the imports, will, until a railroad is built side by side with it, pass through the canal to Chicago.

From Joliet to Dresden[13] we had an interesting ride, and at the latter place we took supper, our Yankee landlady serving us up codfish as a luxury, and hashed potatoes. At a small place called Morris, at half past eleven o'clock, we again stopped to change horses, and remained an hour in the most uncomfortable place you

---

[12] The plat for "Juliet" was recorded in June, 1834, the name being that of the founder's daughter, Juliet Campbell; this name the town bore until 1845, when it was changed to Joliet by act of the legislature.

[13] "A town site near the junction of the Des Plaines and Kankakee, and on the line of the canal." J. M. Peck, *A Gazetteer of Illinois* (2nd ed.; Philadelphia, 1837), 191.

can conceive of; the tavern-keeper and all his people were in bed, but we succeeded, after some difficulty, in getting into the house, and had the luxury of two tallow candles, and a little water, which was warm, and not very palatable. On the opposite side of the road was another still smaller tavern, from which proceeded the sound of a violin. We walked over, and found about twenty persons assembled in a room on the lower floor, trying to learn to dance cotillions; the room was lighted by a solitary dip-candle; the teacher, who was also the musician, was in his shirt sleeves, and wore a shocking bad straw hat; the ladies were two little girls, two old women, and two or three fat, coarse-looking girls, about twenty; one of the male dancers wore a straw hat, two or three were without coats, and the one who was evidently the dandy of the place—for village it could hardly be called—wore a nankin-colored frock coat, and had his blue pantaloons strapped down so tight that he could scarcely move about. We amused ourselves for some time in witnessing the troubles and disasters which befell the instructor in his attempts to make the company go through correctly with the difficult figures of right and left, cross over, and promenade.

The rest of our ride during the night was as uncomfortable as any enemy, if we had one, could desire. We made progress at the rate of less than three miles an hour; the weather was intensely hot, and not a breath of air was stirring; the horses and carriage raised any quantity of dust, which, of course, rose only high enough to fill the carriage; and we were nine inside passengers, a new one having been taken in to replace the lady we had left at Dresden—[*illegible*]. We arrived at Ottawa about six o'clock in the morning, having seen nothing of the country for many miles, but bearing about as indisputable evidence that the road had led through the same soft and fertile soil that we had had during the whole day before. Ottawa is a considerable village, and has a large court-house, pleasantly situated in a square surrounded with thriving acacia, or locust trees, and a number of stores, besides some half dozen bar-rooms, independent of four taverns.

I have spoken of the want of wood on the prairies. The acacia is easily cultivated, and grows very rapidly wherever it is planted; some people are beginning to appreciate its advantage, and when we come to any considerable settlement, we find that they have commenced setting out trees on the borders of the lots; in some places, large groves have been planted, which will, in a few years, be very valuable. Of bridges, we saw few during yesterday, being obliged to ford most of the streams; as we entered Lockport we forded the river Des Plaines, which is an eighth of a mile wide, although there is a ricketty bridge over it. The whole road from Chicago lies through a tract of country which is a sort of valley— if you can call that a valley where there are no hills on either side— which was once evidently the bed of a river. The prairie is in many places undulating, or rolling, and the waters of Lake Michigan once undoubtedly flowed uninterruptedly through to the Illinois river; the stones and rock formations show this, and the course of the former current is distinctly marked on the whole line. We forded a number of inconsiderable streams, which I am informed are sometimes—at the season of the year when the lakes and rivers are at the highest—almost impassable, and the greater part of the wood-land is on the borders of these streams.

After breakfast we took up our line of march, for it could hardly be called anything else, at the rate of two or three miles an hour, on the borders of the Illinois river, and passing by the village of La Salle, arrived at the terminus of the Canal at Peru, about twelve o'clock. Peru is next to Lisbon, in St. Lawrence county, New-York, the most uninviting place I ever saw. It is destined to become a great and growing village, the head and centre of a great trade. It is at the head of the navigation of the river, and already there are a number of stores, grog-shops, a barber's shop, and two taverns. In the early days in the history of the Canal, it was built up with log huts and mud cabins, to accommodate the Irish mud-diggers, and they remain in all their primitive ugliness, and with increased nastiness, the larger part of the village—certainly the most peopled, if we count the dirty children and the independent hogs. I ought to state, however, that a little distance from the bank of the river, on the high bluffs, are some good farms, and several nice dwellings; as I had little time to go into the interior from the main village, my remarks must be considered as applying to the terminus of the canal. Mr. Webster once owned a farm in this vicinity, where Mr. Fletcher Webster was a resident for some year or more, but I believe it has been sold to some one else.[14]

SPRINGFIELD, ILLINOIS
[July 11, 1847]

After waiting three hours at Peru, in the hope of finding a better conveyance, we embarked on board a small steamboat called the *Dial*, to come down the Illinois river. We were loaded with freight and crowded with passengers. The engine was out-doors, on the lower deck, and altogether the prospect of comfort was very small. The captain, however, did his best for the accommodation of every body, and the steward served up a very good dinner. A company of about fifty raw volunteer recruits for the Mexican army were desirous of coming on board, but the captain refused to take them, and thereby deserves our gratitude; for they were excessively noisy and very drunk. We stopped at several small places on the river, to take in more freight, particularly at Hennepin and at Lacon. At this latter place, our friends J. & N. Fisher of Boston, own considerable property, and carry on a large business in packing pork, &c. It is rather a pretty place, and will, like all other places of the kind, share the fate of all in this Western country, and be a place of great trade. We remained at Lacon for nearly three hours, and took on board two hundred barrels of flour and provisions, two hundred bags of wheat, and some wool. We started again after dark, and arrived at Peoria about two o'clock in the morning.

---

[14] Fletcher Webster, 1813-1862, was the son of the renowned Daniel Webster. He was graduated from Harvard in 1833. After studying law with his father, he moved to Peru, Illinois in 1837, where he practiced for three years. He was his father's private secretary during part of the latter's services as Secretary of State; a member of the Massachusetts legislature in 1847; and surveyor of the port of Boston, 1850-1861. He was killed in battle in 1862.

PEORIA IN 1846
From a contemporary painting.

I have heard of flies, and mosquitoes, and bed bugs, and fleas, and sundry other nuisances that are said to infest the Western waters. I have heard of the same kind of troublesome vermin being rather numerous in Mexico, but I never could be brought to believe one half of what I experienced on board the *Dial*. The boat actually swarmed with them after dark. The heat of the weather and the heat of the boat, and the lights, brought them about us, and I should think that they were, in variety, countless as they were in number. The lady who lately so industriously counted the seeds in a fig, and published the results of her labor in the newspapers, would here have been absolutely foiled. They came and they staid; they were brushed off and fell upon the deck, but their places were immediately supplied by an additional increased number. The seeds in a fig would not grow or increase during the process of counting, but the insects were multiplying from dark until daylight. The floors, the state-room partitions, the mast of the boat, the ceiling, the freight, the baggage, and the passengers, were literally covered. We had mosquito nets to our berths, but shutting out the winged insects seemed but to serve as a better chance to allow the creeping things to luxuriate. Some people slept! Happy immobility! I tried segar smoke on the upper deck, and it had a partial effect; but the enemy was invulnerable, and as soon as possible I took my baggage in hand and went ashore at Peoria, and laid down on the steps of the hotel at the top of the hill, to wait for daylight.[15]

Peoria is a beautifully situated town on the right bank of the river, and is already the seat of a great business. It commands one of the most grand and interesting views in the world, and is built or laid out something in the New-England style. It has a large extent of back country to supply, and has increased

---

[15] It is a river trip of sixty-seven miles from Peru to Peoria. The hotel in Peoria was either the Clinton House at the corner of Fulton and Adams, or the Planters House at Hamilton and Adams streets. These hotels were only two blocks from the Illinois River. In 1847, the city did not extend much, if any, above Adams Street, so either may have been at the "top of the hill."

within a few years almost beyond what it would be considered reasonable for me to state. In the little time I remained here, I had little opportunity to see its beauties or to learn of its trade and capacities; but as daylight came gradually on, I saw how it was situated, and soon took a walk around the more settled and business portion of the town. But everybody was asleep. The stores were shut, the night lamps were out or burnt dim, and the early morning dawn only exposed the silent beauties of a landscape without showing vitality. It was a picture of still-life, which any painter might copy, and which, if copied, would be purchased and appreciated by the man of taste, as the richest of his collection.

At four o'clock we took a stage coach for the interior, six inside, in a carriage built to carry but four, and drawn by horses that evidently knew their driver to be bent on making work easy and pay profitable. We crossed the river in a ferry-boat,[16] and then all got out and walked up a long hill, turning every now and then to admire the beautiful scenery, which included the town of Peoria, the river and other objects of interest in the distance.

Our party was again changed. We had two members of Congress from the state of Illinois, one Whig and one Locofoco,[17] and persons of other professions. Query,—Is a member of Congress a professional man or not? We started in a grumbling humor, but our Whig congressman was determined to be good natured, and to keep all the rest so if he could; he told stories, and badgered his opponent, who it appeared was an old personal friend, until we all laughed, in spite of the dismal circumstances in which we were placed. The character of the Western people is in every respect different from ours. Our Locofoco friend is a regular canvasser; he says that he has a way in his district

---

[16] The ferry was owned by William L. May, a member of Congress from 1834 to 1838.

[17] The Whig Congressman was Abraham Lincoln, and the Locofoco was Robert Smith of Alton, Illinois. Smith was a member of Congress from 1843 to 1849 and 1857 to 1859.

of bowing to everybody, of kissing every man's child, and making love to every man's wife and daughter; he regretted that he did not ask "Long John," as everybody calls Mr. Wentworth, how he should behave in Wentworth's district, because the force of habit is so great with him, he feared he might exceed the bounds of propriety—it may be that the fashion with Long John is more abrupt, and in that case he might be going contrary to established usage. For some miles we were in Wentworth's district, and a tolerably poor district it appeared to be.[18]

We breakfasted at Tremont, a very pretty village on a prairie, but the propriety of the name did not make itself manifest, as there were no three hills any where in the neighborhood;—all was level country. Tremont was about twelve years ago an uninhabited prairie, and a gentleman of our party stated that a friend of his, one winter, since 1835, entrusted his wife to his care to go to a town some miles further south. That friend had purchased largely of lands in the present town of Tremont, and had had a lithographic map prepared, exhibiting the squares, and the buildings, and the trees which might thereafter be erected and set out. The wife saw the map and wished very much to go through her husband's town; but when she arrived there she was of course disappointed, as no houses, no squares, no trees, no any thing, was to be seen, but a level and uninteresting prairie.

Now there are houses; trees have been planted, and as every thing that is planted in this soil grows very rapidly, the squares and the streets are sufficiently marked; there is a meeting-house, and a tavern, lots of good farms, and a number of stores, and several mechanic shops, and a saw-mill worked by horse-power.

After breakfast we were fairly launched on one of the great prairies of the state, and I must acknowledge that I did not see a prairie in the neighborhood of Chicago—that is, comparatively speaking. For miles and miles we saw nothing but a vast expanse of what I can compare to nothing else but the ocean itself.

[18] Buckingham was in error; the western boundary of Wentworth's district in 1847 lay some miles to the east of the stage route from Peoria to Springfield.

The tall grass, interspersed occasionally with fields of corn, looked like the deep sea; it seemed as if we were out of sight of land, for no house, no barn, no tree was visible, and the horizon presented the rolling of the waves in the far-off distance. There were all sorts of flowers in the neighborhood of the road, which, by the way, did not appear to be a road, and all the colors of the rainbow were exhibited on all sides,—before, behind, east, west, north and south,—as if the sun were shining upon the gay and dancing waters. We saw the white-weed of our New-England, the wild indigo, the yellow mustard, the mullen, the clover, red and white, the purple nettle, the various colored phlox, numerous yellow, pink and crimson flowers, and almost everything else that is beautiful, that we have ever heard of. Occasionally we passed a cultivated spot, where some person had purchased land from the government, and had made a farm,—cattle, too, are numerous, in herds, and horses in large droves, and swine uncountable. In the distance, we saw at intervals, groves of trees, which looked like islands in the ocean, and we learned that they were planted for the purpose of raising timber. Every thing will grow in this state, and the soil is everlasting, never wearing out, and never needing manure.

Again we came to a settlement, or village, called Delavan, where there was a post-office and a tavern. We changed horses and ordered dinner. Two doctors had offices directly opposite each other, and each kept a sort of apothecary shop; but such shops I never saw before. I went into one of them, and found in one corner a bed, the sheets of which appeared as if they had never been washed. On one side of the room was a case of shelves, on which were paraded half a dozen books, probably comprising the whole library of the worthy practitioner, and twice that number of bottles, labeled—*mirabile dictu!*—with understandable names, and two or three gallipots. In one corner was a pair of saddle-bags, and in another corner a saddle; but the doctor was off at a distance to visit a patient. I think I should be patient for some time before I should send for such a son of

Esculapius—and yet he may be a patient, pains-taking, learned, and very charitable member of his profession. Appearances are often very deceitful, as has been remarked many hundred times before.

We dined. And such a dinner! The table was set in a bed-room, which was neither plastered nor boarded up, the open air, if there had been any, coming through in all directions. If we had had a rain storm to encounter, we should hardly have been protected from it, and for mid-winter there was nothing to keep out the snow. But the landlord was civil, his wife and daughter bare-footed and dirty, and he could only keep off the flies by waving continually over the table a bough which he had cut from one of his locust trees. The table-cloth was stained with the grease of many former meals, if with nothing worse, and his meat, which he called beef, was swimming in fat. The only things palatable were some fried eggs and some hashed potatoes, with some tolerable bread. However, we satisfied our craving appetites, and started in good spirits, with the hope of doing better next time.

How we speed on our journey for the rest of the day, it is unnecessary to relate. It is sufficient to say that we came, in the course of the afternoon, to a more wooded tract of land, forded several streams, and saw more beautiful flowers, several groves of acacias, and in the distance, what appeared to be hills of trees or islands of forests. Towards Springfield the cultivated farms were more numerous, and we passed through miles and miles of tall corn, the bright and beautiful green of which was almost dazzling in the sunlight; some acres of wheat, tall as an ordinary man; and many fields of oats, with some of barley—all of which appeared ready for the sickle.

We were now in the district represented by our Whig Congressman, and he knew, or appeared to know, every body we met, the name of the tenant of every farm-house, and the owner of every plat of ground. Such a shaking of hands—such a how-d'ye-do—such a greeting of different kinds, as we saw, was never seen before; it seemed as if he knew every thing, and he had a kind word, a smile and a bow for every body on the road, even to the horses, and the cattle, and the swine. His labor appeared to be so great, that we recommended to our Locofoco friend to sit on the other side of the coach and assist in the ceremonies; but he thought that that would be an interference with the vested rights of his friend and opponent, and so he declined, although he was evidently much disposed to play the amiable to several rather pretty girls that we fell in with at one of our stopping places. It seems that as there is honor among thieves, so there is etiquette among Western Congressmen.

On the road, during the afternoon, we met three large wagons loaded with wool, and drawn by three yokes of oxen each, on their way to Chicago, the wool being destined for the Boston market. Think of that. Look at the map. See what an extent of country that wool is to pass over, what will be the distance it is to be carried by water through the lakes, round over the northern part of Michigan, through the lake St. Clair, lake Erie, and thence by the Erie canal to Albany, and then by water down the Hudson and over Long Island Sound, or over our Western Railroad, and judge for yourself if the Ogdensburg Railroad would not, if it were now open, save something in time, if not in money, to the owner of that wool.

I have spoken somewhere of the cheapness of butter and cheese and eggs and poultry, in Northern New-York. On our road to Springfield, we saw a first rate roasting piece of beef—the first cut of the rib—weighing sixteen pounds, which was sold to a tavern-keeper for *four cents a pound*, and that was said to be a good price in this neighborhood. Think of that, ye housekeepers in Boston! Of vegetables we are now in the enjoyment of all the luxuries of the season, such as green peas, cucumbers, string and other beans, and new potatoes. Cherries and strawberries are among the things that were.

We arrived at Springfield early in the evening, after the most fatiguing day's ride that, in all my traveling, I ever experienced.

We were all tired and dirty, covered with dust and perspiration, and not in much better humor than we were when we started in the morning. The strangers in Buffalo complained of the impositions, the lies, and the impudence of certain steamboat captains, but I will put an Illinois stage agent or driver against any thing that ever I saw before, in Europe or America, and bet odds upon him for impudence and imposition.

[SPRINGFIELD], ILLINOIS
[July 12, 1847]

Why should I date from Springfield, or from any other town or city, when what I have to say in this chapter of my Diary relates to every thing and every where? Last evening, after a ride of ten miles and back again, through a most excellent country, lined with corn-fields, and oat-fields, and hemp-fields, I was taken *vi et armis* to the house of a new acquaintance, all dusty as I was, to supper. Remonstrance was useless, for he said that Western life and Western customs would excuse every thing. I am very much in the habit of accommodating myself to circumstances, and on this occasion I found little difficulty in making apologies for my personal appearance. The lady was, as she styled herself, a "Western girl," and she was not at all discommoded by her husband bringing home a stranger. We had a hearty meal, and after a long conversation separated for the night.

The ride I have alluded to was through a wooded part of the country, up hill and down dale—but yet it could not be called woods as we talk of woods in New-England and as for hills, we actually rode over none that would compare with the ascent from Congress-street to Washington-street through Water-street. In this neighborhood there is to be found considerable bituminous coal, but it is not used much—in fact, it is not used at all in families, because it makes so much smoke. As far as I can learn, it is about equal in quality to the common sort of Sidney coal, which we use in Boston.

About five miles from the city of Springfield, our old acquaintance, J. Vincent Brown, has established himself as a manufacturer of hemp. We passed by his place, but did not stop, as he was not at home. He has a contract to furnish hemp for the United States government, but his principal building was burnt a few weeks ago, and has not yet been entirely rebuilt. It is said that the hemp manufactured at his establishment is the best, and is packed handsomer than any that is sent from this part of the country.[19]

I have rode again on the prairies some ten miles and back, to the south-east, and have been where there are no roads, riding over the grass, and seeing the hemp, and the corn, and the wheat, and the oats, all of which grow without any cultivation, except that of sowing. With us, corn has to be hoed—but here on the prairies, the ground is ploughed up, the seed deposited, and when it comes up the plough is once more run through the field, and the corn ripens as it stands. Dry weather does not affect it injuriously, as there is moisture enough in the earth to sustain it, and with the least attention that can be bestowed upon it, the yield is from thirty to fifty bushels to the acre; on old farms, fifty bushels is a fair average crop.

I said but little, nothing at all, if I recollect right, about the Illinois river. It is a narrow stream, presenting many pretty views, but nothing very striking, and little variety. The shore is well wooded, and the different towns or landing places which we passed, coming down to Peoria, were built high up on hills, having levees or slopes of land running down to the water-side, with no wharves; in every case where we stopped for freight or passengers, the boat was run bow on to the shore and a plough

---

[19] J. Vincent Brown had a three-year contract with the United States Navy for hemp. Having an aversion to slave labor, Brown came to Sangamon County in 1846 and contracted with the farmers to raise 2,500 acres of hemp. He set up four steam rolling and breaking mills at a cost of $60,000. The building which burned was on Prairie Creek near the Beardstown Road, eight miles northwest of Springfield. Citizens of Springfield and farmers of the vicinity contributed liberally to the rebuilding of the structure. According to naval tests, hemp grown in Sangamon County in 1847 was the finest in the world, but the costs of production were too high for a profit-producing crop.

run out, and when we started again the boat was pushed off by main force into the channel. This is said to be the worst season to see the prairies for the lover of flowers, but I have gathered many that were beautiful. We are now between the spring and autumn, when many of the most brilliant of the plants are generally in the perfection of splendor. I don't know what would become of my enthusiasm if I should be here at those periods, for I am all but enchanted now.

To-day I visited the State House, to listen to the debates of the [Constitutional] Convention.[20] The President is not worth much as a presiding officer, for he understands, or at any rate practises, little of the etiquette necessary for parliamentary government; he seldom rises, never announces the names of the speakers, allows two of them to speak at once, and puts the questions in such a tone of voice that he can scarcely be understood. The chief clerk,[21] who has a tolerably clear intonation, stated the question when I was there this morning, and if it had not been for his assistance, I do not see how the members could have understood what they were voting for. A motion was made and carried, for the Convention to go into committee of the whole, and I expected something better from the new chairman,[22] but he seemed to know but little, if any thing more than the President, and was not any better than that officer in his manner of conducting business. The members of the Convention are to appearance a much more intellectual body of men

[20] The Constitution of 1818 was sadly outgrown; in the election of 1846, both parties favored a revision by large majorities. One hundred and sixty-two delegates began the task on June 7, 1847, and adjourned on August 31. The new Constitution, a series of compromises not too happily received by the leaders of either party, was ratified by a large majority at the polls in March, 1848.

Buckingham's views on Newton Cloud, the presiding officer, were not those of the *Illinois State Register*, Springfield's Democratic newspaper. Commenting on his election it said: "Newton Cloud was the Speaker of the last House of Representatives, and distinguished himself for impartiality, rapid dispatch of business and thorough acquaintance with parliamentary rules and usages. A better presiding officer could not have been chosen."

[21] Henry W. Moore of Gallatin County, the secretary or chief clerk, was Secretary of the Illinois Senate, 1846-1848.

[22] He refers to John Crain of Nashville, Illinois, who had served for ten years in the Illinois Senate and House.

than the members of our House of Representatives; they have generally marked features, and much character. As for discipline and etiquette, I cannot say much for them. Every member who spoke, rose and put one foot in his chair, and one hand in his breeches pocket, and more than half of the whole sat with their feet on the desks before them, tilting up in their chairs. They looked like sensible men, but they want training, from the President down.

The State-House is at present an unfinished building, of stone, and intended to be well-arranged; but the architect has set it too low on the ground, so that it will never be any ornament to the place.[23] It has a cupola built of wood, and stands in the centre of a large public square. By and by it will have a portico, with several large columns, but the columns are to be laid in blocks like the pillars before St. Paul's Church in Boston and will never present an appearance corresponding to the design of the architect. The interior, even, is not finished, and we ascend to the Representatives' hall, where the Convention assembles, by a flight of temporary stairs. The halls of the two houses will be very pretty when they are finished, but I doubt whether they will not want much remodeling before they will give satisfaction, either to members or to the sovereign people, who wish to listen to the debates of their servants.

Near the State-House is a much handsomer building, which was erected some years ago by the State Bank of Illinois: it has columns, and a porch in front, and looks quite classical. The business of the place is done in stores, which are arranged round and in the neighborhood of the square, and it is even now very considerable. A railroad is to be built from Springfield to Alton,[24] which will enable the farmers in the interior of the state to send their produce to a market; at present the only means

---

[23] The State House, now the Courthouse of Sangamon County, was raised a story in 1901. Begun in 1837, the building was not completed until the early fifties.
[24] The first train on the Alton & Sangamon Railroad arrived in Springfield on September 9, 1852. On July 30, 1854, the connection was made with Chicago.

ILLINOIS STATE HOUSE, SPRINGFIELD

Showing the Sangamon County Courthouse (1845-76) and the State Bank Building in the background at the left.

of transportation is by wagons, and this summer it has cost seventy-five cents to a dollar a barrel to send flour to Alton on the Mississippi, on its way to New-Orleans. Wheat cannot be sent, at present, at any price, as the cost of freight would absorb all its value,—the only way it can be sent to market, is in its manufactured state.

The fields of corn—the miles and miles of corn to be seen here—would strike a Massachusetts farmer with astonishment. A farmer in this neighborhood thinks nothing of raising one hundred acres of corn in one lot, and it grows of itself without any assistance. There are large lots of hemp also raised here, as I have before stated, and its greenness at this season, while not so dazzling as the corn, is equally deep and beautiful. As may be supposed, this is a great country for raising cattle, and I am almost afraid to tell you that I saw yesterday, in one drove, eleven hundred head of cattle, besides several hundred horses, and some mules, which were on the way to the East for sale;—they were going by the way of Indiana and Ohio to New-York state, and probably some of them may be found at Brighton before they are slaughtered. Hogs, of course, are plenty, and it is for the purpose of fattening these that so much corn is raised. When I said that Chicago might one day rival Cincinnati as a pork market, I may have been thought extravagant, but the thought is not so very absurd after all, if you will look at the means of raising the material. The animals are marked and turned out into the open prairie, and they come home at night, like the cattle, of their own accord, to be fed with "something warm and comfortable,"—something that they cannot get in their daily wanderings.

In the neighborhood of Springfield, and in the city itself, for I believe it is a city, there are many beautiful residences, and one can hardly believe that fifteen years ago, the place contained but two houses, one of which was a common drover's tavern,—that there was, as lately as 1835, but one mail a week brought here from the South, and but one a fortnight from the

North,—yet such is the fact.[25]

JACKSONVILLE, ILLINOIS
[July 14, 1847]

The weather has been so hot and dry, the crowd has been so intense, and the bustle so great, that I have not as yet gone out of the house to-day. The crowds of people—men, women and children—which have been moving into this town since five o'clock last evening, I cannot pretend to estimate. I am favored with a room fronting on the public square, and can see every thing that is going on. The numbers increase rather than diminish, and the people are coming from every direction, and in all sorts of conveyances. Stage coaches are scarce, but large wagons are plenty. Women ride on horses and on mules. Whole families come in on large wagons, the travelers being seated on straw-bottomed country chairs. The females are dressed in all the colors of the rainbow; but white, or what was white when the dresses were clean, predominates. Parasols are as plenty as blackberries, and are only outnumbered by cotton umbrellas,— every other man, whether on foot or on horseback, and every *old* woman, of whom there are not a few, carrying one of the latter articles.

This day is devoted to the *solemn* duty of depositing in the grave the remains of Colonel Hardin, which have been brought from Mexico for that purpose.[26] The state Convention has adjourned, and came here from Springfield, for the purpose of honoring the dead with the presence of its members, who may be seen in the crowd with extravagant badges of black crape on the left arm of each. But it is in fact *a gala day*. There is no solemnity. A country muster in New England, in old times,

---

[25] Buckingham overstated the rapidity of Springfield's growth, for more than twenty-five years, instead of fifteen, had elapsed since its founding. Springfield had perhaps thirty families in 1823, when the land was put on sale. The 1835 census listed 1,419 inhabitants, and this figure had increased to 3,900 by 1848.

[26] Col. John J. Hardin commanded the First Regiment of Illinois Foot Volunteers. He was killed in battle at Buena Vista on February 23, 1847. The newspapers estimated that the crowd in attendance at his funeral numbered over 15,000.

was as nothing to it. This is a temperance town, and no liquor is allowed to be sold in its precincts, but yet drunken men and boys are abundant, and noisy. Last night, a military company marched into town from Springfield, and to-day it has marched off to the strains of gay music, towards the former residence of the dead, to take up and escort the procession. The engine company is out with its banner. The masons are in full regalia. The Convention has assembled in a body, with black crape and blue scarfs. The square is over-run with mounted marshals, dressed with enormous white sashes, who are curvetting and galloping about in every direction, apparently with no other object in view than to show themselves off, and defeating that very object in a great measure, by raising such a quantity of dust, that it is difficult to see, sometimes, who kicks it up.

After an absence of two hours the people have all returned from the residence of the deceased, in the neighborhood of which—in fact, in sight of its very windows—an oration was delivered and a sermon preached, and other ceremonies per-formed. At the head of the procession rode the chief marshal, on a very gay horse, into whose sides we could see the rider, every minute or two, sticking his spurs, in order to make the animal still more gay. The marshal was dressed in white panta-loons, having a black stripe down the legs, and a sheet tied round his body, and he rode with his hat in his hand, bowing to the multitude like a victorious general making a triumphal entry into the city. The infantry company followed, the band playing Pleyel's Hymn in quick time. After the masons and others, came the black hearse bearing the corpse, and then the horse of Col. Hardin, dressed in mourning. But what was all this to what followed? Next came the family coach, containing the be-reaved widow and orphans! I would not cast a word of censure upon any one who really sorrowed. And it is not for any of us to say who sorrows in this world, where the countenance and the actions so often belie the real sentiments; but what a mockery does this seem to be of grief, to parade it before thousands of strangers—to follow in a gorgeous pageant the decorated hearse, in a march of some miles, through dust and noise, and sur-rounded with mounted marshals and racing cavalcade!

After marching all round the public square, the procession went to the burying-ground, where the body was deposited. After some recess, the multitude again assembled in a grove near Colonel Hardin's house, where a collation was served up to the public, and at which, after the manner of festive occasions, several speeches were made. Those of the returned volunteers who served under the deceased, and who belonged to the town, were treated to a collation at the house, by invitation of the widow!

And this is one scene connected with the Mexican war. It has been got up to gratify a spirit of military ardor, which is quite prevalent in this state, and it can result in nothing but the most incalculable mischief. More volunteers are called for, and regiments are now forming in Illinois. The fruit of to-day's pageant will be the enlistment of at least a thousand new victims to the insatiate ambition of our wicked and unprincipled gov-ernment. The streets are filled with the fathers and the mothers, the brothers and the sisters of volunteers, and yet the whole seem to be afflicted with the military mania.

It is not in Jacksonville alone that this spirit prevails, but I see it in every town and village south of Chicago, and it is more apparent the further I penetrate into the interior of the state. It does not appear to be patriotism, but a sort of ambition to be some thing. I learn, that unlike the volunteers of Massachu-setts and some other states, those from Illinois, with some few ex-ceptions, have been from some of the most respectable families in the state. Those who first enlisted who have not died in Mexico, are now returning; but they express, at present, very little or no opinion at all as to their feelings—they have generally gone quietly to their homes, being for the present apparently satisfied with the glory they have achieved.

Yesterday I met Lieut. Col. Weatherford, and a queerer

specimen of a sucker never yet was seen; a daguerrian picture of him would have made a sketch that no one would believe could have been taken from nature. On him devolved the command of the regiment after Col. Hardin's death.[27] He is now a thin, tall man, very much emaciated by sickness, and darker colored than most Indians. He had on a coarse blue checked cotton shirt, with no collar, and no neck-cloth. He wore a dirty colored linen frock, which has seen much service, and was open in front like a common frock coat. His pantaloons were of the common cheap blue cotton, and were worn through in holes about where his legs probably touched the saddle in riding. He had on shoes nearly worn out, with large spurs strapped on around the instep. We have had descriptions of the uncouth appearance of the Mexican officers, but no description I have ever seen gave me any idea of such a poverty-stricken and miserable specimen of a commander as did the actual appearance of the Lieutenant Colonel of the first regiment of Illinois Volunteers, on this his return from a successful and *honorable* (!) career in the present war. This is no fancy sketch, and it is not in the least exaggerated.

The Lieutenant Colonel talked of the war, and of his deeds in arms, but withal was rather modest. He claimed great credit for his regiment, and expressed great admiration of the character of Col. Hardin. But it is plainly to be perceived, that he is a broken-down man, unfit for further service, and without much hope for the future. He will probably, with scores of others in similar situations, become, if he is not already, a violent politician, an office-seeker and a demagogue.

WHITEHALL, ILLINOIS
[July 15, 1847]

After the festivities of yesterday were closed at Jacksonville, our party started, in an overloaded coach, for the Mississippi River. The country begins to lose that level appearance that it

---

[27] William Weatherford was elected colonel at Buena Vista, February 26, 1847, to succeed Colonel Hardin.

has exhibited before, and, as we proceed to the south, is more wooded, with more up-hill and down-hill. There is, however, still much prairie land to pass over, and the soil is, if possible, richer than it is farther north. Everything will grow here, and the settlers have taken some pains to plant trees, particularly the locust and the rock or sugar maple. In the valleys and on the hill-sides we find oak, and walnut, and the hazel-nut. On the hills are the blackberry and other bushes known in New-England—the mustard, the mullen, the whiteweed, &c. We are now in a part of the country that is "fenced in," and we behold on every side the most luxurious farms, good houses and large barns. As we proceed south, the corn grows, or has grown, taller and taller, with ears, in the silk, higher up in the air than a tolerably tall man can reach. The wheat is harvested, and the oats are about ready. We have seen some beautiful fields of rye, and thick tall grass of the various descriptions. As we pass through a more generally settled district, we find the prairie grass is nearly run out, and in its place is the timothy, and the red-top, and the clover. This is surely a great country, and this is a glorious season for the farmer.

We have stopped for the night at a very pleasant village, situated on a prairie, and at a tavern that would do honor to any good housewife in New-England. Every thing is neat and clean, every body is attentive, the supper has been well got up, and abundant in variety, as well as excellent in quality. The name of the landlord is Tracy, and he and his wife deserve to be remembered, and to be made known to the traveling community. May they become as rich as they wish, and be able to return to their native New-England, well rewarded for their toil and privations.

Late in the evening a stage-coach from Alton arrived, containing several returned volunteers, who were met by about fifty personal friends, who were in waiting. Of course there was much boisterous gladness exhibited on both sides; but the volunteers did not exhibit marks of much prosperity, nor of much elasticity of spirit. They have "seen the elephant," and have very little to say about him. The war is a sorry subject to most of those who have been engaged in it.

I think that it is a sort of duty that a traveler owes to his friends and acquaintances, to point out to them not only the best, but the worst, places on the route. It is not probable that many of my readers will ever find themselves in Jacksonville, as it is not on a direct route to any where that Boston people are likely to seek. But I must warn them to avoid the town until it has a good tavern. It has a *hotel*, which is not fit for a decently-dressed man to set his foot in, and a *house*, where he can find nothing comfortable. Although the town was full of people yesterday, both landlords left their boarders or guests to take care of themselves, and officiated all day as marshals to the procession. At the *hotel* we were overrun with women and children; the breakfast was absolutely nasty, so that I could not be prevailed upon to go to the table at dinner, which proved, I was informed, still more disgustingly dirty.

It seems as if I were doomed to be a victim to the Mexican war, in one shape or another. I was sick of it in Boston, and glad to be absent from all discussions on the subject for several weeks. But now I have again got into a current, and every day, every hour, I hear something about it. We have been bored almost beyond endurance, for one whole afternoon, by a returned volunteer lieutenant, who has described over and over again the battles of which he was a spectator, and sickened with his nonsense about patriotism, and disgusted by his avowed principles. He says he had a brother and a brother-in-law killed by the Mexicans, and he considers it a duty, as well as a pleasure, to kill as many Mexicans as he can. The scoundrel talks, too, of religion, and claims that the present war is favored by the Almighty, because it will be the means of eradicating Papacy, and extending the benefits of Protestantism. I doubt whether he has any more Christianity than knowledge, and his whole talk proves him a fool and a liar.

I give you a short letter to-night, for heat and dust, and the fatigue of incessant travel, have rendered me more fit for the bed than for my usual gossip.

ALTON, ILLINOIS
[July 16, 1847]

We came into this place at a snail's pace, although the road was down hill. The hill was so steep that it would have been dangerous for all of us if the wheels of the coach had not been locked hard enough to oblige the horses to draw. On the top of the last hill I had my first glimpse of the Mississippi river—apparently a calm, sluggish stream, as smooth as plate glass, with a bright polish which reflected the rays of the burning sun with dazzling splendor—it was painful to look at it. I found afterwards, that it was not so sluggish, but that it ran at the rate of about four or five miles an hour. When one is on its banks, it is a much more attractive sheet of water, and although differing from the St. Lawrence in its whole character, is, perhaps, quite as interesting to contemplate. Opposite to the city is a large island which prevents a view of the Missouri shore, but on the bluffs one can see over the low land and its trees, and have an uninterrupted sight of the hills of the neighbor-state.

This place is somewhat celebrated for the abolition riots which occurred here some years ago,[28] and my general impression was, that it was rather a rowdy city. But I find the people of an entirely different character. It is situated much like our New-England towns, and instead of having all the residences collected together near the centre of business, they are scattered all round among the hills, and over an extent of country embracing many miles. The principal portion of the inhabitants are New-England people, and many were originally from Boston—men who came

---

[28] On the night of November 7, 1837, the abolitionist editor, Elijah P. Lovejoy, was killed in attempting, with his friends, to prevent the seizure by a mob of his printing press, stored in the warehouse of Godfrey, Gilman & Company. The incident was broadcast by the press over the United States, many editors condemning the affair as an assault on the freedom of the press and speech even while they condemned abolition.

out to this country some twelve or fifteen years ago, and have, under all the fluctuations of trade, all the changes from rich to poor, and poor to rich, maintained their integrity, and are now, although Alton is not the thriving place it once was, doing good business, and are mostly well off in this world's goods. As a friend remarked a few days ago, Illinois, of all the states in the Union, is the poor man's country. Its resources are unbounded, and wherever an industrious man plants his foot, or digs the soil, he is sure to be remunerated for his trouble. The prairies once presented a vast expanse of waste land, covered with grass, and flowers of all the colors of the rainbow. Only a few years have been devoted to their cultivation, and now they are covered with corn and wheat, and oats, potatoes, hemp, and trees. Time was when there were no trees, except on the borders of the streams— now the locust is to be seen every where, and the farmers have planted that and many other descriptions of trees on the borders of their lots, in groves, and before their dwellings. There are a number of Dutch farmers settled in this neighborhood, and they have profited by the facility which the ground affords to become rich. As we approached Alton, the crops were more advanced than we had seen them in other places, and the large and substantial barns, are getting to be well filled. The Yankee, however, is the thriving man, all the world over, and where he is, there you see evidences of care and neatness, and plenty and prosperity; he may be laughed at, he may be scorned, he may be abused in various, or in all ways, but Jonathan is the man on whom the people, his neighbors, rely for every thing that is stable, every thing that brings or continues civilization, good government, good order, and lasting prosperity.

The state of Illinois, some years ago, and not many years ago neither, was infatuated with a sense of its own natural advantages, its own unbounded resources, and launched forth into the wildest scheme of internal improvement.[29] It projected rail-

---

[29] The Internal Improvement Bill became a law on February 27, 1837. Approximately $10,000,000 was voted for river improvement and railroad building. Many enterprises were begun, but none of them finished. Within three years the

roads and canals in every direction. It borrowed money that it could not pay. It commenced works that it could not finish. It employed engineers to lay out routes, who knew only in theory what the people wished to have constructed by practical men. The consequences are known to the world, and canals and railroads, half or quarter completed, some graded, some half built, are to be met with in different parts of the state. A better day is now dawning, and those who once thought the time for such gigantic operations had not then arrived—the men of reflection—are now moving to accomplish the task which others too soon under took—are destined to reap the benefits which early cupidity came near losing.

A railroad is now to be built from Alton to Springfield, which cannot fail to be an investment of great profit to the stockholders. The company has a very favorable charter, and the state gives its aid in the shape of a free grant, of such portions of a formerly graded road as they may need or can use to advantage. The road will have for its terminus the capital of the state, and will open to the towns and the farms of the interior a means of communication with the seaboard, or rather with navigation, which must be immensely profitable. All along on the line, and I have been over the whole of it, there is a country capable of producing, which does now produce enormous crops of every thing, almost, that will grow in any soil. Alton is so situated that boats of the largest class can come up to its levee and load at all seasons of the year; it is the head of navigation for freighting vessels, and the completion of this railroad will be the means of increasing its trade to an almost incalculable amount. The railroad as at present is intended to be built, will be eighty-eight miles in length; the engineers will undoubtedly shorten it about ten miles. It runs through a country very favorable for construction, and on almost a level grade for the greater part of the line. The

---

craze had run its course, and the state faced a debt of about $15,000,000, with repudiation not an impossibility. No interest was paid on this debt from July 1, 1841 to July 1, 1846. Measures enacted during the administration of Gov. Thomas Ford, 1842-1846, looked toward the ultimate extinction of the debt.

state has a road graded for ten miles at one end, and fifteen at the other, which will be taken by the company, and can be put in order at once for the rails at a trifling expense.

I have, in a former letter, spoken of the Illinois and Michigan canal, which runs from Chicago to Peru. I am not as competent as some others to give an opinion, and it may be great impertinence in me to express one; but I think that every practical New-England man, who makes a personal examination of the route, will agree with me in wondering that the commissioners, who came out here for the English bond-holders, and induced them to advance more money for its completion, did not recommend turning it into a railroad. Since we have established it as a "fixed fact" in New-England, that transportation can be had cheaper on a railroad than on a canal, the expense of lockage and delay are things to be avoided if possible. It will not be many years before a railroad will be built on that route, that will be worth to the public more than fifty canals.

Alton has, in its immediate vicinity, five extensive flour mills, and a large number of stores. The steamboats from the lower part of the Upper Mississippi are continually passing, and last night the snorting and belching of the engines, the ringing of the bells of the boats, was to be heard every four minutes. The ware-houses are built of stone and brick. There is an abundance of lime stone to be found in the town, close down to the edge of the river. The state penitentiary[30] stands on a high bluff overlooking the town, the river, and the neighboring part of the state of Missouri; the prisoners are employed now in manufacturing hemp,—they used to be engaged in all sorts of mechanical labor, but on a remonstrance to the Legislature, setting forth that they underworked the regular mechanics, a law was passed obliging the overseers to put them to a kind of work that would not interfere with the industry of more honest people.

---

[30] The penitentiary at Alton, authorized by the legislature in 1827, was completed in the early thirties. It was used until 1860, when the prisoners were transferred to the new prison at Joliet.

Gen. Semple,[31] the author of the famous post-office report, of which the readers of the *Courier* have heard something before, lives at Alton, but I understand that he is disgusted with politics, and is now devoting his time and talents to the construction of a steam car, that he expects will travel over the prairies with or without the aid of roads.[32] I lost an opportunity to see this new machine a few days ago, in consequence of the forgetfulness of a friend; but I am informed that it is almost as visionary a thing as the report to which I have before alluded. It will probably be able to carry the mails through the Pacific Ocean, as soon as it is ready to carry passengers across the continent of America. The General hates President Polk and the whole administration, and is not by any means chary in his comments upon their want of foresight, in not appreciating his transcendant abilities sufficiently to give him either a high military or civil appointment.

I rode out a few miles in the neighborhood, this afternoon, with a friend, to see the country. The continued dry and hot weather has made the roads very dusty, and every thing now appears to less advantage than usual; but the sites for dwellings, the houses and farms are improved, and the indications of prosperous industry every where apparent, give one a favorable idea of what the citizens may become in a short time. North Alton is at a short distance, and besides being a place of considerable farming, is the residence of a great number of coopers, who make

---

[31] Gen. James Semple, 1798-1866, was born in Green County, Kentucky; he studied law in Louisville; moved to Edwardsville, Illinois in 1818 where he stayed only a short time, returning there again in 1828; Brigadier General in the Black Hawk War. Semple served several terms in the legislature and was twice elected Speaker of the House; he was Chargé d'Affaires to New Granada, 1837-1842, and United States Senator, 1843-1847. He was enthusiastic over the acquisition of Oregon, and in the spring of 1846 brought in two reports to the Senate calling for the establishment of a mail route to Oregon. His second report detailed the possibilities of a route by way of the Isthmus of Panama.

[32] General Semple secured patents in 1845 on what he called a "prairie car." The car was very similar to the old-fashioned locomotive in appearance, but differed materially in its mechanical construction, having a broad wheel to enable it to run over the prairies. The car worked successfully, but General Semple did not have sufficient funds to continue experimentation. Forced to abandon the project, he left the car standing out in the prairie near Springfield, where it gradually fell to pieces and was pointed out to passers-by as "Semple's Folly."

a large quantity of barrels for flour and provisions. It has two churches, which look rather out of character, for want of paint. In this village, on a pretty spot, is situated the college, which was endowed by the late Dr. Shurtleff of Boston, and which bears his name.[33] It is a large brick building, but is not at present very prosperous, in consequence of the want of sufficient funds to procure professors and teachers of the highest talent.

Another regiment of volunteers for Mexico is quartered in camp in this village,—it is not quite full, but another company is daily expected, and as soon as it arrives the election of officers will take place. The most prominent candidate for Colonel is Mr. [Joseph B.] Wells, now Lieutenant-Governor of the state. Col. Baker, formerly member of Congress, who has already served with distinction, was a candidate, but he peremptorily declines, as he thinks he is entitled to a higher rank, and is now an applicant for appointment as Brigadier General.

Yesterday, the packet-boat from St. Louis brought up the bodies of three Lieutenants belonging to this place, who were killed in battle in Mexico, and they were received with some ceremony. Guns were fired by way of salute, the bells tolled, and a speech was made on the levee, to which nobody made any reply. A procession was then formed, and the bodies were carried to one of the churches, where they will lie in state for several days, after which there will be a *celebration* on a small scale, after the fashion of that which I saw at Jacksonville. Discharged volunteers, who have served their year in Mexico, are daily returning by the way of St. Louis, and on the arrival of every boat they are saluted by the firing of cannon, and other demonstrations of respect. A few nights ago, it was rumored that a number were on board one of the packets,—the guns were fired as usual, the crowd collected to see them land, and the chairman or spokesman of the committee of reception mounted a woodpile and made a patriotic speech. But lo and behold! there was no volunteer

---

[33] In recognition of Dr. Benjamin Shurtleff's gift of $10,000 in 1835, the name of Alton College was changed to Shurtleff College in 1836.

on board, except a drunken Irishman, who was astonished, as well he might be, at the eloquence which had been so lavishly thrown away upon him, and he exclaimed, with a hiccup, that it was "very affecting—it almost made me cry."

St. Louis, Missouri
[July 17, 1847]

We took passage, at eight o'clock, on board the steamboat *Luella*, but did not get away from the levee until nearly nine. These levees are the banks of the river graded to a convenient slope, sometimes paved and sometimes left in their natural state, and are either dusty or muddy, according to the weather. Wharves there are none, in this part of the country—or rather there are very few. At Alton, as at other places that I have seen on the Mississippi and on the Illinois rivers, the boats passing down always turn round and come to the levee with the bow upstream; this is done for the sake of convenience, and because there would be much trouble in stopping head-way if they attempted to come to with the force of the current in the same direction in which they are running.

Our passage down the river was very pleasant, for there was a slight breeze blowing from the south. The scenery was beautiful. A short distance from Alton we came to the low land called the American Bottom—which at times, when the river is highest, is generally overflowed; it is rich soil, richer than any other in the world. This bottom-land extends on both sides of the river for nearly a hundred miles, and has proved to be inexhaustible—it never wears out. Other lands will yield large produce, but it is necessary to change the seed from year to year, from corn to wheat and from wheat to oats, &c. &c.; but on the American, or as some people more appropriately call it, the Mississippi bottom, it has been proved that the same kind of crops can be produced every year; and at one place farther south, it is said that corn has been raised every year in succession for one hundred and fifty years.

A few miles from Alton, I believe only three, is the mouth of the Missouri, a yellow-colored water, which empties into the Mississippi, but does not mix with it for miles and miles in its course. The difference in the two streams is marked so strongly, that while one is on the clearer waters of the latter, the waters of the other, running only a few feet distance from the boat, look like a sand-bar extended along the side. After we proceed some miles, the two become united; but after all it is like the amalgamation of milk and molasses, with a streak of light and a streak of dark. The Mississippi, however, never again becomes the clear, bright water that it is in the regions above. The bottomlands are well wooded, and the foliage of the trees is the most dense I have ever seen. I believe that oaks and elms, and maple and locust, and walnut, are the most abundant, although other varieties are interspersed. Occasionally you will see a lombardy poplar, but it is where somebody has planted it—it is not natural to the soil. There are no chestnuts and no pines.

At eleven o'clock, we arrived at St. Louis.[34] We have heard of a "forest of masts," but here, without seeing a mast, we were at once in the midst of a forest of chimneys or smoke-pipes. There may be sailing vessels on this river, but the commerce is carried on by means of steamboats. Like the people of every other place, the people here say we can see nothing now,—it is not the season, there is no business doing, and there are few boats here. But I see enough to surprise my unsophisticated Yankeeism. The number now, dull as the season may be, may very properly be named legion.

The levee is high, with a very steep slope, and is paved with blocks of lime-stone. It is covered with all sorts of produce, and is lined on its upper side with immense warehouses; on its lower, with steamboats. The boats lie in regular order, close together, with their bows run on to the shore, as compactly as they can be placed, and discharge or take in freight and passengers from the bow. I believe there was not a boat lying broad-side to the lev

---

[34] The population of St. Louis in 1847 was estimated at 55,000.

when we arrived, and we were obliged to come to along side of the stern of another steamer, and the passengers crossed her decks the whole length, in order to get on shore.

When we landed, the sun was apparently doing his utmost to burn up all the life and energy that remained, after a week's summer weather, in man and beast. The lime-stone, of which the pavements are composed, and the lime-stone soil of the unpaved streets, is light colored, almost white, and the reflection of the sun upon it is dazzling to the eyes. We have hotter weather in Boston, occasionally, than they have had at St. Louis this summer, but it is only for a few days, and is even then occasionally relieved by intervals of east wind. But here, the heat comes on gradually, and is regular, affording no stopping places, so to speak, although the mercury in the thermometer may not be more than ninety or ninety-four, it is the same from morning to night and night to morning, day to day, burning on and baking the people as by a slow fire. I thought that the heat at Alton was tolerably severe, but at St. Louis I find it intolerable.

The first thing that struck my attention, after the steamboats, was the business-like character of the place. I am writing my first impressions, recollect, and therefore I may say something by and by, or hereafter, that will not correspond with what I say now. As Rochester, a small place, was more bustling to me than Boston, and Buffalo appeared larger and more of a business place than Rochester, so St. Louis, with only about fifty thousand inhabitants, would seem at first glance to do more business than New-York or Liverpool. On the levee were all sorts of goods, and in all sorts of packages. The warehouses are of great height, situated not only on the levee, but in the street above, or in the cross streets which run down to the river, and they all appear to be filled with goods of all descriptions. The drays are numerous, and the draymen, black and white, keep up a constant yelling and shouting that would stun a quiet man.

Hot as it was, a friend induced me in the middle of the day to jump into his buggy and ride around the city, in order to obtain

St. Louis Levee, 1850

a sort of outside view of its magnitude and its character. We did not go off from the paved streets into the suburbs, but we rode round through the principal and some of the minor thorough-fares. The retail trade is extended over the whole city. Large blocks of many storied brick dwelling-houses are in all the streets. Churches and other public buildings are numerous. Hotels are all but uncountable, and bar-rooms are quite so. The sidewalks are paved with brick, and are wide and comfortable. The streets in the upper part of the city are wide and run at right angles, many of them being shaded with trees, which are planted on each side!

Dinner time brought us to the Planters' House, where I have concluded to rest for a day, before I take up my line of march for a new and somewhat unknown region on the Upper Mississippi.

ST. LOUIS, MISSOURI

My notes of St. Louis are meagre, for the heat of the weather, and the fatigue of the last week, rendered it necessary that I should remain in the house nearly all the time I have been here. The Planters' House, at which I am staying, is built after the plan of the Astor House, and is nearly as large. It is kept by Stickney & Scollay, both of whom, I believe, are Yankees. Its situation is the best and pleasantest of any public house in the city, and by favor of good friends, I was enabled to secure an upper room, with a southern aspect, which gave me all the comfort of breeze and freedom from mosquitoes that any one can obtain in St. Louis. The street in front is broad, and appears to be the Broadway of the city. An evening stroll on Saturday night was very pleasant, exhibiting the different retail shops, con-fectioneries, &c. to good advantage. The majority of the business streets are narrow and much cumbered with goods and people. Even in the day-time, and under a broiling sun, it appeared as if the people were all in the streets in the part of the city devoted to traffic. Taverns and grog-shops are abundant, and, like the boot and shoe shops of Montreal, appear to be a very large per centage of the whole number of places devoted to business in some particular neighborhoods. The streets devoted to wholesale trade, exhibit more bustle and activity than those of New-York or Boston, even at this dull season of the year, and one is irresistibly led to the belief that the trade of St. Louis is not only most flourishing, but must be increasing. A gentleman informs me that he has seen five hundred large steam-boats discharging and taking in cargoes at the levee at the same time. There is one cotton factory in the city, which was established and is kept in operation by a German house.

There are several foundries and machine shops, which turn out the very best of work; it is said that some of the machinery manufactured in St. Louis is equal, if not superior, to any that has ever been made at the East. Within a few years, there have been some splendid boats built in this city or its neighborhood, and the improvements which are constantly made, in the strength, speed, capacity, and light draught of those which hail from this port, will, ere long, make this *the* place in the West for ship-building.

On the square, next to the Planters' House, is the Court House, a most uncouth looking building at present; they tell me it is to be altered and improved.[35] It is built in the shape of a square cross, or a square building with four wings. The front of each wing is built as high as the top of the second story, of white limestone; the rest is of brick, including all the space above the second story window caps. It has the air in part of falling to decay, and in part of being unfinished. Good and substantial stone steps lead to the entrances, and an iron fence has been erected partly round the building. When seated in my chamber this morning, I heard the stentorian voice of somebody making a speech, for so long a time that I concluded that I would go down and see what it all meant. Following the direction of the sound, I soon found myself in the Criminal Court. Twelve jurors, most of them with their coats off, one apparently asleep,

---

[35] Little work was done on the courthouse in 1847.

PLANTERS HOUSE, ST. LOUIS, 1865

and all seated in such way as could make them most comfortable, were supposed to be listening to a one-eyed, shaggy-headed lawyer, who was arguing for the defence. The Judge was quite a young man, not more than thirty years of age, and the most gentlemanly looking of all in the room.[36] Three other persons were seated at the tables appropriated to counsel, and they were too much amazed, evidently, with the queer arguments of the person speaking, to talk or write. There were half a dozen spectators, and the whole number of persons present, judge, jury, counsel, prisoners, and spectators, did not amount to twenty-five. It was astonishing to see how a man could work so hard, and talk so loud, and chew so much tobacco, with the thermometer at ninety-six, and not a breath of air stirring. The gentlemen— for all lawyers are gentlemen,—appeared to be trying to make out a case of somnambulism in one of the witnesses, and told us of his having experienced dreadful sensations on several occasions, in consequence of suddenly waking at night, and fancying he saw sights which he did not see; he told how easy it was to be deceived by appearances, and to be frightened at nothing; and he put it to the Jury to say for themselves, whether they had not often made mistakes as to objects which they looked at in the dark. From all his arguments he deduced that the principal witness was half asleep when she saw what she had testified to, and was not half certain of that which she did see—therefore, he claimed an acquittal. Before he concluded I came away.

There are many handsome public buildings in St. Louis, and many blocks of handsome and substantial private houses. But I am astonished to see that, with fifty thousand inhabitants, the streets are not lighted at night.[37] I regretted that I could not see the interior of some of the churches, and still more that I was unable to accept of several invitations of private hospitality, all of which must be deferred till circumstances, as strange as those which brought me unexpectedly here now, shall send me here again.

---

[36] Alonzo W. Manning was judge of the Criminal Court in 1847.
[37] The streets of the business section were first lighted by gas on Nov. 6, 1847.

This is the first hotel I have seen, since I left home, where I could enjoy a breakfast. I have eaten breakfasts every day, but they have only been in the performance of a regular duty. But here, at the Planters' House, a man can come to the table and enjoy an hour in the morning, in comfort. So few people in this busy world know how to live, that half of those who do live only exist. Now men will tell us that every thing depends upon dinner, for which they want "time;" therefore they are up early in the morning, swallow a cup of tea or coffee, bolt half a pound of beef steak or other meat, not properly cooked, a few hot cakes, and off they run to business; before noon, they are half starved, and while the stuff they put into their stomachs in the morning is still undigested, they take a hearty luncheon, that ought to serve a moderate man for his dinner, if it were fit for anybody to eat, and away they run again to business; before they have digested either the breakfast or the lunch, they go to dinner, and "take time for it"—that is, they perhaps sit half or three quarters of an hour at table, without any appetite, very dainty, and pretend to enjoy luxuries which their cooks know not how to prepare for the table, and which they are not in a fit state to appreciate. And yet such men live and grow rich, and before they are sixty, die of apoplexy or of indigestion. If a man would have a good constitution, and be in a proper state of body or mind to do business and enjoy a good dinner, he should spend an hour in the *early morning*, at his breakfast table, with his family and friends—not in eating and drinking, but taking his food in moderation, and sitting with his newspaper or his conversation, or both, until his food begins to digest; he will then be fit for business or pleasure all the rest of the day. Let him avoid a lunch, for he will need none, and he will enjoy his dinner again, as his breakfast, and it will do him good, however humbly it may be served, however scanty or coarse, or devoid of luxuries and variety. Let no one say he has no time in the morning to *waste* at the breakfast table, for if business requires him to be early about, he can get up early enough to take all the time he wants.

At the Planters', as at the Astor House, you can get a good breakfast, and take all the time you wish for.   Of course, I recommend
it to travelers coming this way, as a place where they will not
be hustled out by hurrying servants, before they are half finished,
nor entirely deserted by company.

MISSISSIPPI RIVER

And this is the "mighty father of rivers!"   He is like "linked
sweetness, long drawn out," but he is a small father, after all,
at this end, not being over a mile and a half to a mile and three
quarters wide above St. Louis.   Of course I know nothing of his
rotundity below.   From here upwards, he is slim and shallow.
About twenty miles above St. Louis, the Missouri river empties
in him, as I have already stated, and as the Missouri is the bigger,
if not the better stream, it seems rather a mistake that it should
lose its identity—it would be more appropriate to give the name
Missouri to the whole river below, and to lose the Mississippi.
But this is no affair of mine.

We left St. Louis about half past seven o'clock in the evening,
that is to say, we backed out from the levee at that time, but
we stopped to take some passengers off from a boat just arrived
from Ohio, and to take in some salt from another boat, and the
consequence was that we actually did not get away until nine
o'clock.   The Western people are a queer people in some respects,
and the delays and the stoppages that one meets with in traveling
in their country are rather annoying to our more regular Yankee
travelers.   For instance—three steamboats were advertised to
leave St. Louis on Saturday for Galena, and one on Monday.
On Monday, neither of them had gone, and all were for taking
in freight.   By the advice of those who knew, I concluded to
take passage in the *Kentucky*.   The captain said he should start
at noon, *but*, if he did not, he should certainly go at three, P. M.,
and he would send word to the hotel. Three o'clock came, and no
message was sent.   At half past four I went on board with my
baggage, and, wishing to spend a short time with a friend, asked
if the boat would be ready before the expiration of an hour; I

was told that she certainly would. However, I went off and took an hour and a half, and came back and was obliged to wait, as I have said above, until seven and nine o'clock. Neither of the other boats were ready to leave as soon as we did, and the boat advertised to sail certainly on Monday, a "regular packet," we met about a hundred miles up the river on Tuesday, coming down.

We stopped at Alton during the night, and took in two passengers, but until morning there was not much to be seen, although the twilight was long, and I had my usual luck of traveling by moonlight. The bottom lands which lie along the river for nearly a hundred miles, are not interesting in the matter of scenery, as there is much sameness in them; after they are once seen, they only appear beautiful for their richness of soil and their beautiful supply of produce. The shore is generally bold—sufficiently so for the light draught boats to run up where it pleases the captains, for any purpose whatever, whether it be to shake hands with a friend, to call on a sweetheart, to take in wood, or land or receive passengers, for all of which purposes many captains frequently stop.

We have been five nights and nearly five days on the river between St. Louis and Galena. At the mouth of the Des Moines river, which enters into the Mississippi near a little village called Clarksville, on the Missouri side, we left some freight, and left also the shore of the state of Missouri. We now had on one side Iowa, and on the other Illinois, and I could not help thinking that there was a great difference between the appearance of every thing,—the houses, the barns, and the fields in the free states, and similar objects in the slave states. It may be all imagination; but I have less philanthropy and less pretension than some other people, and yet I think that I have seen more frugality, more attention to the interest of the proprietors of the land by the laborers employed, more economy and more industry displayed by all parties,—the men, the women, the children, the hired, the hirer, the owner, and the tenant—in free states, than

I have ever seen in slave states. The Western people are not as frugal as their Eastern friends, of either time or money. Every thing in this country grows so fast that a farmer can afford to idle away many hours that a Massachusetts man, or any New-England man, would be obliged to spend in toil and labor—the consequence is that he grows indolent. The Yankee who comes out to the West with the best principles and the most industrious habits, in a short time becomes rather careless of many of the niceties which he would have insisted upon at home. Still, you can always tell the farm of a Yankee settler. You can see that there is a difference between the thriftiness, and the care of buildings of a New-England emigrant, and those of a family who came into this country from the South, particularly from a slave state.

At Keokuk, the next stopping place above Clarksville, we were obliged to discharge all our freight into lighters, as the waters of the Mississippi are falling, and it is rather difficult for any boat to pass over the rapids, which extend from this place to Montrose, a distance of about twelve miles. We staid at Keokuk about fifteen hours, and then, drawing only thirty-three and a half inches, the *Kentucky* had hard work to get over the rapids. She struck and struggled and rubbed on the rocks, her engines were put to their hardest work, the passengers and the crew were obliged to go from side to side every few minutes, in order, by their weight, to up her one way or the other. Finally, she pressed herself along, the steam belching and bellowing, snorting and wheezing, as nothing in this world except the steam of a high-pressure engine can do, and we were again safe in deeper water. While we lay at Keokuk, I took some trouble to see what sort of a place it is, but I was not much gratified. It must be eventually a great place, as it is at the foot of the rapids, and will be the headquarters of all the Southern produce which is to come up the river. It is now rather below par, as there is some dispute as to the title to lands, the Indians having sold out their rights to several companies, and squatters having come in and made use of lands that belong of right to other people. Pettifogging lawyers and greedy speculators serve to keep up the impression that no good titles can be obtained, and the consequence is that many persons, who might otherwise be disposed to purchase and settle at Keokuk, are deterred from doing so.

A circus company was performing here this afternoon; and for the purpose of seeing the people of the country, I went to their tent, at the expense of fifty cents. There were about six hundred people present, of all ages, sizes and descriptions, mostly women and children, with a slight sprinkling of a country dandy or so, and it was amusing to witness their expressions of feeling at the performances. So far as the circus company was concerned, the performances were the poorest I ever saw, and the horses and the band appeared to be about equally stupid; but the audience was not only a delighted, but a delightful one—every body was happy, and every body was astonished; the clown could not make too stupid a joke, and the man who turned three summersets was pronounced the wonder of the age. How easy and how cheap it is to make people happy!

I forgot to mention, in its proper place in my narrative, that we arrived at Quincy, in the state of Illinois, a town of much importance, at night, after all reasonable people had gone to bed. It was quite a disappointment to me, as I wished to see Quincy, and learn more of its trade and capabilities than I can learn without some personal examination. Soon after we again started; about two miles from the levee, the boat ran upon a sand-bar, and it took two hours of hard work, much scolding and considerable straining of the engines, to get us off. We did float, however, and sailed along up river for about two miles further, when we were obliged to come to a stand still, in consequence of the pumps being choked with sand, so that they would not feed the boilers. This was in consequence of the wheels having stirred up the bottom of the river while we were on the bar, so as to make the water all muddy and thick. Another delay of five or six hours then took place, after which we started again and arrived safely at Keokuk.

NAUVOO, ILLINOIS

The Holy City of the Mormons has always possessed a certain kind of interest in my mind, and I have had much curiosity to know something about it. But I never expected to spend a whole day in it. Newspaper accounts are generally unsatisfactory, and the events of the last two years have raised up a strong party in opposition to the Mormons, so that it has been almost impossible to learn any thing as to the past or present situation of Nauvoo.[38] The city is situated on the left bank of the Mississippi, in the state of Illinois, on a lot of land gently and gradually sloping down to the water, but extending back over a prairie some two or three or more miles. It has had eighteen thousand inhabitants; it now has eighteen hundred, or at most, two thousand. It appears to have been laid out by somebody, originally, into streets running in squares, and each house is built with regard to the original plan. The families have erected each one their house on their own lot, and of course the dwellings are not compact, but are scattered over a large extent of ground. There is but one block of dwellings, or stores, in the whole city, and that appears to have been left unfinished. Most of them are of brick, two stories and a half high, and square, with a gable roof. There are, however, a number of buildings of wood, and some of them three stories high. Time was, and that not two years and a half ago, when every house was full, and every farm under good cultivation. Now, every thing looks forlorn and desolate. Not half the buildings are occupied, and of these not half are half full. The stores are closed. The farms are running to waste. The streets are overgrown with grass. The inhabitants

---

[38] The Mormons founded Nauvoo in 1838. In 1840, they voted the Whig ticket, in recognition of which the Whig legislature granted Nauvoo a charter of unlimited power. Opposition to the Mormons' political power, their practice of polygamy, the arrogance of their leaders, culminating in the destruction of the *Expositor*, an anti-Mormon newspaper in Nauvoo, brought the imprisonment of Joseph and Hyrum Smith in the jail at Carthage, Illinois. Here the brothers were murdered. Brigham Young then became the leader of the church. In January, 1845, the charter was repealed, and in February, 1846, the great trek of the Mormons to Utah began.

look like any thing but an industrious people, and every thing
tells of ruin instead of prosperity.

Our first object, of course, was the far-famed Mormon temple,[39] which stands upon the top of the hill, and can be seen for
some miles up and down the river. The first sight we had of it
gave us a pang of disappointment, for it looked more like a white
Yankee meeting-house, with its steeple on one end, than a magnificent structure which had cost, all uncompleted as it is, seven
hundred and fifty thousand dollars. But as we approached
nearer, it proved to be something worth seeing. It is nearly a
mile from the landing, the most conspicuous, in fact the only
conspicuous object in the city. It is built of white limestone.
The front is ornamented with sunken square columns of no particular style of architecture, having capitals representing half a
a man's head—the upper half—showing the forehead, eyes and
the top of the nose, and crowned with thorns, or perhaps what
was intended for the points of stars. Over the head are two
bugles or horns, with their largest ends outwards, and the handles,
on the upper side, forming a sort of festoon protection. On all
sides of the temple are similar columns with similar capitals; the
base of each column is heavy, but in good proportion and of a
fanciful design, which it would be difficult to describe. There is
a basement with small windows. Ten steps lead to the front and
only entrance to the main building. Three arches enable you to
enter into a sort of vestibule, from which, by doors, you enter
the grand hall, and at the sides are the entries to the staircases,
to ascend to the upper apartments.

The front of the temple is apparently three stories high, and
is surmounted by an octagonal tower or steeple, which itself is
three stories, with a dome, and having on four sides a clock next
below the dome. There is a line of circular windows over the
arched entrance, ornamented with carved work between each, and

---

[39] The cornerstone of the Temple was laid on April 6, 1841, in the presence of
10,000 people. The Temple was destroyed by fire of unknown origin in November,
1848.

Mormon Temple, Nauvoo
From a lithograph in H. Lewis, *Das Illustrirte Mississippithal.*

over that again a line of square windows.   In this upper row is
a large square entablature, on which is cut the following inscription:—

THE HOUSE OF THE LORD
built by
THE CHURCH OF JESUS CHRIST
OF LATTER DAY SAINTS,
Commenced April 6th, 1841.

HOLINESS TO THE LORD.

A similar entablature is on the front [*illegible*] vestibule, over
the doors of entrance, with the same inscription.   The letters on
each are gilt.

The man in attendance demanded twenty-five cents each as
fee for showing us the Temple, and asked every one to subscribe
a visitor's book. I looked over this book, and saw but two names
of persons hailing from Boston for the last six months, neither of
which was familiar to me.   We were then taken to the very top
of the building, and enjoyed there, for some time, a view of the
surrounding country, which, of itself, well paid for the trouble of
ascending, as the whole valley of the Mississippi for miles and
miles lay exposed to view on the north and south, while the
prairie lands of Illinois, and Iowa, and Missouri, were to be seen
at the east and west, overlooking the few hills lying near to the
shore in the latter state, and showing the tortuous course of the
Des Moines river for some distance.

Coming down, we were ushered into the Council Chamber,
which is a large low room, lighted by one large half circular
window at the end, and several small sky-lights in the roof. On
each side are six small ante-chambers, said to have been intended
for the twelve priests, councillors, or elders, or whatever they
may have been called.   The chamber itself is devoid of ornament,
and I was unable to ascertain whether it was intended to have
any, if it should have been completed.

In the entry, on each side of the door to the Council Chamber,
is a room called the wardrobe, where the priests were to keep

their dresses. On one side was a room intended for a pantry, showing that the priests did not mean to go supperless to bed. Under the Council Chamber was another large hall, with seven windows on each side, and four at the further end.

On the lower floor was the grand hall for the assemblage and worship of the people. Over the windows at the end, was inscribed in gilded capital letters—"THE LORD HAS BEHELD OUR SACRIFICE: COME AFTER US." This was in a circular line, corresponding to the circle of the ceiling. Seats are provided in this hall for the accommodation at one time of thirty-five hundred people, and they are arranged with backs, which are fitted like the backs to seats in a modern railroad car, so as to allow the spectator to sit and look in either direction, east or west. At the east and west ends are raised platforms, composed of series of pulpits, on steps one above the other. The fronts of these pulpits were semi-circular, and are inscribed, in gilded letters, on the west side, P A P, P P Q, P T Q, P D Q, meaning, as the guide informed us, the uppermost one, President of Aronic Priesthood; the second, President of the Priests' Quorum; the third, President of the Teachers' Quorum; and the fourth and lowest, President of the Deacons' Quorum. On the east side, the pulpits were marked P H P, P S Z, P H Q, and P E Q, and the knowledge of the guide was no better than ours as to what these symbolical letters were intended for. Like the rooms above, this was devoid of any but architectural ornaments.

We next descended to the basement, where is the far-celebrated font. It is in fact the cellar of the building. The font is of white lime-stone, of an oval shape, twelve by sixteen feet in size on the inside, and about four and a half feet to five feet deep. It is very plain, and rests on the backs of twelve stone oxen or cows, which stand immersed to their knees in the earth. It has two flights of steps, with iron banisters, by which you enter and go out of the font, one at the east end, and the other at the west end. The oxen have tin horns and tin ears, but are otherwise of stone, and a stone drapery hangs like a curtain

NAUVOO
From an engraving made about 1846.

down from the font, so as to prevent the exposure of all back of the four legs of the beasts. In consequence of what I had heard of this font, I was disappointed; for it was neither vast nor gorgeous; every thing about it was quite simple and unostentatious. The basement is unpaved, and on each side and at the ends are small alcoves, intended for robing rooms for the faithful.

I don't know as I have been able to give an intelligent description of this far-famed temple of the Mormons, but it is correct as far as it goes. The whole is quite unfinished, and one can imagine what it might have been in the course of time, if Joe Smith had been allowed to pursue his career in prosperity.

After wandering about Nauvoo for some time, a small party concluded we would call on the widow of Joe Smith, the prophet, and dine with her—she now keeps a public house, at the sign of the "Nauvoo Mansion." We found her at home, and had considerable conversation with her. She is an intelligent woman, apparently about fifty years of age, rather large, and very good looking, with a bright sparkling eye, but a countenance of sadness when she is not talking; she must have been a handsome woman when some years younger. She answered all our questions as we sat at dinner, although perhaps some of them might have been rather impertinent under a strict construction of the rules of etiquette, with great readiness and great willingness. Our dinner consisted of fresh fried fish and stewed mutton, with vegetables and pastry, to all of which we did full justice, for it was well cooked and cleanly served. After obtaining considerable information, and fully gratifying a not altogether useless curiosity, we separated, highly pleased with our visit.

If any body should wish to go [to] Nauvoo, after this, we advise the taking of a skiff or a row-boat, from a steamboat, and crossing the river from Montrose, which is on the Iowa side directly opposite, rather than put up with the delays, the impudence, and the imposition, which are sure to be encountered by the fellow that manages the regular ferry boat. We advise, also, all strangers to walk over the city, rather than accept of any of the different conveyances for riding, that may be offered on landing. If the drivers or the ferryman insult you, let them know that you are at once able and ready to chastise their insolence on the spot, for if they think you are too tame, they will not cease their impertinences otherwise, from the time you start from the Iowa territory until you get back again.

The history of the rise and progress of the Mormon delusion, of the causes of their downfall, and the means of their extermination—for they are now as a race exterminated—will be, if it should ever be written, a romance of thrilling interest. No one can visit Nauvoo, and come away without a conviction that whatever of rascality and crime there may have been among them, the body of the Mormons were an industrious, hard-working, and frugal people. In the history of the world there cannot be found such another instance of so rapid a rise of a city out of a wilderness—a city so well built, a territory so well cultivated. That they had bad men and bad women among them, is not to be doubted nor denied; but if the authorities of Illinois had acted in good faith,—if Governor Ford had had firmness and moral courage enough to do his duty and sustain the laws, which he pretended, and, I believe, intended to sustain, the race would not have been driven away by mobs to die of starvation, and disease, and of grief. A few are left at Nauvoo, and those are too poor to live honestly, too broken-hearted to work earnestly.

Joe Smith, the prophet-leader, was, although an uneducated man, a man of great powers, and a man who could conceive great projects. One of his errors was the meddling in the politics of the state and country, and by alternately throwing the weight of the Mormon vote in favor of first one political party and then of another, he raised up enemies, who afterwards became embittered towards him, and when he was suspected of moral crimes, such as tampering with justice, projecting robberies, assisting at burglaries, &c. &c., he not only had no friends left out of his own sect, but became a sort of outlaw, against whom it was apparently a virtue for every man to raise his hand; for whom, when he died the death of a dog, by downright murder, no one had pity, and whose cause no one dared avenge.

GALENA, ILLINOIS

We made very good progress after we left Montrose, which is a town of not much importance, on the Iowa side of the river, opposite Nauvoo. The captains of the steamboats seem to think that the inhabitants of Iowa, in this section of the state, are not worth much, and they give Keokuk and Montrose a bad name for thievery and all other sorts of rascality; they are obliged, when the river is low, to spend much time at both places. We discharged all our freight at Keokuk into lighters, which were drawn up, for thirteen miles, over the rapids, by horse-power. There is no tow-path, but the water is so shallow that the horses wade along on the Iowa side, sometimes up to their bellies in the water, and occasionally on the shore, where there is a clear path along the beach, finding a dry passage. Our master of the *Kentucky* entrusted his freight to two lighters, but he put his first clerk on board of one and a trusty man on board the other, to protect the property from thieves, with whom it was possible the lightermen might be in connection, either directly or indirectly.

The scenery on the river is pretty, but it is not particularly striking, and we occasionally met with large rafts of timber, &c., floating down. These rafts are very large, and have crews of from five to twenty men, according to their size;—they have four or six large sculls put out at each end, for the purpose of steering or warping them over to the different sides of the river, according to circumstances and the course of the channel. Sometimes they get hard and fast, while going over the rapids or over the sand-bars, and as they have no means of getting off again, they pull their rafts in pieces, and, wading in the water, form them again into new rafts, on the lower side of the shoals where they have run aground. We stopped during the next night after we left the rapids, to take in wood, and the scene was one of the most picturesque I ever saw. Large pine knots were stuck up on end on board the boat and on shore, and lighted so as to make torches.

As no pine is to be had in this part of the country, these torches are manufactured for the purpose, by binding together several sticks of long wood, which the steamboat people obtain at St. Louis from the boats which arrive at that place from New-Orleans and other directions. At the spot where we stopped to wood this night, the lights and the dark shade of the trees, the half savage appearance of the woodmen, and the glare of light on the placid water of the Mississippi, made every thing appear quite romantic.

About daylight, we arrived at Burlington, which is a pretty place of some importance and considerable trade. I regretted that for the two hours we were there, I could not meet with some friends who had expected to show me some of the advantages of the town, but it would have been cruel to call upon them at so early an hour in the morning. Every thing wore the appearance, in the early twilight, of peace and comfort, and the store-houses and shops evinced a prosperity which it is to be hoped will be increased with the increase of time,—the progress of civilization. Only eighteen years ago, this place was but a wilderness, and now it is a thriving, industrious and growing place of business.

The most beautiful,—not the most grand and romantic, but the most strikingly pretty—scenery, is still further up the river, where are situated on the opposite sides, the towns of Davenport in Iowa, and Stephenson in Illinois.[40] We landed freight and passengers at both places, and I don't know which to describe as the most pleasant. Both are generally built of good substantial brick and wooden houses and stores. The situation of Davenport appears the prettiest as you look up the river upon it, and that of Stephenson the prettiest as you go up stream and look down river to it. Davenport, however, is the place of most business at present. Between the two towns is the island called Rock Island, where is a fort which was the scene of a hard contested battle with the British, in the war of 1812,[41] and where Colonel Daven-

---

[40] The name Stephenson was officially changed to Rock Island in March, 1841.
[41] Fort Armstrong was established at the lower end of Rock Island after the close of the War of 1812. Its garrison was withdrawn in 1836.

port was murdered a few years ago by a parcel of horse-thieves, for the sake of his money. The fort is deserted at present, and the public works are not in good preservation. The farm and farm-house of Col. Davenport on the island exhibit evidences of care, and are in good order. It will be recollected by some readers of the newspapers that Col. Davenport was alone in his house on one 4th of July, and he was attacked, murdered, and robbed of about two thousand dollars by several men, three or four of whom were afterwards caught and hung for the crime.[42] He was a singular man in his character, and was divorced from his wife; he afterwards married his wife's daughter, and the two wives or widows now live on the estate together.

We arrived at Galena about eleven o'clock in the forenoon on Saturday, and found it a much larger, much more of a business place than we expected. The principal street runs along the bank of the river up into a valley, and houses are scattered along on the banks of the hills for some miles. This town is situated about seven miles from the Mississippi, on a shallow winding stream, called Fever River. The river runs in all sorts of directions, and is very crooked,—sometimes to the south, sometimes to the east, sometimes west, and sometimes almost north again. At some seasons of the year it is not navigable, except for rafts or very light flatboats, and about a mile from the village it is fordable at almost all seasons by cattle and persons on foot. Two ferries are maintained by the town, and the village is situated in a valley on both sides of the river.

Our general impression of Galena is, that it is a rough mining town, with hardly any civilization, and no business, except that which naturally grows out of the wants of the miners. But it is a place of much trade, and the centre of what will by and by be a great agricultural country. The hills and fields are favorable for the growth of wheat, and the raising of cattle. A few years ago it

---

[42] Col. George Davenport, born in England, came to America and entered into trade with the Indians. He had lived on Rock Island for some thirty years, acquiring a fortune and a reputation among Indians and whites for his fairness, generosity and kindness to all.

was in reality a wilderness, but now it has a large number of stores, and several meeting-houses, good, substantial, fashionable looking dwelling-houses, and about a dozen good taverns, besides a dozen dashing-looking bar-rooms. The progress of civilization and the great increase of travel has induced farmers to settle in the town, and turn their attention to raising vegetables, fruit and poultry for market, for which they get good prices.

As this is *the* lead region of the United States, from which so much wealth has already been accumulated, I was anxious to visit the mines. On the levee were piled up large piles of lead in pigs, which were going on board several steamers, or waiting for opportunities for shipment to St. Louis. Procuring a guide, I started, after dinner, for the "diggings" and the furnaces. The country is composed of small hills and valleys, and on almost every mound we saw the yellow earth turned up in piles, showing where the miners had been at work. Being Saturday afternoon, few persons were engaged in the operation of digging, but I saw several holes where the men were hoisting with a common windlass the ore and earth from little wells. The land in this neighborhood has all been entered and become private property. The owners have no objection to any one coming on their land and digging for lead. If the operators succeed in striking a vein, they make a bargain with the owner to get out as much as they can, giving him a certain portion—the lion's share, of course—and receiving the rest for their own labor; if they are not successful, they abandon the work, and commence in another part of the lot, no harm having been done, except their own loss of time and money. Some laborers make a great deal by this operation, while others only get about enough to pay them their outfit and day's wages, while the owner is sure to become rich by their labor.

Lead is a cash article, and is worth money the moment it is brought to the surface of the earth. There is no credit system allowed, for it sells for cash, and although not so valuable in market as silver or gold, is quite as readily turned into those commodities, or into bank bills. There are in the neighborhood several smelting

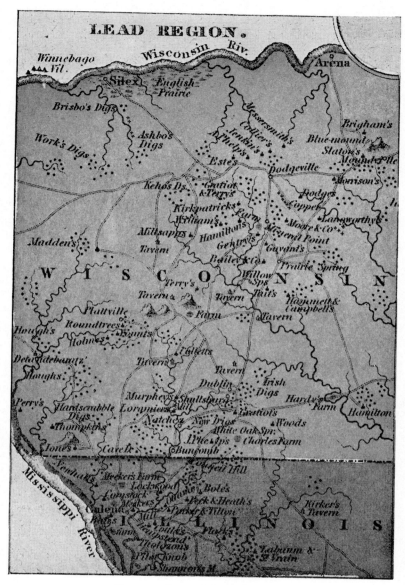

GALENA LEAD MINE REGION
From a map published by H. S. Tanner in 1841.

houses or furnaces. The ore is so pure that it requires little working to make it into pigs. In the furnaces there is no puddling, as
there is with iron. The fire is built of charcoal, or wood, or both,
and the earth thrown into the furnace; as it melts, the ore runs out
as pure as silver itself, from the mouth, into a pot in front, from
which it is scooped up in its liquid state and poured into moulds,
from which it is taken as soon as it becomes cool or hardened, and
thrown into wagons, to be transported to the river side. It appears to be the most easy and the most rapidly transformed metal
in the world. A large lot of dark blue earth, sometimes in large
lumps and sometimes apparently nothing but sand, is shoveled
into the fire, and it runs out pure lead, in a moment. There is a
considerable quantity of dross taken out of the furnaces, from time
to time, but it is not thrown away,—for that, in its turn, is again
subjected to the heat in a differently constructed furnace, and
yields, although not so plentifully, not so rapidly, a large quantity
of the precious metal. At one furnace I saw ore, or earth, as I
should call it, which yielded ninety-five per cent of pure lead, and
dross which, it was said, would yield twenty to twenty-five per
cent more after going through the second process.

CHICAGO, ILLINOIS

Back again! This may be called the first mile-stone on my
road home. When I left Boston, I had no intention of coming
to Chicago; and when I came to Chicago, I had no expectation
or intention of going any further West or South; but every day's
experience proves that all human calculations are in vain, as has
been said and proved millions of times before; and I am sure that
it is best for us not to know "what a day may bring forth." I
have seen a much larger portion of the state of Illinois than
travelers for mere business or pleasure would be likely to see in
a hundred journeys, as my wanderings have not been confined to
the regular stage routes, nor to the direct roads from far-off points
to far-off points. I have walked, and I have sailed, and I have
rode, over farms, and prairies, and rivers, and on lakes;—I have
not only met with all sorts of people, made acquaintance with

all sorts of men, women and children, but I have fallen in with all sorts of relations. I traveled seven days with a gentleman who helped me to ravel out a tangled string of genealogy, and we found at last that we were actually relations;—it was in this wise: His wife was the daughter of a second cousin to my father's grandmother, on the mother's side, and as her maiden name was the same as one of my three names, it must be that we were, in this extensive country, quite near relations; besides this, and to make the connection still more intimate, one of her nephews is a clergyman in Boston, of whose church many of my relatives are members. *Par consequence*, as they say in France, we became quite intimate. Unfortunately, although my far-off relative is reputed to be rich, he has children to inherit his property, and there are so many between him and me, that I have no chance of gaining any pecuniary advantage by the discovery.

Again, I was agreeably surprised, at a town where I had no acquaintances, by a gentleman who introduced himself, after seeing my name on the books at the hotel, as the brother-in-law to the brother-in-law of one of my connections, and I was not only pleased to make his acquaintance, but I received much benefit from the circumstance. Who would not have relations? And yet some men I have met with, are continually complaining that they have too many, because they cannot, in consequence of their relations, be as independent as they please.

A party of seven contracted at Galena for a stage coach with nine seats to take us to Chicago, with the understanding that no one else was to enter or to ride on the coach. We traveled by what is called the lower route, through Dixon, Mount Carroll, across the Winnebago Swamp, the Big Rock, the Little Rock, the Fox River, &c., a distance of about one hundred and seventy-five miles. The country is not as interesting as that of the more Southern part of the state, because the prairies are not so extensively cultivated—there is more waste land; and because the crops, it being in a higher latitude, are not so far advanced. For the first ten miles from Galena we passed hills where there had been hundreds of "diggings," as they are called, for lead, many of which have been successful. Mount Carroll is a thriving village, with considerable water power, and a number of mills. At Dixon, which is a town of considerable pretension, as well as a county site, with a courthouse, we had a miserable breakfast, after a long and tedious night's ride; the place seems to be prolific in nothing but grocery stores and lawyer's offices.

The prettiest town we passed through was Aurora, on the Fox River, and I was disappointed that we arrived too late in the evening to make a more thorough examination into its resources and its advantages. Only nine years ago the country around this village was almost unsettled. At La Fox, as it was then called—now Geneva—were a few families, and within the circuit of perhaps fifteen miles there only lived about twenty families in the whole; now, in that same circuit there are six villages, with an average population of sixteen hundred inhabitants in each! The water-power on the Fox River is great, particularly for the Western country, and every day is adding to the wealth of those who settled in its valley a few short years ago.

After a ride of two days and two nights we arrived at Chicago. We had fared better than I have fared on some other routes, and we ought to have done so, for the expense was higher; but the journey was a very tedious one, and I was glad to find myself once more in a comfortable bed, and undressed. There is nothing rests a man so much as undressing and getting between a pair of sheets, no matter if it be only for half an hour. Those who have travelled much,—and, as they say in the West, I have travelled some during the last twenty years,—know this, and always act on their knowledge when they can get an opportunity.

We found Chicago the same interesting, busy, bustling place it was some weeks ago. The Convention and the traces of the Convention are gone, but there is nothing, it would seem, can deprive the city of its prosperity, its increase, its enterprise. Boats arrive and depart, produce comes in, and goods from the East are imported. The people are industrious, and the people multiply almost beyond belief, and the people must thrive. A gentleman told me to-day that only about ten years ago he had on his hands a lot of Eastern land, which, during the times of speculation, he had taken up as other men did at that time, with the expectation of making a fortune out of it; of course it fell in value, and he considered it almost valueless. One day a stranger entered his office in Boston, and offered, nay entreated, to swap a few lots on the Skunk River in Chicago, for his Eastern land. My friend asked, in his ignorance, where Chicago was, and had to look for some time on the map before he could find it. Finally he contemptuously rejected the idea of throwing away even worthless lands in Maine for these lots in the West. He has since sold his Eastern land for less than five hundred dollars, and now that he has moved out to Chicago, finds that the despised lots which he was offered in exchange for them are almost in the centre of business, and cannot be purchased of the present owners for twenty thousand dollars.

Chicago is the capital or shire town of Cook county. An artificial harbor has been made by building out into the lake two long piers from the mouth of the river, but even now a dredging machine is needed to keep the entrance open sufficiently to allow heavy loaded vessels to enter at all times, and all seasons, and all weathers. This will be remedied in time. Every thing cannot be done in a day, although it appears as if every thing would grow in a day in this country. Sand bars will grow, and so will trees, and wheat, and corn, and pigs, and cattle, and babies, but it appears that some things grow faster than they can be stunted.

CHICAGO, ILLINOIS

Before I leave this place for the East, I must put down a few matters relating to the great West, that I believe have escaped notice in other pages of my diary. The *Great West* is a term that I use in reference to that part of it which I have seen, but they tell me I have as yet seen nothing at all of it. Travelers who return from a voyage to any place whatever, whether it be in America or Europe, the East or West Indies, are always sure to be asked, on their return, if they have visited such or such a spot—have been to such or such a city. If the reply is in the negative, they are sure to be told by some one that has, by accident, seen something that they have not seen, that they *"ought to have gone there;"* and the superior advantage of the traveled gentleman who has, by accident, been thrown in the way of some hitherto unknown curiosity, or unexplored section, is, in his own estimation at least, raised almost immeasurably. I have experienced this many times before, and expect to experience it again on my return, receiving the commiserating looks, if not the more directly expressed pity, of those who have preceded me in their visits to this part of the country.

Before I left St. Louis, a gentleman advised me not to return to Boston without visiting the West! I told him that I was as far West as I thought proper to go at the present time. But he turned up his eyes in wonder at my ignorance, and said, with all the seriousness imaginable, that I had not yet commenced my travels to the West! On considering all the circumstances, I am inclined to think that he was more than half right. If this country goes on increasing in wealth and population a few years longer, the city of St. Louis will be nearly the centre, and we shall have to speak of New-England as the far off *great East*, in the same way that it is customary now all over the country, to speak of Missouri and Iowa, and other now almost unexplored regions, as the *great West*. One becomes lost in wonder in speculating on this subject, and cannot even imagine to what an extent of greatness we may arrive before the expiration of another fifty years. Now the wealth and the power are on the sea-board—the Atlantic sea-board—and the cities of Boston, New-York, Philadelphia and Baltimore on that coast are metropolitan cities; but in that time they are destined to become provincial cities. The one great metropolis of the country, the centre of the wealth and the population and the power of the country, will be on the west bank of the Mississippi river, if not even further off than that. Arguing on these premises, I have not, as my friend said, yet commenced my travels to the West.

I forgot what or how much I have said of the Mississippi river, but I was reminded today, on seeing Banvard's advertisement in a Boston paper, of his "three mile picture," of the wonder with which I listened to his description of its tortuosity.[43] He told us what we all knew before of its crooked channel—we could see by the map that it was crooked,—and I believe he told us of the number of times a boat was often obliged, in the course of a few miles, to cross directly from one point to another. I thought at the time that he might be telling rather an extravagant story, which might be excusable in one who was publicly exhibiting a picture on which he had expended so much time and labor. But now I am satisfied that he did not tell one half of what he might have told. What the navigation may be below St. Louis, I am not able to testify to, but I am sure that no vessel in head wind ever sailed more miles to beat up one, than I sailed in the steamer *Kentucky*, a few days ago, to get half a mile up stream. At times, we shot across to the left bank to within a few feet, hardly leaving us room to turn, and then went directly back again to within a few feet of the bank on the opposite side. Sometimes, by this crossing and re-crossing, we gained a little, and once, I believe, the channel was so twisted, that when we were on the right we were actually lower down the river than we were a short time before when over on the left. This was owing to the shallowness of the river and the sand-bars.

The sand-bars in the Mississippi are continually shifting, and a pilot who does not constantly travel over the route is very apt to become unfitted for his business, and not by any fault of his own. Once we ran upon a sand-bar, which the captain said did not exist when he came down on his last trip. While the mate and engineer were getting the steamer off, the Captain and Pilot took a small boat and went out to take soundings, and find the channel; having found it, they planted buoys for the benefit of whoever might come after them, but without much hope that they would

---

[43] Banvard's panorama was a "magnificent unwinding depicting of the Father of Waters with the scenery along the banks from New Orleans to St. Louis, with all the accompanying incidents of trade and navigation."

be of service for many days. This fact shows the necessity for some action of the national government respecting the Western waters. It is supposed that with a comparatively trifling expense, a clear channel might be kept open all the season, that would allow of much more rapid and safer communication than we now have.

Travelers in the Western country—that is, the West of to-day, do not experience all the inconveniences nor meet with all the amusing incidents that were to be met with some years ago. The country is not so wild, nor are the people so unsophisticated as they were only as lately as 1832; there has been so much immigration that a certain degree of civilization has been attained in the country towns, and to a certain extent some luxuries may be found every where. But the whole people in the interior of Illinois are in a sort of transition state—between rude unsophisticated life and civilized comfort. Almost every where, I found the people had a plenty of ice, which is a luxury to every body, and a necessary article to those of us who have always been accustomed to it. I believe I have already spoken of the want of good taverns on the stage roads, but I have said nothing of the funny incidents which used to take place at log houses, where people slept all in one room, some on beds, some in blankets on the floor, and some on buffalo skins; because no such things came under my notice. But I have seen taverns, first rate taverns too, they were called, where there were four or five beds in the one solitary bed-room,—all double beds, as a single bed would be a luxury not dreamed of at present in those regions—where men, and women, and children are obliged, even at this day, to be all accommodated at once.

The nearest approach to any thing like trouble that I met with, was at a tavern in quite a considerable town in this state, where, after I had got comfortably into bed, one night, the landlord insisted upon my taking in as a companion, a stranger, to sleep with me. I refused, and he said it must be so. I told him I never yet had slept in the same bed with another man, and I never would. The man, too, was determined to come to bed, and mine was the only one in the house that had not two persons in it. So, rather than have a quarrel, I got up, and taking my great coat, laid down on the floor in the corner of the room, with my carpet bag for a pillow, and slept comfortably for the rest of the night, while the landlord accommodated the stranger on my abdicated straw bed; both probably laughing at and despising my fastidiousness.

I had the impertinence,—I suppose some people will call it so,—to doubt, in a former chapter of my diary, the wisdom of those who advised the spending of a large sum of money to complete the Illinois and Michigan Canal. Further examination has convinced me that those who had the direction of that matter, would have done far better to have turned the Canal into a Railroad. It is said now, that although the Canal is almost finished, it will not hold water after it is filled; for the work is so finished, and the soil is so porous, that the water will *leech* through. If this is the case, the money is thrown away, and a railroad will have to be built, on the same route, in order to accommodate the trade from the interior to Chicago. The projected railroad from Alton to Springfield will be built in the course of two or three years, and our Eastern people will not be long in seeing the advantages of connecting that link of communication with Chicago and the lakes, thus securing to New-England the commerce of all Mississippi north of St. Louis, and consequently all the northern trade of the state of Missouri. A canal cannot do the business, and a railroad could.

The trade of upper Missouri, all of Wisconsin, nearly all of Illinois, as well as the northern part of Indiana, must, by and by, come through the lakes, and at the present time the people have all their sympathies and all their plans connected with the East, and in a great measure with New-England, of which Boston is the great head. Chicago is destined to be a place of great export for all the products of the states named, as soon as our facilities of communication are opened, as they will be, by the completion of the Ogdensburg Railroad. It will also be a place of much importance as the port of reception for much of the merchandise, the manufactured and foreign goods which are to be consumed in the West.   I may be thought by some persons a little—perhaps a great deal—in advance of the times, in this my speculation, but as a certain noted politician says, "We shall see."

I leave this place to-morrow for Buffalo, to go again through the lakes.

CAMPAIGN LIVES OF ABRAHAM LINCOLN
1860

AN ANNOTATED BIBLIOGRAPHY OF THE BIOGRAPHIES
OF ABRAHAM LINCOLN ISSUED DURING THE
CAMPAIGN YEAR

By ERNEST JAMES WESSEN

The biographies of Abraham Lincoln which were issued as campaign documents in 1860, form the cornerstone of one of the largest branches of American bibliography. Those drab little books played an important part in the election of Lincoln to the presidency. It is to them that we must turn if we are to read the first published life of the greatest American.

The publication of the campaign lives was not, per se, indicative of the obscurity of the candidate, as has so often been suggested. Neither in the number published, nor in the sparsity of their content was there anything unusual about them. In their preparation a simple and time-honored formula was followed: The brief sketch of the life of the candidate served as a vehicle to carry the speeches which had won him recognition.

This type of campaign literature saw its heyday in that colorful "Log Cabin and Hard Cider" campaign of 1840, when over thirty different lives of William Henry Harrison had been published. Campaign lives were issued in all subsequent presidential campaigns, and by 1860 had become an established quadrennial source of income for enterprising publishers, and their hack writers.

Certainly 100,000 and possibly as many as 200,000 copies of Lincoln's biographies were distributed during the campaign of 1860. Some were substantially bound in cloth, and are now quite common. By far the greater number were bound in paper wrappers—if bound at all—and comparatively few of these have been preserved.

Advertised by the publishers as "Cheap Campaign" editions, these unimpressive little pamphlets and paper-bound books became so much campaign debris following the election, and were destroyed accordingly. For half a century, dealers and collectors have sought for and combed promising hiding places; yet, at this late date, several of the lives are known only because unique copies have turned up. The scanty supply of the more common ones is thinly spread out among a large number of private and public collections and no public or private library has ever contained a complete set.

Hence, this bibliographical check list of the campaign lives of Abraham Lincoln could not have been prepared without the generous coöperation of librarians and private collectors. I am deeply indebted to Mr. Paul M. Angle of the Illinois State Historical Library, Miss Esther C. Cushman of the Brown University Library, Dr. Harry E. Pratt of the Abraham Lincoln Association, and last but not least Dr. Louis A. Warren of the Lincoln National Life Foundation. Judge James W. Bollinger of Davenport, Iowa, Mr. R. D. Packard of Cleveland, Ohio, and Mr. H. M. Povenmire of Ada, Ohio have also given most welcome aid.

There is much to be said in favor of an alphabetical arrangement of the check list. On the other hand, dyed-in-the-wool Lincolnians will ask: "Which was the first of the campaign lives to be issued?" No discussion of these books would be complete without the introduction of that most controversial subject. I have spent considerable time in exploring available evidence bearing on the matter, and have succeeded in learning the actual dates upon which a number of the lives were published. By intercalation it is possible to place the others with a fair degree of accuracy. Accordingly, I have arranged the citations in the chronological order in which the first editions probably appeared.

THE WIGWAM EDITION

The "Wigwam Edition." / [*Rule*] / The / Life, Speeches and Public Services / of / Abram Lincoln, / Together with a Sketch of the Life of / Hannibal Hamlin, / Republican Candidates for the Offices of President and Vice- / President of the United States. / [*Publisher's device*] / New York: / Rudd & Carleton, 130 Grand Street / (Brooks Building, Cor. of Broadway). / M DCCC LX.　　　　　　　　　　　　　　　　　　　　[1]

Collation: [1], blank; [2], portrait; [3], title-page; [4], copyright notice; [5]-117, text; [118], blank; i-ii, advertising matter.

Variant:

(A) A copy has been noted in Brown University Library with advertising matter on the verso of page 117. This, I believe, is a late issue.

Binding: Paper wrappers. Noted in shades ranging from bright salmon to brown. Printed in black: "The Wigwam Edition" / Price] [25 cts. / The / Life, Speeches, and Public Services / of / Abram Lincoln. / [*Portrait of Lincoln*] / New York: / Rudd & Carleton, 130 Grand Street. / M DCCC LX. Spine printed: Life of Abram Lincoln. Advertising matter on verso of front wrapper, and on both sides of back wrapper.

Page size: 7⅜ by 4⅝ inches.

Variants:

Upon the front wrappers of some copies the following additional imprints have been noted. The location of the associate publisher, followed by the name, is in a single line set immediately below the regular imprint of Rudd & Carleton:

(B) Portland, Maine.　　Bailey & Noyes.
(C) Boston.　　A. Williams & Co.
(D) Chicago.　　McNally & Co.
(E) Providence, R. I.　　D. Kimball.

Publication Date: June 2, 1860.

Rudd & Carleton were one of a half-dozen publishing concerns who announced, on May 19, the day after the nomination, that they had lives of Lincoln "in press." Among the firms making that claim were two who, we now know, had not so much as engaged their authors. Nevertheless, within a week every one of them was advertising a life of Lincoln as "now ready"—misleading, but typical preliminary advertising of the period, designed not to sell books which did not exist, but to build up staffs of selling agents. In determining date of publication, little weight can be assigned to advance notices of this character.

THE WIGWAM EDITION
The first campaign life of Lincoln.

On June 2, Rudd & Carleton changed their tune. No longer did their advertisement read "now ready." In the *New York Tribune* of that date appeared their advertisement, reading: "Published this morning, *The Wigwam Edition Life, Speeches, and Public Services of Abraham Lincoln* . . . first in the field. . . ." In seeking evidence bearing upon this matter, a really intensive search has been made. Contemporary newspapers of Boston, New York, Chicago, and a number of other cities have been carefully examined. Everything which I have found lends support to the claim that the Wigwam Edition was indeed the "first in the field."

Source: The author drew his material for the biography from an article which appeared in the *Chicago Press and Tribune* on May 19. There is every reason to believe that that article had been prepared well in advance of the nomination, and sent out to Republican editors in much the same manner as the present day "political handout" is handled. On the same day, May 19, the article was printed in a number of eastern metropolitan dailies, and usually under one of the following captions: "Honest Old Abe," "The People's Candidate for President," "Rails and Flatboats," "Log Cabins and Hard Cider Come Again," "Biographical Sketch of Abraham Lincoln." Obviously the author spared no pains in his attempt to paint his subject as a true son of democracy.

I believe that a variant of that release went out from Chicago—a version in which other catchwords, slogans, and diminutives were included, with the hope that they might catch on, and become popular. In the *Chicago Press and Tribune* version, as well as that which appeared in the *New York Tribune*, the Christian name "Abraham" was used throughout. On the other hand, in the articles printed in the newspapers of Detroit, Cleveland, and Columbus, there is a significant uniformity in the occasional substitution of "Abram" for "Abraham." These articles were published under the credit line of the *Chicago Press and Tribune*, and, identical in content, they show no evidence of local editing. The disgruntled Bennett published a highly condensed version in his *New York Herald*, and used the name "Abram" throughout.

When writing his biography, the unknown author of the Wigwam Edition obviously had before him one of the versions in which both "Abram" and "Abraham" appeared. The publisher was pressing him for copy. He had to make a choice, and he chose the wrong name. The error has provided at least three Lincoln bibliographers with a little amusement. It does not seem to have occurred to them that the blunder in itself might have some bibliographical significance.

On May 19, the firm of Derby & Jackson advertised the forthcoming Bartlett life, and that announcement read "Abram" Lincoln. By Monday, May 21, they had learned the candidate's correct name, and changed their advertising copy accordingly. Consequently, Bartlett's life appeared with the correct name.

Rudd & Carleton were top flight publishers. Surely they would not have permitted their book to appear with this glaring error had they learned of it before the book was "in press." The error is, per se, evidence of the hasty preparation and printing of the book. The publishers enjoyed the impetus given to the sale of the book, by reason of its having been "the first in the field." Within a week after its appearance 12,000 copies had been sold. And, despite the error, it enjoyed a brisk sale throughout the campaign.

Undoubtedly the Wigwam Edition was the most popular life issued during the campaign. To this day it retains its popularity among Lincoln collectors, and is rightfully the keystone to any collection of Lincolniana.

BARTLETT, DAVID VANDEWATER GOLDEN

The / Life and Public Services / of / Hon. Abraham Lincoln, / by D. W. Bartlett, / Washington Correspondent of the New-York Independent and Evening Post / and Author of "Lives of Modern Agitators" Life of "Lady / Jane Grey," "Joan of Arc," etc. / [Rule] / New-York: / H. Dayton, Publisher, / No. 36 Howard-Street. / [Rule] / 1860.   [2]

Variant:

(A) The book also appears with the imprint of Derby & Jackson, 498 Broadway. Priority has not been established, and probably never will be. On the morning of May 19, 1860, both publishers announced their intentions of publishing a life of "Abram" Lincoln, to be written by the veteran political writer, D. W. Bartlett, and to be issued "in a neat duodecimo in cloth for one dollar." I am inclined to believe that they had engaged Bartlett, and arrived at a preconvention agreement to publish jointly the life of the Republican nominee, whoever that nominee might be. Dayton applied for the copyright.

Collation: [i], title page; [ii], copyright notice; [iii], preface dated June 1, 1860; [iv], blank; v-vi, contents; [15]-150, text.

Binding: Paper wrappers, noted in the following colors: pale blue, buff, tan and light brown. Printed in black: Price Twenty-five Cents. / Life and Public Services / of / Hon. Abraham Lincoln / [Portrait of Lincoln] / by D. W. Bartlett, / Washington Correspondent of the N. Y. Evening Post, and N. Y. Independent. / [Rule] / New-York: / H. Dayton, Publisher, / 36 Howard-Street. Advertising matter on verso of front wrapper, and upon both sides of back wrapper. Spine printed: Life of Hon. Abraham Lincoln.

Page Size: 7 3/16 by 4 3/4 inches.

Variant:

In the above-mentioned variant (A), published by Derby & Jackson, the imprint on the wrapper is as follows: New-York: / Derby & Jackson, / 498 Broadway. The text of the advertising matter is different, covering, naturally, their own regular publications. The printing on the spine reads: Life and Public Services of Abraham Lincoln.

Publication Date: June 4, 1860.

In the columns of *Harper's Weekly* for June 9, 1860, Derby & Jackson ran a conspicuous advertisement under the caption, "first in the field." Naturally the copy for that advertisement had been placed ten or fifteen days prior to June 9, and it so happened that the book they described as "one handsome 12mo, Gilt Back, Price $1.00" had not yet reached the market. Up to this time, neither publisher had mentioned an edition in paper wrappings.

On June 4, both publishers were advertising the "neat duodecimo bound in cloth." Dayton promised it for delivery on June 11, and his associates, Derby & Jackson, announced that it would be ready on June 12. This was in the columns of the *New York Tribune*, and other metropolitan dailies. Strangely enough, on the same day, June 4, several selling agents were advertising Bartlett's campaign life as "on hand," and for sale at twenty-five cents.

All of the several publishers who issued clothbound campaign lives suffered disappointing delays in getting their books on the market. With the Wigwam Edition enjoying a brisk demand, and with two other cheap campaign editions in the immediate offing, I believe that Bartlett's publishers issued this book in short form and in this format, in order to meet competition—if not to keep their agents appeased until the $1.00 edition was ready. Hence, I believe that the present book was in the hands of the agents on June 4. Three days later it was on sale in the midwest, according to an advertisement in the *Cleveland Leader*.

The usual chapter on Hamlin was not included in this short-form issue; hence the book cannot be deprived of the distinction of being the first book devoted exclusively to Abraham Lincoln.

Sources: Bartlett, like the unknown author of the Wigwam Edition, drew heavily upon the *Chicago Press and Tribune* article. The author of that article was, no doubt, John Locke Scripps. He had taken the so-called Fell autobiography of December 20, 1859, and added such anecdotes as would lend color to the biography. Among the anecdotes was the story of the loss of Lincoln's surveying instruments through a sheriff's sale. It has an important bearing upon the identification of at least two first editions; hence the excerpt below is quoted from the columns of the *Press and Tribune*: "He learned the art of surveying, and prosecuted that profession until the financial crash of 1837 destroyed the value of real estate and ruined the business—the result of which was that young Lincoln's surveying apparatus was sold on execution by the sheriff."

In the Wigwam Edition the incident was covered as follows: "At this time he was a land surveyor, but so poor that in 1837 his instruments were sold under execution." Nothing particularly offensive in that. But, abjectly enough, Bartlett copied the story from the *Press and Tribune* release, word for word. Hence, in this book appears the unadorned statement that Lincoln had once defaulted, and lost his property through sheriff's sale—the sort of thing which might prove to be loaded with political dynamite.

Obviously some jittery politician must have felt that way about it; for the presses were stopped, stereotype plates changed, and the book was reissued with that story deleted. Bearing in mind that the publication of this book was a private venture, it would seem that powerful pressure must have been brought to bear upon the publishers or a valuable consideration offered, to induce them to make such a change in the midst of the campaign.

It is interesting to note that about the time we believe the change was made, Horace Greeley took this book under his wing, and frequently listed it in his *New York Tribune* as an "authentic Republican campaign document." Further, it should be noted that the revised edition of the book bore the notation, "Authorized Edition."

Note: Comparatively few copies of this book could have been issued before the revision was made, for that edition is quite rare.

SECOND (REVISED) EDITION

[Authorized Edition.] / [*Rule*] / The / Life and Public Services / of / Hon. Abraham Lincoln, / by D. W. Bartlett, / Washington Correspondent of the New-York Independent and Evening Post / and Author of "Lives of Modern Agitators" Life of "Lady / Jane Grey," "Joan of Arc," etc. / [*Rule*] / New-York: / H. Dayton, Publisher, / No. 36 Howard-Street. / [*Rule*] / 1860.

NOTE: It also appeared under the imprint of Derby & Jackson.

Collation: Two white flyleaves; title page with copyright notice on verso; [15]-150, text.

Note: The dated preface is not present in this edition.

Binding: On copies bearing the Derby & Jackson imprint, the top line of the printed matter on the front wrapper reads: Price] Authorized Edition. [25 Cents. In all other respects the binding is the same as that of the first edition.

Page Size: 7 ¼ by 4 ¾ inches.

Publication Date: About June 15, 1860.

Source: In revising the book, Bartlett had before him the third-person autobiography said to have been given to Scripps, by Lincoln, early in June. From page [15] to page 26, the text has been completely revised. The reference to Lincoln's experience as a surveyor now appears as follows: "The surveyor of Sangamon offered to depute to Lincoln that portion of his work which was in his part of the county. He accepted, procured a compass and chain, studied Flint and Gibson a little, and went to it. This procured bread, and kept soul and body together."

See No. 7.

THAYER & ELDRIDGE

The / Life and Public Services / of / Hon. Abraham Lincoln, / of Illinois, / and / Hon. Hannibal Hamlin, / of Maine. / [*Rule*] / Boston: / Thayer & Eldridge, / 114 and 116 Washington Street. / 1860.

[3]

Collation: Frontispiece; [1], title page; [2], copyright notice; [3]-5, table of contents; [6], blank; [7]-12, introductory; [13]-102, text; [103], second title page: Life and Public Services / of / Hon. Hannibal Hamlin, / of Maine.; [104], portrait of Hamlin; [105]-106, introductory; [107]-128, text.

Note: This, the first edition, is distinguished by running heads and page numbers at the tops of the pages.

Binding: Green paper wrappers. Printed in black: Price 25 Cents. / Life and Public Services / of / Hon. Abraham Lincoln / of Illinois. / [*Portrait of Lincoln*] / and / Hon. Hannibal Hamlin / of Maine. / [*Rule*] / Boston: / Thayer & Eldridge, / 114 and 116 Washington Street. Advertising matter on verso of front wrapper, and on both sides of back wrapper.

Page Size: 7 3/8 by 4 5/8 inches.

Publication Date: June 7, 1860, or later.

The nomination of Lincoln found this enterprising firm in no position to create production records in publishing his campaign life. They gambled heavily on the nomination of Seward—and lost. Their campaign life of Seward was so far advanced in production that they could not abandon it. It was published, and appeared on the market before their Lincoln volume was ready.

On May 28, 1860, Thayer & Eldridge announced, in the *New York Tribune*, that this campaign life of Lincoln was "now ready." I am afraid they were drawing a long bow, in their efforts to attract agents. The anonymous author quoted, on page 18, from an article in the *Cleveland Leader*, which did not appear in that paper until May 22. It is extremely doubtful if that article was in our author's hands before May 24. He was rather more leisurely than other authors in compiling his life of Lincoln. He quoted from a number of newspaper articles, and indulged in at least some original research. I do not believe that all of this author's copy was in the hands of his printer before May 28.

A Boston agent advertised this book as "on hand" on June 7, 1860. Apparently an agent in Worcester, Massachusetts, and several in New York City, had the book in stock on June 9. If, as I believe, the book was actually published on June 7, then the production record was a creditable one.

Parenthetically it may be noted that one writer[1] has held that the book was published on May 28, 1860, because that was the date upon which it was registered

---

[1] William E. Barton, "The Lincoln of the Biographers," *Transactions of the Illinois State Historical Society for the Year 1929* (Springfield, 1929), 62.

for copyright. Unfortunately, available copyright data has shed no light upon our problem. May 28 was the day upon which the publisher filed the title page of his projected work. Thus he was protected while the book was in the process of production. Under the then-existing law, that publisher still had ninety days in which to complete the copyright, and file the completed book. Obviously, the relation of the filing date to the date of publication depended upon the whim of the individual publisher. He not only could, but often did register a title page before the author had completed his work. On the other hand, the copyright was sometimes completed in a single operation by filing the completed book with the original application.

Source: Here, again, was an author who had drawn heavily upon the *Chicago Press and Tribune* article. With the exception of a word or two, the story of the sheriff's sale was lifted without alteration. This author delved into old newspaper files, and he drew also from that mighty campaign arsenal, the *Lincoln-Douglas Debates*. As a result of this research his book contained several passages which may have appeared dangerous to the captious politician. However, as to the political impropriety of one passage there could be no doubt.

On page 33, the resolutions which, our author tells us, were adopted at a mass convention in Springfield in October, 1854, appear in full. Douglas had made the same error in the Ottawa debate. In that debate and some of those which followed, Lincoln had found the matter a bothersome one. It is well known that these radical resolutions had been adopted at a Republican meeting in Kane County, and were in no sense the resolutions of the Illinois Republican State Convention of October, 1854. They had no place in a campaign document issued in the interests of Abraham Lincoln.

Once more came that pressure from a now unknown source, and this time the biographical section of the book was literally emasculated. The sketch of Lincoln's life was reduced to a pitifully scanty affair, requiring barely eight pages, and speeches were inserted to compensate for the deleted material.

SECOND (EMASCULATED) EDITION

The / Life and Public Services / of / Hon. Abraham Lincoln, / of Illinois, / and / Hon. Hannibal Hamlin, / of Maine. / [*Rule*] / Boston: / Thayer & Eldridge, / 114 and 116 Washington Street. / 1860.

Collation: Frontispiece; [1], title page; [2], copyright notice; [3]-4, table of contents; [5]-8, introductory; [9]-101, text; [102], portrait; [103], second title page; Life and Public Services / of / Hon. Hannibal Hamlin, / of Maine.; [104], blank; [105]-106, introductory; [107]-128, text.

Note: In this edition there are no running heads, the page numerals being in the top-center of the pages.

Page Size: Same as first edition.

Publication Date: Probably late in July. It is somewhat scarcer than the first edition.

Source: See note under first edition.

See No. 8.

WASHBURNE, HON. E. B.

Caption Title: Abraham Lincoln, / His Personal History and Public Record. / [*Rule*] / Speech / of / Hon. E. B. Washburne, of Illinois. / [*Rule*] / Delivered in the U. S. House of Representatives, May 29th, 1860. / [*Rule*]. In the lower margin of the first page appears the following: Published by the Republican Committee. Price 50 cents per Hundred.   [4]

Collation: [1]-8, text.

Binding: Unbound.

Page Size: In uncut state approximately 9 ¾ by 6 ⅛ inches.

Publication Date: Undetermined. The writer is in possession of a copy bearing an inscription dated: "Philadelphia, June 11th, 1860." It probably appeared at an earlier date. Washington printers were well-equipped, and were experienced in getting out pamphlets of this character upon short notice.

Source: This, in subject matter the most meritorious of the campaign lives of 1860, was drawn partly from the *Chicago Press and Tribune* article, but principally from the author's own intimate knowledge of Lincoln's career.

A warm friend of Lincoln, and a shrewd politician and seasoned political orator, Washburne saw no danger of political repercussions in the story of the sheriff's sale; so he wrote that Lincoln "was compelled to surrender up his mathematical and surveying instruments to the sheriff, to be sold on execution."

Note: During the preparation of this work there arose the question as to whether this pamphlet could properly be considered a campaign life. Biographical in character, and sold as a campaign document, it is most certainly a campaign life of Abraham Lincoln.

CODDING, ICHABOD

A / Republican Manual / for / the Campaign. / [*Rule*] / Facts / for / the People: / [*Rule*] / The / Whole Argument / in / One Book. / By I. Codding. / [*Rule*] / Princeton, Illinois: / Printed at the "Republican" Book and Job Printing Office. / [*Rule*] / 1860.   [5]

Collation: [1], title page; [2], blank; [3], preface; [4], blank; [5]-94, text; 95-96, index.

Binding: Olive green paper wrappers, printed in black: A / Republican Manual / for / the Campaign. / [*Rule*] / Facts / for / the People: / [*Rule*] / The / Whole Argument / in / one Book. / By I. Codding. / [*Rule*] / Princeton, Illinois: / Printed at the "Republican" Book and Job Printing Office. / [*Rule*] / 1860.

Page Size: 8⅜ by 5 inches.

Publication Date: Undetermined. I am led by the text, however, to believe that this pamphlet appeared not later than the week of June 11.

Source: The *Chicago Press and Tribune* article is reprinted in its entirety, and appears on the first six pages of the text.

Note: Of extraordinary scarcity, a copy in the Illinois State Historical Library and another in my possession are all that I have been able to locate. Physically, a well-made, substantial pamphlet, it is difficult to account for its rarity. It cannot be dismissed as an ephemeral pamphlet issued for local consumption. On the contrary, the text clearly demonstrates that the author, a radical abolitionist, prepared this pamphlet for the purpose of attracting fellow radicals to the banner of Abraham Lincoln. He apologizes for Lincoln's stand on the subject of racial equality and presents a thorough treatise in support of abolition. Codding was one of the founders of the Republican Party in Illinois.

I am inclined to believe that this work was suppressed. Is it not probable that fellow Republicans went to him and, pointing out that his radical views might be misunderstood and might alienate the votes of many who were inclined to support Lincoln, prevailed upon him to withdraw the book from circulation?

VOSE, REUBEN

Cover Title: The Life / and / Speeches / of / Abraham Lincoln, / and / Hannibal Hamlin, / [*Rule*] / Edited and Published by / Reuben Vose, / No. 45 Maiden Lane, / New York. / [*Rule*] / Hilton, Gallagher & Co., Printers, / 24 & 25 Ann St., N. Y.   [6]

Collation: iii-li, text—at this point the publisher changed from Roman to Arabic numerals, and erroneously numbered the next page "42;" 42-71½, text; blank page, not included in pagination; 72-118, text; four pages of advertising matter on same stock as the wrappers, and lettered A to D.

Binding: Tan paper wrappers. Verso of front wrapper bears copyright notice. Advertising matter on both sides of back wrapper.

Page Size: 4 ⅝ by 2 ⅞ inches.

Publication Date: Week of June 11, 1860.

On May 26, L. Shear's "Lightning News Express" advertised in the *New York Tribune* that Vose's life of Lincoln at fifteen cents would "be ready on May

30th." (Ready within four days, although he had not yet determined the number of pages the book would contain!)

In his efforts to attract agents, Vose advertised, on May 31, that 10,000 copies were "now ready," and further, that the book would contain 128 pages, and sell at fifteen cents; and finally, that the "Irrepressible Edition" would "be ready June 5th, or 6th, at 20c." The "Irrepressible Edition" was also to contain 128 pages, and one wonders what it had to offer for that extra five cents. We will probably never know, for no copy is known; in fact I do not believe it was ever published.

Instead of increasing his publicity with the alleged appearance of the pamphlet—as one would expect him to do—Vose does not seem to have advertised again until June 11, and then inserted only one or two brief notices. I believe that the few copies that were published appeared with the resumption of advertising, during the week of June 11.

Source: Probably the *Chicago Press and Tribune* release.

Note: Long the despair of the collector, this little book possesses nothing to commend it, aside from its great rarity. Copies are in the Lincoln National Life Foundation, and the Henry E. Huntington Library. A third copy is owned by a private collector who wishes to remain anonymous.

BARTLETT, DAVID VANDEWATER GOLDEN

The / Life and Public Services / of / Hon. Abraham Lincoln, / with a Portrait on Steel. / To Which is Added A Biographical Sketch of / Hon. Hannibal Hamlin. / By D. W. Bartlett, / Washington Correspondent of the New-York Independent and Evening Post, / and Author of "Lives of Modern Agitators," Life of "Lady / Jane Grey," "Joan of Arc," etc. / [*Rule*] / New-York: / H. Dayton, Publisher, / No. 36 Howard-Street. / 1860.   [7]

NOTE: It also appeared under the imprint of Derby & Jackson.

Variant:

(A) A copy has been noted bearing, on the title page, the following imprint beneath that of H. Dayton: Indianapolis: Asher & Company.

Collation: Yellow end paper; two white flyleaves; frontispiece; [i], title page; [ii], copyright notice; [iii], preface, dated June 1, 1860; [iv], blank; v-vi, contents; [15]-354, text; two white flyleaves; one yellow end paper.

Binding: Cloth. Noted in the following colors: Black, olive green, and brown. Some copies have a blind-stamped conventional design on front and back covers.

Page Size: 7¼ by 4¾ inches.

Publication Date: June 12, 1860.

Source: The section devoted to Lincoln's biography was printed from the same plates as were used in producing Bartlett's campaign life in wrappers (the first edition of No. 2 above). Accordingly, it was subject to the same criticism as that book and was rewritten.

SECOND (REVISED) EDITION

[Authorized Edition.] / [*Rule*] / The / Life and Public Services / of / Hon. Abraham Lincoln, / with a Portrait on Steel. / To Which is Added a Biographical Sketch of / Hon. Hannibal Hamlin. / By D. W. Bartlett, / Washington Correspondent of the New-York Independent and Evening Post, / and Author of "Lives of Modern Agitators," Life of "Lady / Jane Gray," "Joan of Arc," etc. / [*Rule*] / New-York: / H. Dayton, Publisher, / No. 36 Howard-Street. / [*Rule*] / 1860.

NOTE: It also appeared under the imprint of Derby & Jackson.

Variants:

Copies have been noted with the following single imprints:

(A) New York: / A. B. Burdick, / No. 115 Nassau-Street.

(B) Cincinnati: / Broaders & Company, / 51 Fourth Street, Cor. of Walnut.

(C) Philadelphia: / J. W. Bradley. (Note: I have not seen this issue; hence I am not certain that the imprint as recorded above is complete).

(D) Indianapolis: Asher & Company.

Collation: Yellow end paper; two white flyleaves; inserted frontispiece; title page; copyright notice; [v]-vii, contents; [viii], blank; [15]-354, text; one white flyleaf; yellow end paper.

Variant:

(E) A copy containing 357 pages has been noted. The letters of notification and acceptance appear upon the added pages. I have not seen this issue, but am reliably informed that no other change in collation is involved. It has been noted with the Dayton imprint only. There seems to be no reasonable ground for Fish's contention that this was "an earlier edition."

Binding: Cloth. Noted in the following colors: black, blue, green, brown, tan, and maroon. Spine lettered in gilt: The Life of Abraham Lincoln. Various conventional designs are blind-stamped on front and back covers.

Variant:

(F)   Copies have been noted with a varying number of pages of advertising matter following page 354, the end of the text. They have most interesting bindings, noted in the following colors: maroon, green, and brown pebbled cloth. The front and back covers are blind-stamped in a rustic design. On the spine, in gilt, appears: [*Rule*] / Honest Old Abe / [*Rule*] / Bartlett / [*Rule*] / [*An axe*] / [*Portrait of Lincoln surrounded by a wreath*] / Derby & Jackson. / [*Rule*].

Note: This variant has not been noted with the Dayton imprint.

Page Size: Same as first edition.

Publication Date: Probably early in July.

Source: The section devoted to Lincoln's biography was printed from the same plates as were used in producing the second (revised) edition of Bartlett's campaign life, in wrappers.

WIDE-AWAKE EDITION

Wide-Awake Edition. / [*Rule*] / The / Life and Public Services / of / Hon. Abraham Lincoln, / of Illinois, / and / Hon. Hannibal Hamlin, / of Maine. / [*Rule*] / Boston: / Thayer & Eldridge, / 114 and 116 Washington Street. / 1860.   [8]

Collation: Yellow end paper; white flyleaf; frontispiece; engraving on stee by Buttre (portrait of Lincoln); [1], title page; [2], copyright notice and printer's imprint; [3]-5, table of contents; [6], blank; [7]-12, introductory; [13]-102, text; engraving on steel by Buttre (portrait of Hamlin); [103], second title page: Life and Public Services / of / Hon. Hannibal Hamlin, / of Maine.; [104], portrait; [105]-106, introductory; [107]-128, text; [129], third title page: Speeches / of / Hon. Abraham Lincoln, / of Illinois.; [130], blank; [131]-320, text; white flyleaf; yellow end paper.

Binding: Cloth.   Noted in black, brown, green, and plum colors.   Spine lettered in gold: Lives / and / Speeches / of / Lincoln / and / Hamlin / [*Rule*] / Wide Awake / Edition. / Followed by four blind-stamped, broad rules.   Blind-stamped on the front and back covers is the publisher's device, "T and E" within a chamfered square.

Page Size: 7 ⅜ by 4 ¾ inches.

Publication Date: June 25, 1860.   On June 16, the publishers announced this book as "nearly ready."   I find the advertisements of sales agents, announcing the book on hand, dated June 25, 1860.

Source: The first 128 pages of this book are identical with those of the campaign life in wrappers, issued by these publishers (No. 3 above).   Internal evidence indicates that, while the first edition of the life in wrappers was being run off from the original type forms, stereotype plates had been prepared from which the pages referred to were being printed. The book contains, of course, all of the objectionable matter found in the first little edition in wrappers.

The original matter was padded with the addition of 200 pages of speeches. Steel engravings of both Lincoln and Hamlin were added, and the woodcut of Hamlin was permitted to remain on the verso of the second title page. This with the incongruous result that two portraits of the vice-presidential candidate were provided, and but one of Lincoln.

Note: It is possible that the publishers revised the text as in the case of their campaign life in wrappers, and issued a second edition of this book. I have been unable to locate a copy of such an edition.

Though not uncommon, the book is considerably scarcer than the clothbound books by either Bartlett, Barrett, or Howells. This fact leads to the conclusion that the book did not enjoy the popularity of the works by those authors. For this reason the publishers may have felt that they were not justified in issuing an emasculated second edition.

HOWELLS, WILLIAM DEAN

Lives and Speeches / of / Abraham Lincoln / and / Hannibal Hamlin. / [*Rule*] / Columbus, O: / Follett, Foster & Co. / 1860.
[9]

Collation: [1], half title page; [2], blank; [3], title page; [4], copyright notice, printer's and stereotyper's imprints; [5], list of illustrations; [6], blank; [7], index; [8], blank; [9], subtitle page: Life / of / Abraham Lincoln. / By / W. D. Howells. / 2; [10], blank; [xi]-xii, preface; [xiii]-xv, contents; [xvi], blank; [17]-94, text; [95], blank; [96], woodcut of the Republican Wigwam at Chicago; [97], subtitle: Memorabilia / of the / Chicago Convention. / 9; [98], blank; [99]-111, text; [112], blank; [113], subtitle: Speeches. / 10; [114], blank; [115]-153, text; [154], blank; [157]-170, text (Life of Hannibal Hamlin).

Note: Though portraits of the candidates are listed, they were not issued in this edition. Pages 155-56 were omitted in all copies examined; however it is quite possible that copies will be found with a subtitle page at this point.

Binding: Light buff-colored paper wrappers, printed in black: Life of / [*Woodcut portrait of Lincoln*] / Abraham Lincoln. / [*Rule*] / Columbus: / Follett, Foster & Co. / 1860. Advertising matter on verso of front wrapper, reading in part: 20, 416 Sold! The Debates in Illinois between Stephen A. Douglas, and Abraham Lincoln.

Variant:

(A) We have been unable to locate a copy of this book reported to bear, upon the front wrapper, the imprint, Cincinnati, Rickey, Mallory & Co., 1860., in lieu of the above described imprint.

Page Size: 7⅜ by 4⅝ inches.

Publication Date: June 25, 1860.

Follett, Foster & Company published the *Lincoln-Douglas Debates* before the nomination. Indeed, on May 21, 1860, their advertisements announced that this book was then in its fourth edition. Certainly it was destined to become the "best-seller" of 1860.

The demand for the *Debates* literally swamped the publisher's printing plant and bindery within a few days after the nomination. On May 23, they announced in the columns of the *Ohio State Journal* the acquisition of two new "Williamson" presses, and in the same paper they advertised for "feeders." Before the end of that week they had announced the preparation of two new sets of stereotypes.

The *Debates* were advertised for sale in two formats: clothbound at fifty cents, and "stitched" at thirty-five cents. Today the "stitched" copies of the *Debates* are exceedingly rare, while the issues bound in cloth are very common—mute testimony to the willingness of their public to pay the additional fifteen cents for the cloth binding. And therein lay a production problem of major proportions.

In every instance, there was a lag between the early announcements of publication dates of clothbound campaign lives and the actual appearance of the books, amounting to anywhere from ten to thirty days. Seemingly the demand for clothbound campaign material was greater than the nation's binders were prepared to meet. Conditions were especially critical in the active publishing centers of Cincinnati and Columbus, Ohio. The many variant bindings of the *Debates* attest the fact that Follett, Foster & Company must have farmed out the work to all available binders. I believe it will be shown, beyond reasonable doubt, that this condition was responsible for the very existence of the edition of Howells' campaign life of Lincoln, now under consideration.

The publishers were among those who, on May 19, advertised a campaign life of Lincoln as "in press." Specifically naming Howells as the author, on May 28 his book was announced as "in press will soon appear." The book was described as being "bound in cloth. Price $1.00," and, in small letters, "campaign edition in paper at 25c."

Generous buyers of advertising space in newspapers, probably their best available medium was the use of advertising inserts in the rapidly selling *Debates*, and the enterprising publishers were not long in taking advantage of this. All but the very early issues and editions of the *Debates* have several pages of advertising matter bound in at the front of the books. One of these pages was always devoted to advertising Howells' volume. The earliest appearance of this advertisement read, in part: "Will have ready June 12th," and, towards the bottom of the page: "Also, a Campaign Edition, *without the Speeches*. Paper cover. 25 Cents."

Shortly after this appearance of the *Debates*, the advertising matter in newspapers underwent an interesting change in the copy. No mention was now made of the cheap edition in paper. In the next issue of the *Debates*, the advertisement of Howells was changed to read: "Will have ready June 20th." But, of greater significance, the announcement near the foot of the page now read: "Also, a Campaign Edition of the Lives of Lincoln and Hamlin, entirely distinct from above. Paper Cover. Price 25 Cents."

Apparently the idea of issuing Howells' volume in wrappers had been abandoned. What had happened? At this stage, the newspapers were announcing 9,000 copies of Howells' book as being "already sold," although it had not yet emerged from the press room—or, at least, the bindery. Of course, the reference was to advance orders. With heavy advance orders for the $1.00 edition, the publishers, feeling that the sale of the cheap campaign edition would substantially reduce the demand for the more profitable $1.00 edition, abandoned the former. However, competition cried aloud for the publication of a "cheap, campaign edition."

Close at hand was a young man vastly impressed with his own ability, one James Quay Howard, who had aided Howells in gathering his material. From what little I have been able to learn about Howard I am quite certain that he would be one to resent the use of his material by another. Though but a young law student, he felt quite competent to write his own campaign life of Lincoln, and under the circumstances experienced little, if any, difficulty in persuading Follett, Foster & Company to publish it. This is the life which I believe the publishers had in mind when they advertised in the *Debates*, the "Campaign Edition of the Lives of Lincoln and Hamlin, entirely distinct from above," for these same publishers issued Howard's book—see No. 13 below.

In the interim, newspaper advertisements continued to announce that the Howells life would be ready on June 20, but that day rolled around, and the advertising copy was again changed; this time it read, "will be ready, June 25th." In the meantime, various eastern publications were finding their way into the local markets. In the neighboring city of Cincinnati, the harassed publishers of Barrett's life were sparing no effort in trying to get their book on the market ahead of Howells'. The various selling agents for the *Debates*, who had enthusiastically signed up for the Howells volume must, by this time, have been clamoring for their books. Howard was nowhere near ready. His prefatory note is dated June 26, and his book did not appear until weeks later. It is quite possible that there existed contractual obligations with some of the selling agents, which had to be met.

Yielding to the attendant pressure, Follett, Foster & Company probably issued this edition of Howells' to meet a very real emergency. Although this book carries a stereotyper's imprint, it was not printed from plates. On the contrary, it was printed directly from the type from which the plates for the complete edition were made. In the copy before me the impression is so heavy as to puncture the paper at places.

The complete Howells edition contains over 400 pages, while, as we have noted, the present book consists of but 170 pages. Nor is this the cheap campaign issue described by the publishers, in their early advertisements, as being "without the speeches," for a substantial part of this book is devoted to speeches. The publishers removed as much material as was practicable from the original forms, reset the new pagination, and issued the book in great haste—unannounced.

In the advertisements inserted by the publishers in the *Ohio State Journal*, mention was made of the number of copies of the *Debates* sold to that date. On June 25, the number sold was 20,416 copies, coinciding with the number given in the advertisement on the verso of the front wrapper of this book.

However, of greater evidential value is the advertisement of Rickey, Mallory & Company, which appeared in the *Cincinnati Daily Press* on June 25, 1860, for the first time, announcing that they had "now on sale" a supply of Howells' life of Lincoln, in paper, at twenty-five cents.

See No. 11.

BARRETT, JOSEPH HARTWELL

Barrett's Authentic Edition. / [*Rule*] / Life / of / Abraham Lincoln, / (of Illinois). / With a Condensed View of His Most / Important Speeches; / Also / a Sketch of the Life of / Hannibal Hamlin / (of Maine). / By J. H. Barrett. / [*Rule*] / Cincinnati: / Moore, Wilstach, Keys & Co. / 25 West Fourth Street, / 1860.

[10]

Collation: Yellow, or pink end paper; one white flyleaf (end paper and flyleaf not present in issue bound in wrappers); frontispiece; [i], title page; [ii], copyright notice; [iii], preface; [iv], blank; [v]-viii, contents; 9-193, text; 194, caption: Sketch / of the / Life of Hannibal Hamlin.; plate (lithographed portrait of Hamlin); 195-216, text; one white flyleaf; yellow or pink end paper (flyleaf and end paper are not present in issue bound in wrappers).

Note: The lithographed portrait of Lincoln appears in its earliest state in those issues of this book which were bound in wrappers. In the first state, the imprint on the portrait reads: Middleton, Strobridge & Co. Lith Cin. O. In the second state, as issued in copies of the book bound in cloth, the imprint reads: Middleton, Strobridge & Co. In clothbound copies, intermediate states of the frontispiece are occasionally noted, in which evidence of the erasure of "Lith Cin. O." from the stone is visible to the naked eye. (The portrait of Hamlin appears only in its earliest state in the paper-bound issues of this book, while it appears in both states in the clothbound copies).

Binding (wrappers): The earliest appearance of this book was in salmon-colored paper wrappers, printed in black: Life / of / Abraham Lincoln, / (of Illinois). / With a Condensed View of his Most Important Speeches; / Also, / a Sketch of the Life of / Hannibal Hamlin, / (of Maine). / By J. H. Barrett. / [*Rule*] / Cincinnati: / Moore, Wilstach, Keys & Co. / 25 West Fourth Street / 1860. The spine is printed: Barrett's Authentic Edition. Advertising matter appears on verso of front wrapper, and on both sides of back wrapper.

Binding (cloth): Various shades and textures of cloth. Blind-stamped ornaments within triple-ruled border on front and back covers. Spine lettered in gilt: [*Three parallel rules*] / Life / of / A. Lincoln / [*Rule*] / Sketch of / H. Hamlin / [*Rule*] / Barrett / [*Three parallel rules*].

Variant:

(A) A copy of the clothbound book has been noted with the following imprint on its title page: Indianapolis: / Asher & Company . / Cincinnati: / Moore, Wilstach, Keys & Co. / 1860.

Page Size: In wrappers: 7⅜ by 4¾ inches. In cloth: 7⅝ by 4⅞ inches.

Publication Dates: In wrappers, probably June 27, 1860. In cloth, probably July 2, 1860.

The publishers were among those who, on May 19, 1860, announced a forthcoming campaign life of Lincoln. On May 24, 1860, they advertised in the *New York Tribune* that they had a life of Lincoln "in active preparation." It so happened that on that very day their author, Barrett, and a photographer were engaged in obtaining a portrait of Lincoln. On May 31, 1860, the publishers promised that this life would "be ready in a few days." On June 8, they announced in the *New York Tribune* that the book would be ready "next week." And, on June 12, the advertisement again read: "ready next week." All of this was publicity, designed to attract agents. For, if we are to accept the date on the preface of the book, the author did not complete his work until June 18, 1860.

From the first the book had been announced to sell: "In cloth, 50c. In paper, 25c." It was advertised in the *Cleveland Leader* as on sale "at 25c" on June 27, 1860. On the next day, the twenty-five cent book was being offered in Columbus and Cincinnati. No earlier offerings have been found, and I believe June 27 to be the day upon which the issue in wrappers was placed on sale. In Pittsburgh, one James McMillen offered the clothbound book on July 5, 1860. The earliest announcement of the clothbound book by an Ohio retailer, which I have been able to find, was dated July 10. Copies of the book bound in wrappers are excessively rare.

Source: Barrett had been a delegate to the Chicago convention, and seems to have been closely associated with Lincoln for several days after its adjournment. Years later he wrote: "He [Lincoln] readily gave such facts as my inquiries invited or suggested."[2]

Nor was Barrett content with the material which he obtained directly from Lincoln. He sought to provide an accurate background, and to this end turned to Filson's history of Kentucky, Judge Scott's gazetteer of Indiana, and to other source books. The result was a commendable work, the first of a long series which was to issue from the pen of this author.

---

[2] Joseph H. Barrett, *Abraham Lincoln and his Presidency* (New York, 1904), I: iii.

HOWELLS, WILLIAM DEAN
Complete Edition

Lives and Speeches / of / Abraham Lincoln / and / Hannibal Hamlin. / [*Rule*] / Columbus, O: / Follett, Foster & Co. / 1860.

[11]

Collation: Pink end paper; white flyleaf; [1], half title; [2], blank; frontispiece not included in pagination; [3], title page; [4], copyright notice, and imprints of printer and stereotyper; [5], list of illustrations; [6], blank; [7], index; [8], blank; [9], subtitle: Life / of / Abraham Lincoln. / By / W. D. Howells.; [10], blank; [xi]-xii, preface; [xiii]-xv, list of contents; [xvi], blank; [17] -94, text; [95], blank; [96], woodcut (the Republican Wigwam at Chicago); [97], subtitle: Memorabilia / of the / Chicago Convention; [98], blank; [99]-111, text; [112], blank; [113], subtitle: Speeches; [114], blank; [115]-304, text; frontispiece to Hamlin section, not included in pagination; [305], subtitle: Life and Speeches / of / Hannibal Hamlin. / By / John L. Hayes.; [306], blank; [307]-406, text; two white flyleaves; pink end paper.

Variants:

Copies bearing the following imprints on the title page below that of Follett, Foster & Company have been noted. (In the case of these multiple imprints a minor correction has been made on the title page, a period being added to the abbreviation for Ohio, thus: Columbus, O.):

(A)   Cincinnati: Rickey, Mallory & Co.

(B)   Boston: Brown and Taggard.

(C)   Chicago: S. C. Griggs & Co. Pittsburgh: Hunt and Miner. Cleveland: Ingham & Bragg.

(D)   Detroit: Putnam, Smith & Co.

(E)   Boston: Crosby, Nichols, Lee & Co.

(F)   New York: M. Doolady.

Binding: Pebbled cloth of various textures, and in a wide range of colors. Among the colors noted are: black, red, several shades of brown, plum, green, blue, maroon, and tan. Lettered in gilt on the spine: [*Four parallel rules*] / Lives of / Lincoln / and / Hamlin / [*Broken rule*] / Howells & Hayes / Follett, Foster & Co. / [*Four parallel rules*].

In our discussion of the short-form edition of Howells' life[3] of Lincoln, we pointed to congested bindery facilities in Ohio. I believe that, because of this condition, books printed in that state were sent in sheets to W. A. Townsend of New York, and bound in that city.

Variant:

(G)   Imprint: New York: / W. A. Townsend & Co., / Columbus: Follett, Foster & Co. / 1860. In this issue the end papers are lemon yellow, and the en-

---

[3] See *ante*, 202-205.

graved portraits of the two candidates are gathered and bound between the front flyleaf and page [1], the half title. Lettered in gilt on the spine: [*Rule*] / The Lives / and / Speeches / of / Lincoln / and / Hamlin / [*Rule*] / Illustrated. / W. A. Townsend & Co. / [*Double rule*].

Priority of Imprints: Undetermined. A copy with the single imprint of Follett, Foster & Company, and bearing an inscription dated July 8, 1860, is in the writer's possession. The Sam Parks copy[4] which, beyond reasonable doubt, was in Lincoln's hands in July, 1860, had the single imprint. It is probable that copies bearing the single imprint were issued locally, and also sent out to prominent Republicans, before those with multiple imprints were sent on to associate publishers.

Copies are distinguished by certain typographical variants; however these are without evidential value. We know that the publisher worked from two sets of stereotype plates, and no one is qualified to say from which set of plates the earliest copies were printed. Uncorrected typographical defects simply demonstrate which was the earliest plate to be cast.

For instance, the letter "i" is missing from the word "importance" in the last line of the text on page 46, in all copies bearing the single imprint. In copies bearing the multiple imprints, that letter "i" has been restored from another font of type of slightly bolder face. But, in the last edition of the book to be published, and under the single imprint of Follett, Foster & Company, that letter "i" is still missing, although textual corrections have been made. Obviously, the mat from which the plates were cast, and which, in turn, was used in the printing of the issues with the single imprint, was made before the absence of the letter was noticed. The letter was then missed and an "i" inserted by the founders and another mat drawn off, from which another set of plates was cast. All of which has nothing whatever to do with the vicissitudes of the sheets in the hands of the printers and the binders.

Page Size: 7⅜ by 4¾ inches.

Publication Date: Published on July 5, 1860, and reviewed the following day in the editorial columns of Howells' own paper, the *Ohio State Journal*.

Source: Among the letters of William Dean Howells, we find the author's own story:

"It was the expectation that I would go to Springfield, Illinois, and gather the material for the work from Lincoln himself, and from his friends and neighbors. But this part of the project was distasteful to me, was impossible; I would not go, and I missed the greatest chance of my life in its kind, though I am not sure I was wholly wrong, for I might not have been equal to that chance; I might not have seemed to the man I would not go to see, the person to report him to the world in a campaign life. What we did was to commission a young law-student of those I knew, to go to Springfield and get the material for me. When he brought it back, I felt the charm of the material; the wild poetry of its reality was not unknown to me; I was at home with it, for I had known the belated backwoods of a certain re-

---

[4] See *post*, 210.

gion of Ohio; I had almost lived the pioneer; and I wrote the little book with none of the reluctance I felt from studying its sources."[5]

That "young law-student" was James Quay Howard. Whether the material that he brought back from Springfield was too scanty, or whether Howells felt that it was a bit drab, does not appear at this late date. But of one thing we are sure: Howells did not stick closely to the material supplied Howard by Lincoln. On the contrary, he drew from previously published biographies; and, as we shall see, one story lifted from the Thayer & Eldridge life (see No. 3 above) got him and his publishers into hot water.

On June 8, 1860, Follett, Foster & Company advertised Howells' life of Lincoln in the *Ohio State Journal*, under the caption: "Authorized by Mr. Lincoln." I have been unable to locate other advertisements carrying that claim; hence do not know how widely it was disseminated. If true it would mean a luscious plum for the publishers. Possibly Barrett's publishers, in Cincinnati, instituted some inquiries; or maybe Republicans wondered if this personally authorized biography was to be adopted by them as official; in any event, the announcement seems to have created something of a stir in Columbus political circles.

On June 15, Samuel Galloway, a prominent member of the Ohio Republican State Central Committee, wrote Lincoln, who replied on June 19, 1860. Because it provides us with an illuminating picture of Lincoln's attitude towards campaign biographies in general, the letter is quoted in full:

SPRINGFIELD, ILLINOIS, June 19, 1860.

My dear Sir: Your very kind letter of the 15th is received. Messrs. Follet, Foster & Co.'s *Life* of me is *not* by my authority; and I have scarcely been so much astounded by anything, as their public announcement that it is authorized by me. They have fallen into some strange misunderstanding. I certainly knew they contemplated publishing a biography, and I certainly did not object to their doing so, *upon their own responsibility*. I even took pains to facilitate them. But, at the same time, I made myself tiresome, if not hoarse, with repeating to Mr. Howard, their only agent seen by me, my protest that I *authorized nothing*—would be *responsible for nothing*. How they could so misunderstand me, passes comprehension. As a matter, *wholly my own*, I would authorize no biography, without *time* and *opportunity* to carefully examine and consider every word of it; and, in this case, in the nature of things, I can have no such time and opportunity. But, in my present position, when, by the lessons of the past, and the united voice of all discreet friends, I can neither write nor speak a word for the public, how dare I to send forth, by my authority, a volume of hundreds of pages, for adversaries to make points upon without end? Were I to do so, the Convention would have a right to reassemble, and substitute another name for mine.

---

[5] *Life in Letters of William Dean Howells*, edited by Mildred Howells (Garden City, N. Y., 1928), I: 36-37.

For these reasons, I would not look at the proof sheets. I am determined to maintain the position of truly saying I never saw the proof sheets, or any part of their work, before its publication.

Now, do not mistake me. I feel great kindness for Messrs. F., F. & Co.—do not think they have intentionally done wrong. There may be nothing wrong in their proposed book. I sincerely hope there will not. I barely suggest that you, or any of the friends there, on the party account, look it over, and exclude what you may think would embarrass the party, bearing in mind, at all times, that I *authorize nothing*—will be *responsible* for *nothing*.

Your friend as ever,   A. LINCOLN.[6]

Upon receipt of this letter, the publishers immediately changed the offending caption to read "accurate and reliable." It does not appear that Galloway followed Lincoln's suggestion to look it over and exclude embarrassing matter, for, from a political standpoint, a most serious blunder had been committed by Howells, and was allowed to appear in the early issues of the book.

Thus forcibly brought to his attention, we may be sure that Lincoln carefully conned the first available copy. What must have been his feelings when, after noting several minor errors, he turned to page 74, and found that his emphatic refusal to sponsor the book had been fully justified! For there appeared the same error, with reference to the Ottawa debate, which the unknown author of the Thayer & Eldridge life had made—an error out of which Douglas had made forensic capital, time and again, during the debates. "It is true," wrote Howells, "that a Mass State Convention, with a view to forming a permanent organization, had been held at Springfield, in October; but many anti-Nebraska men, who still adhered to old names, had not taken part in it. The following resolutions were adopted at this Convention. . . ." A bulletin of the Abraham Lincoln Association is devoted to a discussion of that priceless and most desirable of all campaign biographies, the copy of Howells' life which Lincoln corrected in his own handwriting, and gave to his friend, Mr. Samuel C. Parks. On the flyleaf of that copy, Mr. Parks wrote: "This life of Lincoln was corrected by him for me, at my request, in the summer of 1860, by notes in his handwriting, in pencil in the margin."[7]

We cannot read the Galloway letter, and believe that Lincoln took it upon himself to correct a campaign life (it is his own unmistakable handwriting), and pass it on to an acquaintance as a mere gesture of friendship. I believe that Lincoln made those corrections, and turned the corrected book over to Parks—a trusted and prominent Republican worker—with the sole idea that the matter would be brought to the attention of the publishers, and the necessary corrections made.

With a single exception—previously noted—none of the errors were of any

LINCOLN'S LETTER DISCLAIMING RESPONSIBILITY FOR A CAMPAIGN BIOGRAPHY.
Original letter owned by Illinois State Historical Library.

political importance. The publishers took immediate steps to correct that error, but not until thousands of copies of the book had been distributed.

Issue With The Errata Slip

Title page, collation, binding, and page size: No changes.

An errata slip is inserted at page 74, reading:

"The resolutions said to have been passed at a Convention at Springfield, and found on page 74, were not passed. They were a political trick, intended by the Democrats, to defeat Yates, candidate for Congress. See Douglas and Lincoln Debates, pages 90, 97, 98, 182, 189, 195, 199, 200. The error, in the hurry of going to press, crept in. On page 75, it will be seen, Mr. Lincoln is shown to have had no connection with the resolutions."

But two copies of this issue are known: one is in the collection of Gov. Henry Horner, Springfield, Illinois, and the other in the writer's possession.

Note: Both of the known copies are of the issue bearing the single imprint of Follett, Foster & Company.

SECOND (COMPLETE) EDITION

Title Page: Variant B—Boston; Brown and Taggard.

Collation: No change down to page 406; from there on the collation is: one white flyleaf; eight pages of advertising matter; white flyleaf; pink end paper.

Binding: Brown cloth.

Textual Change: The text at page 74, beginning with line 3, has been changed to read: "It was charged by Douglas that a Republican Convention met at Springfield and passed the resolutions found below. This was an error. No Convention was held at Springfield, but the resolutions were offered at a small meeting in Kane County of which Lincoln knew nothing."

The only known copy of this edition is in the collection of Gov. Henry Horner, Springfield, Illinois.

See No. 9.

SCRIPPS, JOHN LOCKE

Caption Title: Life / of / Abraham Lincoln.   In the lower margin of page [1], appears the following: Entered according to Act of Congress, in the year 1860, by the Chicago Press and Tribune Co., in the Clerk's / Office of the District Court for the Northern District of Illinois.   [12]

Collation: [1]-32, text, in double columns. The lower two-thirds of page 32 is devoted to advertising matter.

Binding: Stitched, without wrappers.

Page Size: 8⅞ by 5⅝ inches.

Publication Date: About July 15, 1860. A notice in the *Illinois State Journal*, July 24, 1860, reads: "We are in receipt of a copy of the Campaign Life of Lincoln written by Mr. Scripps and issued at the Chicago *Press and Tribune*. It is one of the best campaign documents we have yet seen."

Advertising Matter: In the first edition of this life, the advertising matter, on page 32, is set in two columns, from the same agate type as is used in the text, with the exception of the captions; the latter are set in the usual display faces, then in vogue in newspaper composing rooms. The text of this advertising matter begins: "The *Press and Tribune* office is prepared to furnish to Republican Clubs and individuals, the following important documents at the low rates annexed. . . ." At the end is the following: "Money in registered letters may be sent at our risk. Address: *Press and Tribune*, Chicago, Illinois."

Typographical Errors: The last word in column 2, line 23, page 32, reads, "thel" and the last word in the following line reads, "wil." The terminal letter of line 24 had slipped up into the preceding line. It so appears in all editions of this work, thus proving that all were printed from stereotypes cast from the same type form.

Source: Early in June, 1860, Scripps was given new biographical material by Lincoln. This, the so-called third person autobiography, is printed in full, in the *Complete Works of Abraham Lincoln*, edited by Nicolay and Hay, under the heading: "Short autobiography written at the request of a friend to use in preparing a popular campaign biography in the election of 1860."[8] The actual date of this autobiography is unknown. Nicolay and Hay approximate its date as June 1; they are probably correct. Howard returned to Columbus, Ohio on June 7, and he either brought with him a copy of that autobiography, or notes drawn directly from a copy. Both Scripps's and Howard's principal, Howells, used a quaint phrase drawn from the autobiography: the store "winked out." So unusual was the expression that Howells felt called upon to explain it was the "idiom of the region."

NEW YORK EDITION

Caption Title: Tribune Tracts. — No. 6 / [*Rule*] / Life / of / Abraham Lincoln. In the lower margin of page [1] appears the following: Entered according to Act of Congress, in the year 1860, by Horace Greeley & Co., in the Clerk's Office of the / District Court of the United States for the Southern District of New York.

---

[8] *Complete Works of Abraham Lincoln*, edited by John G. Nicolay and John Hay (Gettysburg ed.), VI: 24.

Webster's, but is unlike either. It is very large, and phrenologically well proportioned, betokening power in all its developments. A slightly Roman nose, a wide-cut mouth, and a dark complexion, with the appearance of having been weather-beaten, complete the description.

In his personal habits, Mr. Lincoln is as simple as a child. He loves a good dinner, and eats with the appetite which goes with a great brain; but his food is plain and nutritious. He never drinks intoxicating liquors of any sort. He is not addicted to tobacco in any of its shapes. He was never accused of a licentious act in his life. He never uses profane language. He never gambles. He is particularly cautious about incurring pecuniary obligations for any purpose whatever; and, in debt, he is never content until the score is discharged. We presume he owes no man a dollar. He never speculates. The rage for the sudden acquisition of wealth never took hold of him. His gains from his profession have been moderate, but sufficient for his purpose. While others have dreamed of gold, he has been in pursuit of knowledge. In all his dealings, he has the reputation of being generous but exact, and, above all, religiously honest. He would be a bold man who would say that Abraham Lincoln ever wronged a man out of a cent, or ever spent a dolla that he had not honestly earned. His struggles in early life have made him careful of money, but his generosity with his own is proverbial. He is a regular attendant upon religious worship, and, though not a communicant, is a pew-holder and liberal supporter of the Presbyterian Church in Springfield, to which Mrs. Lincoln be-

belongs. He is a scrupulous teller of the truth—too exact in his notions to suit the atmosphere of Washington, as it now is. His enemies may say that he tells Black Republican lies; but no man ever charged that, in a professional capacity, or as a citizen dealing with his neighbors, he would depart from the scriptural command. At home, he lives like a gentleman of modest means and simple tastes. A good-sized house of wood, simply but tastefully furnished, surrounded by trees and flowers, is his own; there he lives, at peace with himself, the idol of his family, and for his honesty, ability and patriotism, the admiration of his countrymen.

If Mr. Lincoln is elected President, he will carry but little that is ornamental to the White House. The country must accept his sincerity, his ability, and his honesty, in the mould in which they are cast. He will not be able to make so polite a bow as Franklin Pierce, but he will not commence anew the agitation of the slavery question by recommending to Congress any Kansas-Nebraska bills. He may not preside at the Presidential dinners with the ease and grace which distinguish the "venerable public functionary," Mr. Buchanan; but he will not create the necessity for a Covode Committee and the disgraceful revelations of Cornelius Wendell. He will take to the Presidential Chair just the qualities which the country now demands to save it from impending destruction—ability that no man can question, firmness that nothing can overbear, honesty that never has been impeached, and patriotism that never despairs."

CAMPAIGN DOCUMENTS FOR SALE.

The PRESS and TRIBUNE officials prepared to furnish to Republican Club and individuals, the following important documents at the low rates annexed:

1. CAMPAIGN LIFE OF LINCOLN.—A 52 page pamphlet, stitched and trimmed. Price per 100, $2.50; per 1,000, $20.

2. IMPORTANT FACTS FOR THE PEOPLE.—A pamphlet on ten subjects, viz.:
I.—Letter of Hon. Edward Bates, of Missouri, in support of Lincoln.
II.—The three National Platforms.
III.—The Wickliffe (slave cod) Resolution, with extracts from the Dred Scott Decision, from Douglas's "Grand Jury" Speech; from Col. Forney's Addresses.
IV.—Herschel V. Johnson's Slave Code Record.
V.—Squatter Sovereignty as the Slave Trade.
VI.—What "Popular Sovereignty" has done—Extract from Mr. Douglas's Speech in the Senate.
VII.—Slavery in New Mexico—Serfdom of White Laborers.
VIII.—Slavery in Nebraska—Efforts of the Republicans to abolish it; Successful Exertions of the Democracy to Preserve and Retain it.
IX.—All votes cast for Douglas are given practically to Breckinridge or old Jo. Lane.
X.—Lincoln's and Hamlin's Letters of Acceptance. Price $1 per 100 copies.

3. DOUGLAS'S RECORD ON THE SLAVERY QUESTION—A document of 16 pages—embracing his Remarks in favor of a Sedition Law, in the Senate, January 23d, 1860.... Senator Davis' Reply in Defence of the Freedom of Speech and Opinion....Mr. Douglas's Letter to J. B. Dorr, of Dubuque, Iowa....Points of Difference between the House and Senate Homestead Bills, together with the record of the defeat of both measures....The Non-Admission of Kansas by Congress....Important Measures of Legislation defeated by the Democrats in the last session of Congress....The Defeat of John Brown's Invasion of Virginia, as shown by the Report of the Senate Harper's Ferry Committee.... Corruptions of the Administration....The Kidnapping Business in Illinois, etc. Price $1 per 100 copies.

4. PROCEEDINGS OF THE NATIONAL REPUBLICAN CONVENTION—A verbatim report, embracing the official roll of delegates, with the post office address of each—44 pages. Price 5 cents per copy; 40 cents per dozen.

5. THE DRED SCOTT DECISION in full—16½ pages. Price 20 cents per copy.

6. THE DEBATES OF LINCOLN AND DOUGLAS IN 1858—268 pp. Price (bound) 50 cents, unbound 35 cents.

7. REPUBLICAN PLATFORM, on elegant paper, and handsomely printed. Price 66 cents per 100.

SPEECHES.

[8 Pages 50 cents per hundred; 16 Pages, $1.00 per hundred; 32 Pages, $2.00 per hundred.]

EIGHT PAGES.
Lincoln's Cooper Institute Speech.
Free Homes for Free Men—G. A. Grow.
Shall the Territories be Africanized—James Harlan.
The Aggression of Slavery—Owen Lovejoy.
The Homestead Bill—M. S. Wilkinson.
Douglas and Popular Sovereignty—Carl Schurz.
Southern Fee Soil—John Hickman.
Protection to American Industry—Alexander H. Rice.
Revenue and Expenditure—John Sherman.
Bill and Report Repealing the Slave Code of New Mexico—John A. Bingham.

8 XTEEN PAGES.
The Republican Party the Conservators of the Union—Speech of Wm. H. Seward in the Senate, February 29th, 1860, together with Trumbull's reply to Douglas on the same occasion.
The Calhoun Revolution—Its Rise and its Progress—J. R. Doolittle.
Federalism Unmasked—Daniel R. Goodloe.
Thomas Corwin's Great Speech.

THIRTY TWO PAGES.
Success of the Calhoun Revolution: "he Constitution Changed and Slavery Nationalized by the Usurpations of the Supreme Court—James M. Ashley.
The Barbarism of Slavery—Charles Sumner.
Wesley's Thoughts on Slavery.

GERMAN SPEECHES.
EIGHT PAGES.
Lincoln's Cooper Institute Speech.
Free Homes for Free Men—G. A. Grow.
Shall the Territories be Africanized—James Harlan.
Douglas and Popular Sovereignty—Carl Schurz.
The Homestead Bill—M. S. Wilkinson.
The Aggression of Slavery—Owen Lovejoy.
Southern Sectionalism—John Hickman.

THE CHICAGO WEEKLY PRESS AND TRIBUNE

is published on a large imperial sheet, every Thursday, and contains Editorials on the important topics of the times, the news of the week, interesting correspondence from all parts of the country, the Chicago and New York Live Stock and Produce Markets, interesting and reliable Political and Agricultural Articles, etc., etc.

One copy, one year	$1.50
Three copies, one year	4.00
Four copies, one year	5.00
Five copies, one year	6.00
Ten copies, one year	10.00
Twenty copies, one year	20.00

Any person sending us a Club of Twenty, or more, will be entitled to an extra copy. Money, in all cases, required in advance. Subscription may commence at any time.

CAMPAIGN PRESS AND TRIBUNE.

The Campaign PRESS AND TRIBUNE will give a full and complete current history of the Presidential Canvass, including reports of speeches, debates, and mass meetings. It will be sent in clubs until the close of the Campaign, at the following reduced rates:
To one address:

Three copies	$1 00
Twelve copies	3 00
Twenty-one copies	5.00
Fifty copies	12.00

Furnish the Postmaster with a list of the names, and, by a recent law of Congress, he is obliged to deliver the papers from a bundle sent to one address.

Money in registered Letters may be sent at our risk.

Address PRESS AND TRIBUNE,
CHICAGO, ILLINOIS.

EARLIEST STATE OF PAGE 32, SCRIPPS'S *Life of Lincoln*.
First Edition.

Collation: [1]-32, text in double columns. The lower two-thirds of page 32 is devoted to advertising matter.

Binding: Stitched, without wrappers.

Page Size: 8¾ by 5¾ inches.

Typographical Errors: Same as in first edition, thus proving that these two editions were printed from plates cast from the same type forms. It seems a safe assumption that the advertising matter and Chicago copyright notice were removed from the forms, a mat was then made and sent on to New York where the new advertising matter and copyright notice were patched in, and the plates for this edition cast.

Advertising Matter: This matter, on page 32, is set in a single column—full-page spread—under the caption: "The New York Tribune." Two captions, "The New York Semi-Weekly Tribune," and "The New York Weekly Tribune" are set in boldface, sans-serif, display type; this seems to have been a favorite in the composing room of the *New York Tribune*, for we find it frequently used in the advertising columns of that newspaper during the year 1860.

SECOND CHICAGO EDITION

Title, Binding and Collation: The same as in the first edition.

Page Size: Approximately the same as the first edition.

Typographical Errors: The same errors persist in this edition, proving that this edition was also printed from plates cast from the original type forms.

Advertising Matter: Here we find a radical difference between the two editions bearing the Chicago imprints. In this edition, the advertising matter on page 32 is set in a single column—full-page spread—and under the caption: "The Chicago Press and Tribune." The general layout closely follows that of the New York (second) edition; so closely, in fact, that I am quite convinced that both were products of the composing room of the *New York Tribune*.

More conclusive, however, is the character of the display type used in one of the captions. All of the type used in the captions of the advertising matter in this edition was characteristic of the *New York Tribune*, rather than the *Chicago Press and Tribune*. However, the type used in the lowest caption, "The Chicago Press and Tribune," was the same boldface, sans-serif, display type, which was noted in the two captions in the New York (second) edition.

While this type—as has been pointed out—was used frequently in the advertising columns of the *New York Tribune* during the year 1860, not once during that period did it appear in the columns of the *Chicago Press and Tribune*. The Chicago composing room possessed an equivalent face, but the letters "S," "P," "R," etc., were slightly chamfered[9] while the same letters in the New York font were smoothly rounded. All of this points to the inevitable conclusion that this edition, al-

---

[9] See the name "S. W. Ripley" in the *Chicago Press and Tribune*, May 19, 1860, editorial page, col. 9.

though bearing a Chicago imprint, was printed in the plant of the *New York Tribune*.

Experienced typographers who have examined the copy of the first edition, now laying before me, are of the opinion that it was printed direct from type. Not all are in agreement on this point, however. If they are correct in their belief, then it would seem that the first edition was hurriedly printed from the type in Chicago, mats made and rushed to New York, and subsequent Chicago requirements supplied by the *New York Tribune*.

HOWARD, JAMES QUAY

The Life / of / Abraham Lincoln: / With / Extracts from his Speeches. / [*Rule*] / By J. Q. Howard. / [*Rule*] / Columbus: / Follett, Foster and Company. / 1860.   [13]

Collation: [1], title page; [2], copyright notice; [3]-102, text; one white flyleaf; eight pages of advertisements.

Binding: Light buff, paper wrappers, printed in black: The Life / of / Abraham Lincoln: / With / Extracts from his Speeches. / [*Rule*] / By J. Q. Howard. / [*Rule*] / Cincinnati: / Anderson, Gates and Wright. / 1860. Advertising matter on verso of front wrapper, and upon recto of the back wrapper. On the verso of the back wrapper appears the woodcut of the Republican Wigwam at Chicago, which was used in Howells' life.

Variants:

(A) Persistent reports of copies bearing the imprint of Follett, Foster and Company, on the front wrapper, have been received, but I have been unable to locate such a copy.

(B) The book was also issued with a portrait of Lincoln on the front wrapper. I have not seen this variant. Howard wrote a letter to McLellan which read, in part: "I have examined several copies of the book printed with and without the Cincinnati pictorial cover, and both seemed to me to be genuine." This letter is now in Brown University Library.

Page Size: 7⅝ by 4⅞ inches.

Publication Date: Its appearance was first announced in the columns of the *Ohio State Journal* on July 26, 1860, to sell at ten cents. The late appearance of this life may have been due to the fact that Howard had incorporated in his copy some of the errors which he had passed on to Howells, and was required to rewrite the book. However, the preface is dated June 26, and thirty days was not a bad production record for his harassed and overloaded publishers.

Discovery: The discovery of this life was one of the most colorful episodes in the history of Lincolniana. That genial and lovable veteran bookman, Charles P. Everitt, was operating a bookstore on Twenty-third Street, New York City, in the

Webster's, but is unlike either. It is very large, and exceedingly well proportioned, betokening power in all its developments. A slightly Roman nose, a wide out mouth, and a dark complexion, with the appearance of having been weather-beaten, complete the description.

In his personal habits, Mr. Lincoln is as simple as a child. He loves a good dinner, and eats with the appetite which goes with a great brain; but his food is plain and nutritious. He never allows intoxicating liquors of any sort. He is not addicted to tobacco in any of its shapes. He was never accused of a licentious act in his life. He never uses profane language. He never gambles. He is particularly cautious about incurring pecuniary obligations for any purpose whatever; and, in debt, he is never content until the score is discharged. We presume he owes no man a dollar. He never speculates. The rage for the sudden acquisition of wealth never took hold of him. His gains from his profession have been moderate, but sufficient for his purposes. While others have dreamed of gold, he has been in pursuit of knowledge. In all his dealings, he has the reputation of being generous but exact, and, above all, religiously honest. He would be a bold man who would say that Abraham Lincoln ever wronged a man out of a cent, or ever spent a dollar that he had not honestly earned. His struggles in early life have made him careful of money, but his generosity with his own is proverbial. He is a regular attendant upon religious worship, and, though not a communicant, is a pew-holder and liberal supporter of the Presbyterian Church in Springfield, to which Mrs. Lincoln belongs. He is a scrupulous teller of the truth—too exact in his notions to suit the atmosphere of Washington, as it now is. His enemies may say that he tells filthy Republican lies; but no man ever charged that, in a professional capacity, or as a citizen dealing with his neighbors, he would depart from the Scriptural command. At home, he lives like a gentleman of modest means and simple tastes. A good-sized house of wood, simply but tastefully furnished, surrounded by trees and flowers, is his own: there he lives, at peace with himself, the idol of his family, noted for his honesty, ability and patriotism, the admiration of his countrymen.

If Mr. Lincoln is elected President, he will carry but little that is ornamental to the White House. The country must accept his sincerity, his ability, and his honesty, in the mould in which they are cast. He will not be able to make so polite a bow as Franklin Pierce, but he will not commence anew the agitation of the slavery question by recommending to Congress any Kansas-Nebraska Bills. He may not preside at the Presidential dinners with the ease and grace which distinguish the "venerable public functionary," Mr. Buchanan; but he will not create the necessity for a Covode Committee and the disgraceful revelations of Cornelius Wendell. He will take to the Presidential Chair just the qualities which the country now demands to save it from impending destruction—ability that no man can question, firmness that nothing can overbear, honesty that never has been impeached, and patriotism that never despairs."

SECOND STATE OF PAGE 32, SCRIPPS'S *Life of Lincoln.*
Second Edition.

fall of 1901.   During his absence one day, an unidentified man dropped into the store, and told the boy who had been left in charge that he would ship Mr. Everitt a box of books, providing that Everitt would pay the express charges.   Such an agreement was made.   From here on the story is best related in Mr. Everitt's own words:

"A few days later I came in and found that the books had arrived and were un-packed.   They were utterly worthless.   I picked up the cover of a pamphlet, Howard's *Life of Lincoln,* and asked the boy what that was.   'That was the packing used to keep the books tight,' he replied, 'I threw the rest of them into the base-ment.'   I told him to throw the books into the basement, and bring the packing upstairs.   There were twenty-eight copies, two different imprints, and one copy in German.   This latter was bought by Colonel McLellan, and is now in Brown Uni-versity."

Up until that time the book had been unknown.   Howard certainly owed Everitt a debt of gratitude for dragging him out of obscurity.   After considerable effort, Everitt located Howard working in the Library of Congress, and promptly wrote him inquiring as to the origin of the book.   Howard replied: "I suppose you want my autograph, if so send two dollars."   The still small voice of gratitude! Source: See No. 9.

COMPOSITE WORKS

The campaign lives of various candidates, such as those we have described, were sold largely in metropolitan centers, by book agents, and from newsstands.   Composite works, impartially set-ting forth the platforms of all parties and providing the biogra-phies of the different candidates, were prepared for distribution in thinly settled rural sections.   They were, in brief, shotgun campaign documents, aimed to hit readers of every political faith. All such were published late in the campaign; in one instance a speech made as late as July 8, 1860 was quoted.

WELLS, J. G.

Part I

Wells' / Illustrated National / Campaign Hand-Book / for 1860. / [*Rule*] / Part First. / [*Rule*] / Embracing the / Lives of all the Candidates for President and / Vice-President: / Including / John Bell and Edward Everett, / Candidates of the National

Union Party. / Abraham Lincoln and Hanibal Hamlin, / Candidates of the National Republican Party. / Steph. A. Douglas and Herschel V. Johnson / Candidates of the National Democratic Party. / John C. Breckinridge and Joseph Lane, / Candidates of the National Democratic Party. / Sam Houston, / Independent Candidate for the Presidency. / With / Portraits of Each, / Engraved Expressly for this Work from Ambrotypes / Taken from Life. / [*Rule*] / 57 Illustrations. / [*Rule*] / New York: / J. G. Wells, Cor. Park-Row and Beekman Street. / Cincinnati, Ohio: / Mack R. Barnitz, 38 and 40 West Fourth Street. / 1860.

Part II

Wells' / Illustrated National / Campaign Hand-Book / for 1860. / [*Rule*] / Part Second. / [*Rule*] / Embracing a / Complete Compendium / of the / Political History of the United States. / From the / Original Formation of the Government / to the Present Time. / [*Rule*] / New York: / J. G. Wells, Cor. Park-Row and Beekman Street. / Cincinnati, Ohio: / Mack R. Barnitz, 38 and 40 West Fourth Street. / 1860.   [14]

Collation (Part I): Yellow end paper; two white flyleaves; [3], pre-title; [4], frontispiece; [5], title page; [6], copyright notice and printer's imprint; [7], table of contents; [8], blank; [9], list of portraits; [10], blank; [11], portrait; [12], blank; [13]-199, text; [200], blank.

(Part II): [3], blank; [4], frontispiece to part II; [5], title page to part II; [6], blank; [7]-[8], contents; [9]-159, text; [160], blank; two white flyleaves; yellow end paper. Twenty-six plates.

Binding: Black cloth. Spine lettered in gilt: Wells' / Campaign / Hand / Book / [*Rule*] / 1860.

Page Size: 7⅝ by 4⅞.

[ANONYMOUS]

The Lives / of the Present / Candidates / for / President and Vice-President / of the United States, / Containing a Condensed and Impartial History of the Lives, / Public Acts, and Political Views of the Present Candidates, / with the Platforms of the Parties they Represent, Their / Portraits from Life, Their Letters of Acceptance, etc. / [*Rule*] / Cincinnati, — H. M. Rulison, / Queen City Publishing House, 141 Main Street. / Philadelphia, — D. Rulison, / Quaker City Publishing House, 33 South Third Street. / St. Louis — C. Drew & Co., / No. 125 Locust Street. / Geneva, N. Y. — J. Whitley, Jr., / Davis' Block, Water Street.

[15]

Variant:

(A) In Brown University Library is a copy with the following imprint: 1860 / Published by Mack R. Barnitz, / Book, Map and Chart Publisher, / 38 and 40 West Fourth St. / Cincinnati. / Agents wanted.

Collation: [i], title page; [ii], copyright notice; [3]-139, text; [140], blank; two pages of advertising matter, numbered [1] and [2].

Binding: Buff paper wrappers, printed in black like title page, but with a different border. Coats of arms of thirty-three states are on inside front cover, and on both sides of back cover.

Page Size: 8¾ by 4⅞ inches.

[ANONYMOUS]

Portraits / and / Sketches of the Lives / of / All the Candidates / for the / Presidency and Vice-Presidency, / for 1860. / Comprising / Eight Portraits Engraved on Steel, Facts in the Life of Each, / the Four Platforms, the Cincinnati Platform, / and / the Constitution of the United States. / [*Rule*] / New-York: / J. C. Buttre, 48 Franklin Street. / [*Rule*] / 1860.   [16]

Collation: [1], title page; [2], blank; plate (portrait of Lincoln); [3]-4, text; plate (portrait of Hamlin); [5]-8, text; plate (portrait of Bell); [9]-10, text; plate (portrait of Everett); [11]-13, text; [14], blank; plate (portrait of Douglas); [15]-16, text; plate (portrait of Johnson); [17]-19, text; [20], blank; plate (portrait of Breckinridge); [21]-22, text; plate (portrait of Lane); [23]-25, text; [26], blank; 15-32,[10] text; two leaves of advertising matter.

Binding: Buff paper wrappers. Printed in black: Price Fifty Cents. / Portraits / and / Sketches of the Lives / of / All the Candidates / for the / Presidency and Vice-Presidency, / for 1860. / omprising [*sic*] / Eight Portraits Engraved on Steel, Facts in the Life of Each, / the Four Platforms, the Cincinnati Platform, / and / the Constitution of the United States. / [*Rule*] / New-York: / J. C. Buttre,

---

[10] The erroneous pagination at this point seems to have escaped the attention of bibliographers, for the book is usually described as having but thirty-two pages.

48 Franklin Street. / [*Rule*] / 1860. Verso of front wrapper blank. Advertising matter on both sides of back wrapper.

Page Size: 8⅛ by 5¾ inches.

Note: On June 8, 1860, Buttre had the effrontery to advertise this book in the *New York Tribune* as "now on sale at all news-stands," although several of the candidates had not then been nominated. This beautiful pamphlet was issued late in July.

Buttre engraved the portraits for the Wide Awake Edition, and yet another set of plates was engraved and supplied to Follett, Foster & Company for Howells' life of Lincoln.

CAMPAIGN LIVES IN WELSH AND GERMAN

As a group, these are the rarest of all Lincolniana. So widely distributed are the few surviving copies it has been impossible to make firsthand examinations of most of these rarities. The citations which follow are provided through the kind coöperation of the few fortunate owners.

[ANONYMOUS]

Das Leben / von / Abraham Lincoln, / nebst einer kurzen Skizze des Lebens von / Hannibal Hamlin. / Republikanische Candidaten für Präsident und Vice-Präsident der Vereinigten Staaten. / [*Printer's device*] / Die Constitution der Ver. Staaten, Unabhängigkeits-Erklärung, / und die / Platformen / der / verscheidenen politischen Parteien & c. / [*Rule*] / Chicago, Ill. / Druck von Höffgen und Schneider. / 1860.   [17]

Translation: The life of Abraham Lincoln, with a short sketch of the life of Hannibal Hamlin, Republican candidates for president and vice-president of the United States. The Constitution of the United States, the Declaration of Independence, and the platforms of the various political parties.

Collation: Title page, verso blank; printed page, unnumbered, verso blank; 4-108, text.

Binding: The only known copy is in the Illinois State Historical Library. This copy is bound in mottled boards, with cloth backstrip and corners. The front wrapper has been preserved; hence it is safe to assume that it originally appeared in paper wrappers. Printed in black: Das Leben / von / Abraham Lincoln / [*Portrait of Lincoln*] / nebst einer kurzen Skizze des Lebens von / Hannibal Hamlin. / Chicago,

1860, / Druck der "Illinois Staats-Zeitung." Verso: quotation from Lincoln.
Page Size: 6⅝ by 4¼ inches.

HOWARD, JAMES QUAY

Das Leben / von / Abraham Lincoln, / nebst / Auszugen aus
seinen Reden. / [*Rule*] / Aus dem Englischen von J. Q. Howard, /
Uebersezt druch / Professor Wilhelm Grauert. / [*Rule*] / Columbus: / Follett, Foster und Compagnie. / 1860.   [18]
    Translation: The life of Abraham Lincoln, with extracts
from his speeches. From the English by J. Q. Howard, translated by Professor Wilhelm Grauert.

    Collation: [2], 57.
    Binding: Printed wrappers.
    Page Size: 7 by 4⅞ inches.
    Publication Date: First announced in the *Ohio State Journal* on July 26, 1860.
There exists not a shred of evidence with which to support the contention that this
was "the first Lincoln biography printed in any foreign language." Bartlett's life—
see No. 19 below—was being offered for sale two weeks earlier.
    Note: But two copies are known: one is in the collection of Gov. Henry Horner,
and the other in Brown University Library.

BARTLETT, D. W.
VOSE, REUBEN

Leben, Wirken und Reden / des / Republikanischen / Praesi-
dentschafts-Candidaten / Abraham Lincoln. / Nach den besten
amerikanischen Quellen: D. W. Bartlett, / Reuben Vose u. A.
deutsch bearbeitet. / New-York, 1860. / Bei Friedrich Gerhard.
                                                                [19]
    Translation: Life, works and speeches of the Republican
presidential candidate, Abraham Lincoln. From the best American authorities. D. W. Bartlett and Reuben Vose. Translated
into German. Rev.

    Collation: Pp. 106.
    Binding: Printed wrappers.
    Page Size: 7⅜ by 4¾ inches.
    Publication Date: On July 16, 1860, it was first advertised in various New
York City newspapers, as being "on sale."

[ANONYMOUS] WELSH (UTICA IMPRINT)

Hanes Bywyd / Abraham Lincoln, / o Illinois, a / Hannibal Hamlin, / o Maine, / yr ymgeiswyr gwerinol am yr arlywyddiaeth a'r islywyddiaeth; / yn nghyd a'r / araeth draddododd Mr. Lincoln yn Cooper's Institute, N. Y., / ar y 27 o Chwefror, 1860. Hefyd, / yr esgynlawr gwerinol, yn nghyd a chan etholiadol. / [*Double Rule*] / Utica, N. Y.: / David C. Davies, Argraffydd a Chyhoeddydd. / 1860.   [20]

Translation: Life history of Abraham Lincoln of Illinois and Hannibal Hamlin of Maine, the Republican candidates for the presidency and vice-presidency; together with the speech Mr. Lincoln delivered in Cooper's Institute, N. Y., on the 27th of February, 1860. Also the Republican platform with the election song.

Collation: [1], title page; [2], song and music; [3]-16, text. A cut of Lincoln appears at the beginning of the text on page [3].
Binding: Unbound, stitched.
Page Size: 9⅜ by 5¾ inches.
Note: The only known copy is in the Library of Congress.
See No. 21 for Pottsville, Pennsylvania imprint.

[ANONYMOUS] WELSH (POTTSVILLE, PA. IMPRINT)

Hanes Bywyd / Abraham Lincoln, o Illinois, / a / Hannibal Hamlin, o Maine; / yr / ymgeisyddion gwerinaidd am arlywydd ac islywydd yr Unol Dalaethau, / Erbyn yr Etholiad yn tachwedd, 1860; / yn nghyd a / Golydiadau ac egwyddorion y gwerinwyr, &c. / [*Portrait of Lincoln*] / [*Rule*] / [*Quotation*] / [*Rule*] / Pottsville, Pa.: / Argraffwyd gan B. Bannan, swyddfa y "Miners' Journal," / 1860.   [21]

Literal Translation: Life History of Abraham Lincoln of Illinois and Hannibal Hamlin of Maine, the Republican candidates for president and vice-president of the United States, for the election of November, 1860; together with the views and principles of the Republicans, etc. [Portrait and quotation].

Collation: [1], title page; [2]-16, text.
Binding: Unbound, stitched.
Page Size: 8¾ by 5½ inches.

OFFICIAL PROCEEDINGS

1937

REPORT OF THE SECRETARY

To the Directors of the Illinois State Historical Society:

GENTLEMEN:

I present herewith a summary of the activities of the Illinois State Historical Society since the last annual meeting, May 15, 1936.

The Society held its usual Illinois Day meeting in Springfield on December 3, 1936, with James A. James presiding. The speaker of the occasion was Dr. Joseph Schafer, Superintendent of the State Historical Society of Wisconsin, who took for his subject, "Was the Frontier a Safety Valve for Labor?" After the address, a reception was held in the Illinois State Historical Library.

A year ago I reported that the membership of the Society had dropped to the lowest point in many years—697. I take pleasure in reporting the admission of fifty-three new members during the past year. After deducting losses by deaths and resignations, our membership shows a net increase, the first gain to be recorded in recent years.

However, all indications are that we have barely begun to attract to the Society those who are potential members. In recent months the membership committee has been actively at work, and is planning to send out several thousand invitations during the coming fall. Directors and members of the Society can contribute to this end by furnishing the names of persons likely to be interested in membership. The committee believes a membership of 1,000 to be a goal which can be attained in the near future. The advantages which will accrue to the Society from an interested and growing membership are obvious.

During the past year nine historical markers have been erected by the Society. This is a smaller number than was reported a year ago, but other demands upon the Secretary's time have been heavier, and besides, suitable sites for markers are no longer as numerous as they were at the beginning of this undertaking.   If the experience of the past year is indicative of the future, little can be done on the Society's historical marker program unless one or two qualified persons are added to our permanent staff.

The committee on popular publications, appointed at the last annual meeting, has made an investigation of the subject and has decided tentatively upon a list of titles, but two factors have prevented any further accomplishment.   The first has been the difficulty of obtaining persons qualified to write both popularly and authoritatively, and inducing them to undertake to produce manuscripts for inadequate compensation; the other is the necessity of securing the approval of the Trustees of the Illinois State Historical Library, since funds for publication must come from this source.   No difficulty is anticipated in this respect, but as yet there has been no opportunity to present the proposal to the Trustees.   As to the merits of the plan, daily experience supports my conviction that almost nothing the Society could do would serve a better purpose or attract more favorable attention.   Experience, however, also indicates that to be successful these publications must not be too restricted in scope; that in a word they must be truly "popular."

You will remember that in 1932 the format of the Society's *Journal* was radically changed.   The format adopted at that time has proved to be greatly superior to that which it superseded, but experience has shown that it also possesses disadvantages. A blue cover, for example, has a tendency to fade.   Moreover, sometimes it has been impossible to obtain identical cover stock, with the result that we have used four different cover stocks in the past five years.   In addition, there has been frequent criticism of the extended feature of the cover.   The initial appearance is good, but it is easily defaced, and difficult to stand upright on book shelves.

These disadvantages could be eliminated simply by substituting a stock cover of a different shade, and trimming the edges flush with the text, but in my opinion, more substantial changes are desirable. In content as well as appearance I think the *Journal* could be changed with profit. At present it is a dignified, and sometimes dull, historical magazine of the traditional type, but I believe firmly that it can be made more sprightly and more interesting without lowering in the least the standard of scholarship which must characterize it.

The publication of a state historical society should not be edited solely for the benefit of the academic historian; it should also be directed towards the person to whom the history of the commonwealth in which he lives is an avocation. This means that articles accepted for publication should deal with subjects having a fairly broad appeal, and should deal with them in an interesting manner. It means the inclusion of more illustrations, and perhaps the addition of one or two departments designed to catch the interest of a reader rather than to make a negligible "contribution" to an obscure point. The demands which such a publication make upon an editor are relatively heavy, and can be met only through the coöperation of a group of highly competent contributors, but the effort is worth making.

The present format of the *Journal* hardly lends itself to the departures which I am recommending. Like every well-designed publication, its appearance fits its content perfectly, and if the content is changed, a certain lack of harmony will be immediately perceptible. I recommend that provision be made for redesigning the *Journal*, both to eliminate the practical disadvantages which I have outlined and to make it a more suitable vehicle for more varied and interesting content.

I regret exceedingly the necessity of announcing the death, on January 15, 1937, of Paul Steinbrecher, one of our most faithful and active Directors. In addition to his connection with this Society, Mr. Steinbrecher was one of the Trustees of the Illinois State Historical Library, a leader in civic and cultural activities both in Chicago and the state, a discriminating collector of Americana, and an indefatigable student of history and literature. His death has meant a heavy loss to the Society and a personal bereavement to many of its members.

In the general membership of the Society, the following deaths have occurred during the past twelve months:

Joseph B. Bacon....................................Macomb
John S. Felmley....................................Griggsville
O. A. Harker......................................Urbana
Sidney Kuh.......................................Chicago
Tracy W. McGregor......................Washington, D. C.
J. G. Mulcaster....................................Hines
Clifford R. Myers.......................Charleston, W. Va.
Louis Seidel......................................Chicago
W. E. Shastid.....................................Pittsfield
Tryggve A. Siqueland.............................Chicago
William T. Vandeveer...........................Taylorville
L. O. Williams....................................Clinton

Respectfully submitted,

PAUL M. ANGLE.

ANNUAL BUSINESS MEETING
ILLINOIS STATE HISTORICAL SOCIETY
GALESBURG, ILLINOIS, MAY 14, 1937

The annual business meeting of the Illinois State Historical Society was held at the Henry M. Seymour Library, Knox College, Galesburg, on May 14, 1937.

A quorum being present, the meeting was called to order by President James A. James.

The Secretary read the minutes of the last meeting, which were approved as read.

Dr. James notified the Society that the terms of five Directors—Paul M. Angle, Carl E. Black, George C. Dixon, Theodore C. Pease, and Clint Clay Tilton—had expired. On the motion of Mr. East, seconded by Mr. Townley, these Directors were re-elected for three-year terms by acclamation.

On the motion of Clint Clay Tilton, seconded by Mrs. English, Jewell F. Stevens of Chicago was elected a Director for the balance of the unexpired term of Paul Steinbrecher, deceased.

Mr. East, from the committee on publicity and membership, reported that the committee had decided upon the form of a membership invitation to be sent to several thousand prospective members, but that in view of the fact that the invitations could not be ready for mailing before summer, it had been decided to defer further action until the fall. Various members present promised to supply lists of persons likely to be interested in joining the Society.

Dr. Pease, from the committee on popular publications, reported that the committee had decided tentatively upon a list of titles, but that definite plans must await the decision of the Trustees of the Illinois State Historical Library, by whom funds for printing would have to be made available.

Mr. Angle proposed that the format of the *Journal* of the Illinois State Historical Society be changed to eliminate a number of objections, and that certain changes be made in the content in an effort to make it of greater general interest. After discussion, the subject was referred to the committee on publicity and membership with power to act.

On behalf of the McLean County Historical Society, Mr. Townley invited the Society to hold its next annual meeting in Bloomington. The invitation was accepted, subject to unforeseen contingencies which might make a different location advisable.

There being no further business, the meeting adjourned.

MEETING OF THE BOARD OF DIRECTORS
ILLINOIS STATE HISTORICAL SOCIETY
GALESBURG, ILLINOIS, MAY 14, 1937

Present: James A. James, Paul M. Angle, Ernest E. East, Mrs. Henry English, John H. Hauberg, Henry J. Patten, Theodore C. Pease, Clint Clay Tilton, and Wayne C. Townley.

By unanimous vote the Directors elected the following officers: President, James A. James; Vice-Presidents, Evarts B. Greene, New York City; John H. Hauberg, Rock Island; Frank O. Lowden, Oregon; Theodore C. Pease, Urbana; George W. Smith, Carbondale; Frank E. Stevens, Springfield; Secretary-Treasurer, Paul M. Angle.

The Directors adopted a budget for the next fiscal year, and then adjourned.

INDEX